Dogfella

Dogfella

How an Abandoned Dog Named Bruno
Turned This Mobster's Life Around

A MEMOIR

JAMES GUILIANI

with Charlie Stella

Da Capo Press
A Member of the Perseus Books Group

Designed by Jack Lenzo
Set in 10.5 point Janson by the Perseus Books Group

Cataloging-in-Publication data for this book is available from the Library of Congress.

First Da Capo Press edition 2015
ISBN: 978-0-7382-1807-6 (hardcover)
ISBN: 978-0-7382-1808-3 (e-book)

Published by Da Capo Press
A Member of the Perseus Books Group
www.dacapopress.com

Note: Certain names and identifying details of people associated with events described in this book have been changed. Any similarity to actual persons is coincidental.

Da Capo Press books are available at special discounts for bulk purchases in the U.S. by corporations, institutions, and other organizations. For more information, please contact the Special Markets Department at the Perseus Books Group, 2300 Chestnut Street, Suite 200, Philadelphia, PA, 19103, or call (800) 810-4145, ext. 5000, or e-mail special.markets@perseusbooks.com.

10 9 8 7 6 5 4 3 2 1

I dedicate this book to all the animals who have graced my life, to include those who have passed and those I couldn't save. From the moment I found an abused and abandoned shih tzu who I named Bruno, animals have blessed my life. They saved me when I most needed saving. For the gift of life they gave me, I dedicate the rest of my life returning the favor—to rescue and care for animals.

I have been all things unholy. If God can work through me, He can work through anyone.

—Saint Francis of Assisi

Until one has loved an animal, a part of one's soul remains unawakened.

—Anatole France

Contents

Author's Note

This book is based on my life and I recorded it all as faithfully as possible, drawing on my recollection of personal experiences. I did change some names and identifying details of people and places in the book. These minor changes were simply intended to protect the privacy of the people involved. With these necessary exceptions, the stories in this book are true.

Chapter 1

Bruno

"The construction should be finished in another week or two," Lena said. "It'll be fine."

"And the bar we could've opened in two days," I said.

I was in a pissy mood because I was about to go into a business I knew nothing about, a business I'd bankrupted my pension to start. Lena was doing her best to keep me calm. She was familiar with my MO: when James gets upset, he goes on a bender for days at a time.

We were having our morning coffee at Cafe Sorrento on Eighteenth Avenue in Brooklyn, just a few blocks from where our first business venture, an animal boutique, was under construction. It was a dreary, shitty day in May 2006. The sky was gray and the air was thick and muggy. I'd been relatively good the last few nights, at least coming home after I was finished drinking in local bars, but I was still holding onto my original idea for a business, to open a gay bar someplace in Manhattan. I still had street connections that could make a place like that swing, but Lena knew better. She reminded me of it before I took another sip of espresso.

"I can't believe you're still talkin' about a bar," she said.

"Not just a bar," I said. "A gay bar. Those people spend. They like to party."

Lena rolled her eyes.

"Look at me," I said. "If we opened in the right location, it'd be a winner."

"You're delusional," she said.

"We opened a gay bar, I wouldn't have to clean up cat shit all day."

"Like you clean it up now."

"Hey, they're your cats," I reminded her. "It's a good thing they use that box you gave them."

"It's called a litter box," Lena said.

"Whatever."

She'd had a dozen or more cats when I moved in with her three years earlier. She also had one dog, a pug she'd named Brock. The poor bastard. Imagine—a dozen cats, you're the only dog? I kind of bonded with one of her cats. I liked it when Sniffles rubbed up against my ankles in the morning.

I'd never been an animal person, but I eventually got used to having Lena's brood around. I wasn't the type to talk to them, or play with them, but I did like Sniffles. I grew used to them, except for having them in our bed. Lena had let them sleep with her before I moved in. I'd put an end to that day one.

"In the meantime, we have to pay the electrician two thousand today and the plumber six hundred tomorrow," Lena said. "And we have some decisions to make on stock."

I had about two grand in cash in my pocket from a cocaine sale she had no idea about. "I have the electrician," I said.

"And we'll need for the plumber tomorrow."

"I'll get it."

"And the stock we have to talk about."

"Like I have a clue about that shit."

"Why you need to pay attention."

I shook my head and downed an espresso.

"Do we want to accept the dog beds?" Lena said. "They're expensive."

"Dog beds," I said. "The guys inna' joint could hear this conversation, fuhgeddaboudit."

"The guys in the joint are probably all dead now. That was almost twenty years ago. Get over it."

"I already took the plastic off one of the beds, so I guess accept them. At least that one."

"You could've waited to take the plastic off, James. You know, discuss it first?"

"What is this, break James's balls day? You should've warned me, I would've brought a bottle of vodka."

"And I would've broke it over your head."

It was how we sometimes started our day. Until I had half a dozen espressos in my system, I was fuckin' cranky. Lena could only put up with so much before she got cranky, too. That morning she was trying to take care of business, but I was still waking up and I wasn't thrilled about our dog boutique.

"So?" she said.

"What?"

"The beds?"

"I don't know, Lena. Do whatever you want."

"Hey, you need to take an interest, James. I can't do everything by myself."

"You can break my balls by yourself."

"Asshole."

I had to laugh. Getting her to curse at me was also part of our morning routine. Once I accomplished that, we could move on.

I said, "We took them on consignment, right? If we can't sell them, we'll ship them back. That way we don't have to eat them."

Lena winked at me.

"What?" I said.

"I knew you could do it," she said. "Good boy."

We could get crazy with one another, but there was never any doubt about loyalty. She'd once saved me from killing myself.

"Leashes," she said.

"What about them?"

"There are so many different kinds, but the retractable ones I don't wanna sell."

I had no idea what she was talking about. "Why not?"

"Because they're dangerous. You can get burns and cuts from them."

"They sell?"

"What?"

"Do they sell? Do people buy them?"

"Yes, people buy them, but I don't want to sell them. Not those or choke collars, no way."

I shook my head. I didn't get it. To me it was business. If people were willing to buy it, you sold it. It was how I operated when I sold stepped-on blow to make enough money to feed my own cocaine habit. If there were suckers willing to pay for the diluted shit I was selling, I wasn't about to worry about them. Buyer beware. I had a habit to feed.

"We looking to make money with this store or jerk ourselves off?" I said.

"Sometimes you're very eloquent, James, you know that?"

I had an idea what *eloquent* meant, but I wasn't sure. I also knew that she was being sarcastic. I pumped the air with a fist for emphasis.

"Eloquent this," I said.

"And sometimes you're a real moron," she said.

"Just sometimes?"

Lena ignored the line I fed her. "We'll still make money, don't worry about that," she said. "Just make sure once we're open, you don't order any of that stuff if somebody asks for it. I'll make you a list of what we won't sell. You can keep it up at the counter."

I closed my eyes and saw myself behind a counter in a pet boutique. *Fuck me*, I thought. I huffed.

"What?" Lena said.

"I'm picturing myself in the store," I said. "Like a big jerkoff."

"And I picture you behind a bar drinking."

"You forgot the cocaine," I said.

"No, you'd probably snort first and then turn to the booze."

I couldn't let her have the final word. I reached for my cigarettes and said, "We'd've made real money with that bar."

Lena raised both arms up to the sky. "Please, God, do something with him." She stared at me a long moment. "You need divine intervention, I swear it."

"Fuck you talkin' about?"

"We really need to go over this again? Seriously? You're an alcoholic, James. And a coke fiend. And you were taking steroids, what, six months ago? How you hurt your back, right, doing blow and steroids together? I'm afraid you'll kill yourself with those steroids as it is. You can't own a bar. You can't go near a bar, never mind own one. What's wrong with you?"

I was still in denial. I didn't want to hear what I couldn't do. "This would've been different," I said. "If I owned it, I wouldn't drink."

Her head snapped back. "Oh, right, sure. Of course not. Please, you couldn't operate a bar without drinking, okay? Or without doing coke, so forget that shit. We'll have a pet boutique to run as soon as they finish the construction, so snap out of it."

I reached for my second espresso and spilled some of it on my sweat suit. "Fuck me," I said. "Look at this shit. All over my leg. Now I gotta go home and change."

"I told you to wear the gray one," Lena said. "Who wears white to a construction site?"

I poured some water from a glass onto a napkin and rubbed at the coffee stain on my right thigh. "Don't break my balls, Lena," I said. "I'm gonna have to have these dry-cleaned now. Shit."

"God forbid you have a stain," she said. "Maybe you should get another haircut while you're at it. When's the last time you went, two days ago?"

I waved her off as I finished whatever espresso was left. Lena turned away from me and was looking toward the street when I saw her brow furrow.

"What?" I said.

She pointed. "What is that in front of the vet's office there?"

I turned and looked in the direction she was pointing.

"James, go look," Lena said. "I think it's an animal."

It was about eleven in the morning. Aside from booze and drugs, I was also addicted to caffeine. I needed half a dozen espressos before noon to operate. Otherwise I'd walk around with a massive caffeine headache. I was thinking I needed another cup of espresso when Lena became impatient.

"James, please!" she said.

Lena had been an animal lover all her life. But me? I could care less about dogs and cats. To me they were more trouble than they were worth. They took time and money, neither of which I was willing to give away. I had my own needs, addictions that left me too selfish to worry about anything else.

"I think it's next to the parking meter, James," Lena said. "Please hurry. Go see."

If there was an animal involved, I wasn't going to win. I gave up and started across the street. The closer I came to the parking meter, the more I squinted. At first I thought it was a rug, but then I could see it was a dog, a sick dog. A thick rope like the ones used to tie boats to docks was wrapped around his neck. The other end was tied to the parking meter. When I bent down for a closer look, I could see the dog's hair was tangled, flat, and knotted. His eyes looked dead, and his jaw seemed crooked. He was spotting blood from his ass, and his coat was a putrid greenish-yellow, which I would later learn was the result of being confined in a tight space where he was forced to sleep in his own piss and shit.

"What the fuck," I said.

As a junkie and alcoholic, I'd left myself in similar situations more than a few times. I'd use cocaine to stay up for days on end, finally drinking myself into a stupor. Sometimes I woke up on the sidewalk outside of a strange bar, my pants drenched in my own piss, my face beat to a pulp. The difference, of course, was I'd put myself into those situations. Nobody had abandoned me the way somebody had obviously left this dog to die on his own. It pissed me off.

I waved for Lena to cross the street. She ran.

"I can't believe somebody left this thing like this," I said as I removed the rope from his neck.

"Maybe they thought someone from inside the vet's office would take him," Lena said.

"They even open?"

Lena stepped up close to the door and read the hours off the sign. "Since nine o'clock."

I picked the dog up and could feel his skin moving. It was then I noticed he was covered in maggots.

"Holy shit," I said.

When Lena saw the maggots, she became hysterical. "Oh, my God, James! Oh, my God! Bring him inside. Come, fast. Here."

Lena ran to the door, opened it, and I carried the dog inside. I wasn't thinking about whether someone from inside the veterinary office had seen the dog on the way to work. I couldn't imagine anybody ignoring it, but then as I approached the reception desk, a middle-aged man in a white jacket held up a hand.

"Don't bring that dog in here unless you have the money to pay for it," he said.

"He's not our dog," I said. "He was tied to a parking meter outside. He's sick."

"Unless you intend to pay for it, bring it right back where you found it."

I looked at him as if he were crazy.

"You heard me," he said.

At that point it took all of my restraint not to hop over the reception desk and put his head through a wall. This guy was a doctor? A veterinarian? How the fuck could he ignore the dog?

"I'm not gonna go tie him back to the parking meter," I said. "He's sick and you're a fucking vet. Help the dog."

He was a tough cocksucker, this vet. He engaged me in a stare-down, something most people wouldn't think of trying. "This is a business," he finally said. "We're not a charity here. If you don't have the money, take the dog back outside."

"Bullshit," I said, then handed the dog to Lena. I pulled out a roll of cash and held it up. "How much? This enough, you prick?"

"You'll need to leave a credit card," he said.

"I don't have a fuckin' credit card," I said. I didn't. I'd operated my entire life on a cash basis. "What's wrong with cash?"

"I don't know what the dog will require yet," the prick said. "Leave a credit card and I'll take care of the dog."

Lena had already pulled out her American Express card. She handed it to the receptionist. "Here," she said, then looked at the piece-of-shit doctor. "Now please take care of the dog."

We were told they'd call us when the dog was ready to be picked up. Lena left her phone number and we spent the next several hours at home. I was still crazed that somebody, a vet, could ignore a sick animal the way that prick had ignored that dog until Lena handed over her credit card. It was a matter of principle. He was supposed to care about animals. He should've taken the dog inside and fixed him up without thinking about money.

All I could think of was how I wanted to handle the doctor after the dog was treated. I saw myself breaking his greedy fingers with a hammer or punching his teeth down his throat with a fistful of quarters. I know what had stopped me inside the office. It was the dog—he needed treatment. Still, it bothered me that I didn't break the prick's jaw. How could I let that guy get away with the shit he pulled?

The waiting was making me crazy. I'd dealt with people like that doctor before. If there wasn't anything in it for them, they weren't getting involved. Fine. I promised myself I'd deal with him later.

Then my anger shifted to how we'd found the dog. How could anybody, for whatever reason, leave him alone like that? How could they leave him, as sick as he obviously was, tied to a fucking parking meter? Did they try to go inside the office first? Had they called first and been told not to bring him in unless they could pay for him? The prick doctor must've known the dog was outside his office. He had to have known.

There were other choices they could've made, whoever left him to die like that. At the least they could've treated him with some dignity. People make choices, animals can't. Animals are voiceless.

I slammed the dining room table with a fist. "Motherfucker!" I yelled.

My mood switched from anger to rage. Lena must've seen my wheels turning, because suddenly she was sitting across the table from me and pointing a finger.

"Hey, don't even think about it," she said. "Get it out of your head right now. We'll just pay the prick whatever he wants and take the dog home."

"Bullshit," I said.

"I mean it," she said. "You do anything crazy and you'll wind up back in jail. Then what?"

"Then I'll come out and break his other fuckin' leg," I said. "How's that?"

Lena had seen me lose it for a lot less bullshit than what that doctor pulled. I once broke some loudmouth jerkoff's wrist for giving me the finger from his car. I followed the tough guy for six blocks until I had him trapped and then jumped out of my car and smashed his window to grab his left arm. I intended to break his middle finger, the one he'd flipped at me, but he turned the wrong way when I grabbed his wrist and then it cracked.

Like I said, Lena knew exactly how and what I was thinking.

"You can't do that," she said, "go after the guy. He's a prick, so what? We have plans, remember? The store'll be ready in another two weeks. You get in trouble now and that's the end of the store. The vet is a piece of shit. He's not worth ruining our lives over. Think of the dog. Hopefully he'll be okay and we can take him home today."

I did my best to ignore the doctor, but it wasn't easy. Fifteen years ago, I might've beat the shit out of him right there in his office, all the while knowing he never would've shown up at my arraignment because somebody would've warned him to stay the fuck away. That was one of the benefits of

"Give me the dog," Lena said.

"What? Why?"

"Because I'm afraid you'll kill him."

I had to smile. "Are you kidding me?"

"James, those beds. We can't sell them now!"

"Who gives a fuck?"

Once again I'd left her in shock. Money was what I needed to eat, get high, and drink. I wouldn't have considered throwing any away on a dog bed.

"You're scaring me," she said.

"I'm still worried about the bleeding, don't get me wrong," I told her. "This gonna stop or what?"

"The doctor had said his bleeding would stop over time, but might start again as the tumors rupture from his defecating," Lena said.

What an image. What a bright fucking future. "Every time he shits?" I said.

"For a while, yeah."

"That jerkoff doctor should bleed from his ass every time he breathes, the prick."

"Enough about the doctor already."

She was right. At least now he was looking and feeling a lot better than when we found him. I let Bruno lick my grille again a few minutes before moving the destroyed dog beds out to the car. When I returned, Lena reminded me of a bill we had to pay.

"You have money for the plumber?"

"Shit," I said. "I forgot."

"Because you were playing with your new pal."

"I will hug him and squeeze him and love him."

"Cute. Ask him if he has the six hundred."

"I'll be right back."

I drove back to the cafe and looked to see who was around. Some of the old men playing cards there carried cash. A few were old-time gangsters enjoying their retirement. I saw one old-timer I'd borrowed from in the past, an old man you'd think was destitute if you saw him on the street. He was no more than five foot five, two hundred pounds, with a pot belly he could use for a table. He wore gray pants and shoes and he smoked a De Nobili cigar, what we used to call "guinea stinkers." I tapped my pocket twice and he nodded. Five minutes later he handed me $1,000 at three points a week; I'd owe him $30 in vig (interest) every week on the principal, whatever the balance. Loan-sharking is one of the more lucrative businesses on the street. A guy could pay that thirty bucks for a year, more than fifteen hundred bucks, and still owe the original grand. Put fifty grand on the street at three points a week and you're looking at fifteen hundred a week in interest alone. Not a bad business if you could hold onto your cash.

I never carried loans longer than the time it took me to make another cocaine sale, so the most this guy would earn off of me was $30. I'd pay him back $1,030, but all in one shot. Still, I appreciated the instant access. Loan sharks are like ATMs to street guys, always available.

On my way out, I handed the girl behind the counter a twenty and told her the old man's coffees and cannoli were on me.

I returned to the store a few minutes before the plumber. I paid him and still had almost $400, enough to get high for a few days. Normally, I'd hit the road and find trouble in some bar, but that day I was content hanging out with my new pal. He hadn't cured me of my demons, but at least I wasn't looking ahead to my next high.

And then there was Lena I'd have to answer to if I disappeared so close to our opening. A year ago I'd gone missing a few days. I'd been on a three-day cocaine bender that ended with me drinking a fifth of vodka and passing out in a friend's basement. I'd been out of work a few months from a back injury and was collecting worker's compensation, but I'd usually piss the money away as soon as I could cash the check. When I finally made it home after a few days, Lena welcomed me with a short right cross that broke my jaw. It was a lucky punch, but it hurt like hell and she'd made her point.

I went in and out of rehab a few times over the next few months until we came up with the idea of a business. I was still thinking the gay bar would've worked, but Lena knew better. I agreed to the pet boutique because of all the shit I'd put her through, and maybe because underneath all my denial, I knew she was right; a junkie-alcoholic had no business going near, never mind owning, a bar.

Somehow the $300-plus remained in my pocket for the rest of the day. I had a steroid connection scheduled for the next day. I had a guy who wholesaled me steroids for a few muscle freaks I was still friendly with from my days lifting weights. If all three muscle heads showed up the next day,

I stood to make about fifteen hundred. If I did what I said I'd do and paid back the thousand, I'd have even more scratch than I was already carrying to get high.

My junkie thought process kicked in. I could buy enough cocaine to keep myself stocked a week or two, and I'd still have enough left over to step on a few times to sell to the suckers hanging out at the clubs, which would lead to more money to repeat the process—wash, rinse, recycle.

The game plan was in the back of my head, but it was sidetracked when we tried to take Bruno back to the house again. We were hoping that Brock would get used to the new kid on the block, but it wasn't going to happen. Brock growled as soon as he spotted Bruno. I had to take the little guy back to the store, and I felt as if I were abandoning him all over again.

I made sure his bed of towels was in place and I set out a few more treats for him to pick on during the night. I went down on my knees and let him kiss my face before I said good night, but then he followed me all the way to the front door, his tail wagging as if he were coming along for the ride back home. I couldn't remember ever feeling so shitty. Looking at him like that killed me.

When I sat behind the wheel of my Cadillac, I adjusted the rearview mirror and looked at my eyes. They were red.

"The fuck is wrong with you?" I said. "It's a fuckin' dog."

Then I forced myself to be the tough guy I was supposed to be and I drove home.

The next day I was up early again, but I had to hustle if I wanted to score the steroids. I picked up my espressos-to-go and drank them in the car as I headed to the store. I was going to check on and feed Bruno, and then head out. All morning I'd been thinking like a junkie again—get my hands on some money and go buy drugs, but when I went to open the door and saw Bruno on the other side, his tail wagging like I was the best thing he'd ever seen in his life, I forgot all about the steroids and the drugs.

Bruno proved to be the second stage of a cure for my demons. The first stage had started three years earlier when I met Lena. She'd talked me out of committing suicide during a six-hour telephone conversation, and then we'd met and clicked. We've been together ever since. She understood my street roots and was willing to tolerate some of my crazy behavior up to a point. She didn't ask questions about how I made my extra money, and she'd always been there for me. She couldn't stand the bingeing I sometimes did when I fell off the wagon for days at a time, but again, she was always there for me when I came home with my tail between my legs, genuinely sorry for being a fuckup.

What she'd never done, at least to this point in our relationship, was abandon me the way somebody had obviously abandoned Bruno.

I still needed the steroid money to pay back the old man, so I took an early lunch and did what I had to do. I bought steroids from one guy and sold them to the three juicers hoping to make it into the big leagues of bodybuilding someday, something I knew a bit about because my uncle had been a successful bodybuilder who'd made it into Arnold Schwarzenegger's film *Pumping Iron*. My brother Anthony was also a bodybuilder, which he continued to do after serving in the US Marines and does to this day.

I made my runs, paid off the old man, and made it back to the store within a few hours. Maybe it was from loyalty to Lena or because I had Bruno to take care of every day, but I managed to avoid executing my initial junkie plan to sell the steroids to secure drugs for myself. I avoided falling off the wagon. I didn't drink or do cocaine, or do anything else that would take time away from Bruno or cause Lena any extra anxiety.

Then we learned that Bruno's tumors were cancerous and that he wouldn't live a long life. Upset as I was at the news, I refused to abuse whatever time we had left together by getting high or drinking myself into another stupor.

Two weeks passed and The Diamond Collar had its grand opening, with Bruno right beside me. This was our first Diamond Collar, on Seventy-sixth Street and Thirteenth Avenue. It was a great day. I was sober, and I had Bruno there. We hoped to hire a few dog groomers, but it would take some time before we could afford the extra expense. There was a dog groomer up the block, competition we didn't even consider when we planned the business. We also didn't consider the hours we'd have to put in. At least I never considered it. If it was Lena's plan to keep me occupied most of the day running the store, it was a good one. There was no way we could afford to hire counter help yet, so it was Lena or me to handle the business, except we had a house full of animals Lena had to take care of,

as well as all the record keeping for both the business and our home. One day she showed me the various regulations small businesses had to comply with or face fines. It was crazy. In dollars and cents, it would cost us almost seven grand to stay abreast of small-business laws and regulations. In time, with all the paperwork involved, it would take Lena the equivalent of two forty-hour workweeks.

That left me, "James the jerkoff," I told her after the first week of business. "I guess we're playing tag and I'm it."

Lena was laughing. "So, it's a business," she said. "It takes time to get off the ground and its hard work. Welcome to reality, James."

"Look at me," I said. "I'm telling you right now, it wasn't for Bruno, I would've gone to lunch and come back two weeks from now."

"Oh, yeah?" Lena said. "And when you came back there would've been locks on the doors over there and over here. We have eighty grand tied up in this business now. You start fucking up again and you might as well go to jail."

I shook my head at her, but I knew she was right. It was like a nightmare; one night I went to bed a street-savvy, knock-around guy, and the next morning I woke up Mr. Fuckin' Rogers.

I had carried a Laborers' Union book for twenty-three years. I'd been laid off from time to time, but mob connections had always kept me employed until I hurt my back in the gym and ruined any chance of working construction again. All I had was my reputation, some connections from my days with the Gambino crew, some street smarts, but not enough sense to avoid the crazy shit that could put me away again.

So, what am I doing standing behind a counter selling dog and cat food, leashes and collars? That's the question some of my best friends asked me.

Ralph Salzano: "The fuck are you gonna do in a pet store?"

"It's not a pet store," I told him. "It's a boutique."

"The fuck is that?"

"I don't know, don't break my balls."

"You should've opened a gay bar," Fat George DiBello told me, but he was purposely breaking them. He knew about my gay-bar conversation with Lena and was having some fun at my expense.

"How about I open your head?" I said.

"What are you, a Dogfella now?" Mike Murphy said.

Fat George broke into hysterics. I flipped Mike the bird.

Whatever was going on in my head, it was keeping me straight, and there was no denying the fact that I looked forward to seeing Bruno every morning. I still felt like shit when I had to leave him behind at night, so either I was turning soft in the brain or the heart. I wasn't sure which, but I wound up making Bruno his own little Murphy bed after the store opened, so he felt special when he was left alone for the night.

By the third week of business, I was getting into the routine of going to the store to work instead of some bar to get drunk. I was still selling cocaine and steroids, but I wasn't taking big risks. Bruno and the store came first. I was becoming an animal lover without knowing it.

Still, after a few months, we were a new business, and I was as clueless about the operation as I would've been trying to fly a rocket ship. Right around then, a guy from the neighborhood approached me with a litter of beagles. He said, "Put them in the window and we'll split the money."

What the hell did I know? I saw a score, so I put the beagle puppies in a cage in the window. I sold two of them before the end of the day for a nice profit—a lot more than we were making selling leashes and collars.

Nice, I thought. Maybe this business was a good idea after all.

The next day I decided we should have some curtains on the windows to keep out the light when the sun was too bright for the pups, so I went to a local fabric store. De Crescenzo Bros. had been on Thirteenth Avenue forever. I walked in and told them about my new store, that I had beagle puppies for sale, and that I wanted to provide them some shade, and so on. The attractive middle-aged woman behind the counter told me that her son was a veterinarian. *Great*, I thought. *Maybe he could give me a few pointers.*

A few days later, her son showed up at The Diamond Collar and introduced himself. Dr. Salvatore Pernice, trained in Milan, Italy, a *paisano* (countryman). What could be better? Dr. Pernice belonged to the Brooklyn Veterinary Group (BVG) over on Seventy-seventh Street and New Utrecht Avenue, just a few blocks away. He asked me what I intended to do when the puppies I was selling became sick.

"I don't know," I told him. "Take them to you, I guess. You or somebody like you."

He shook his head. "You won't do that," he said.

I was confused. "Why not?"

"Because you'll be out of business in three months."

Still clueless about where he was going, I said, "What do you mean? How?"

"It's too expensive," he said. "You'll do what most pet stores do. You'll put the sick animals down."

I became angry. "The fuck are you talkin' about?" I said.

"Think about it," he said. "One puppy gets sick, they all do. Whether it's kennel cough or canine parvovirus type 2, once one dog has it, they'll all get it. And it isn't cheap to treat the animals once they have it. Frankly, a lot of pet-store owners will send the dogs back to the puppy mill they bought them from, and there they'll just put the dogs down. It's cheaper than treatment."

I was shocked. "You're kidding me."

Dr. Pernice shook his head. "It's what they do. If they're in it for business . . . "

I immediately remembered the piece-of-shit veterinarian who refused to treat Bruno without a credit card he could charge. He was all about business, too.

"That's insane," I said. "I'd never do that."

"You keep selling puppies, you'll have to. Either that or go out of business."

I lifted Bruno up to the counter and told him how we'd saved him. Dr. Pernice looked the dog over and said, "He was abused."

"Yeah, and I only wish I could find the scumbag did that to his jaw and return the favor."

"Listen, you went into your pocket to save an abandoned dog, you obviously love animals. Don't sell the puppies. Do something else. Puppy mills are in business because people don't realize how these dogs are treated. You'd get sick if you ever visited one."

And that's all I needed to stop selling animals. We sold the rest of the beagles and hoped to hell that the people who bought them would treat them right. I gave the local guy half the money for the litter and that was it—we were out of the pet-selling business. When I returned home later the same day and explained what had happened to Lena, she was impressed. She could tell that Salvatore Pernice hadn't become a veterinarian to make money. He was a true animal lover. I didn't know it then, but that day was the start of a friendship I will forever treasure. We can never repay Dr. Pernice for his generosity, time, and skill, but we both, Lena and I, hold him dearest in our hearts. He is a truly beautiful man.

The next two-plus months I was up earlier than usual, but it was only to get to the store and hang out with Bruno. It was a blast to spend the day with him. If we weren't in the store together, I was taking him for walks. Even when the occasional asshole would make a wisecrack about Bruno's crooked jaw or the way he sometimes had to stop and take a rest before moving again, I remained proud to have him at my side.

I probably became a bit too protective, because sometimes the wisecracks got to me. Bruno's jaw remained misaligned because the scumbag who'd abused him had let it set that way. I could care less about how he looked. He was my dog, so when somebody was ballsy enough to make a comment I could hear, I'd wheel on them and either confront them directly or shoot them my best death stare—the one I used to use to shake down a slow pay when I collected for shylocks and bookmakers.

Then one day when some punks were hanging out on Thirteenth Avenue trying to look tough, one of them said something about "that ragged-ass dog," but it was a little too loud for me to ignore.

I walked over to him and said, "I could make your face look a lot worse and it won't take longer than it takes this dog to take a shit. How about that, tough guy?"

He nearly choked trying to apologize, "Sa-sa-sorry, mister."

I was too pissed off to leave it there. "Fuck you," I said, then watched his Adam's apple bob as he swallowed.

I finished walking Bruno and made damn sure to pick him up and kiss his head a dozen times when we were on our way back to the store. If that punk had half a brain, he learned a valuable lesson; to keep his wisecracks to himself. I knew he'd remember me and Bruno for the rest of his life, and putting a little fear into his life might've kept him from being a jerkoff in the future. Frankly, I could care less what happened to him down the road. I'd stood up for my dog and that's all I cared about.

When I told Lena what happened, she suggested letting someone else walk Bruno, but there was no way that was going to happen.

"And suppose you get into a fight with somebody?" she said. "Then what? You get arrested again and what happens then?"

She made sense, but I wasn't about to let anybody abuse Bruno in whatever way possible ever again. I had his back 100 percent.

As for the loudmouths who got their rocks off making fun of Bruno, fuck them. I wouldn't piss on those assholes if they were on fire.

Fortunately, that was as bad as it got. Maybe the punks spread the word to leave the ugly dog alone, especially if the big guy with the tattoos was walking him. Who knows and who cares?

I didn't have a trained eye to know when or if Bruno was feeling sick. Most days he seemed lively and full of steam. He always greeted me when I opened the store with his tail wagging from excitement. I'd pick him up and he'd kiss me like he hadn't seen me in years. Then he'd stay right alongside me while I sat behind the counter. To me he was fine. On the days when he seemed a little less enthusiastic, I chalked it up to Bruno having a bad day. People had good and bad days all the time, and I assumed Bruno was no different.

On Memorial Day 2006, I opened the store, but Bruno wasn't there to greet me.

I ran to the back of the store, and there he was lying on the little Murphy bed I had built for him. All the treats I'd left him the night before remained untouched. I knew something was wrong. Bruno could barely look at me when I got down on all fours.

"Bruno?" I said. "Hey, buddy."

His tail barely wagged. He managed to stick his tongue out just enough to let me know he was trying to kiss me, but I became terrified that he was dying. I called Lena and asked her to find a veterinary hospital. She reminded me that it was Memorial Day.

"Shit," I said. "There has to be someplace open."

"Manhattan," she said. "I'll call and find out."

"Call me when you know," I told her. "I'll head into the city in the meantime."

I picked Bruno up and ran out to my car. Lena called me back as I pulled onto the Brooklyn-Queens Expressway. She gave me the name and address of the Fifth Avenue Veterinary Specialists on Fifteenth Street. I drove like a madman into Manhattan, then ran lights until I pulled up and double-parked in front of the place. It took me less than fifteen minutes from the time Lena called me with the address.

Lena had also called the office before I got there with Bruno. The people were great. A technician took Bruno into an examination room and a female doctor gave him her immediate attention. She told me it would take a few hours and recommended leaving Bruno overnight. I called Lena, but she didn't like the idea of leaving Bruno.

"I don't want him to stay with strangers," Lena told me. "He was abandoned once. Not again."

I hadn't thought about it that way, but once Lena said it, I agreed. There was no way I was leaving Bruno with anybody. If anything, I'd spend the night with him. Lena told me to pick her up while they examined Bruno. I headed back to Brooklyn to get Lena, then raced back to Manhattan. I was there and back within forty minutes.

This time when the doctor approached us, she said, "He's very sick. You really should let him spend the night here."

"No way," Lena said. "Either he's coming home with us, or we'll stay here."

I paid the bill for $400 in cash. It included medicines and a number of tests that suggested he was in a bad way, but I agreed with Lena and didn't want him left with strangers. I took Bruno out to the car and as soon as I sat behind the wheel, he projectile vomited all over the place. The dashboard, steering wheel, seats, carpeting, and my clothes were covered with Bruno's vomit. I held him up, but Bruno went limp in my hands. Lena was screaming. I thought he was dead.

I ran back inside the veterinary office with Bruno against my chest. My sweat suit was covered with vomit as I handed Bruno back to the technicians.

"Please call the doctor," I said. "My dog is dying."

Another hour of waiting drove me insane. My stomach was in knots. I couldn't stop seeing Bruno limp in my hands. I could still feel his lifelessness. It felt like the day my brother Joseph suffered a massive heart attack. Four of us were waiting to use the bathroom when he clutched his chest and dropped to the floor. All of us gasped, but the look on my mother's face was pure horror.

If I closed my eyes, I saw Bruno's limp body in my hands. If I kept them closed too long, I saw my mother's face, the face of a parent watching her child die.

I jumped out of my seat when the doctor finally came out to the reception area. Bruno was still in the examination room.

"Mr. Guiliani," she said, "your dog is in a very bad way. He needs to spend the night here."

I pulled out the cash I was holding, about $2,000. I set it on the reception desk. "Here," I said. "Take it all. I'll go get more if you need it. Just tell me that my dog is going to be okay. Tell me that and I'll give you whatever you want. Just don't lie to me. Please don't lie to me."

The doctor frowned, looked up at me, and shook her head. Compassion replaced business. She took a moment. I could see her eyes well up, and I felt a sudden hollowness in my chest.

"What would you do if this was your dog?" I said. "Please, tell me the truth."

"I'd let him go," she said. "He might not last the night."

Tears poured from my eyes. I managed to thank her for being honest. Then I told Lena and she agreed that we shouldn't let Bruno suffer.

A few minutes later, I was led into the examination room. Bruno was in another room I could see through a glass partition. As soon as he saw me, he stood up and his tail wagged, as if nothing was wrong. He was excited to see me. He had life in his eyes again.

He must've thought he was going home. I felt an immediate resurgence of hope. How could I let him go now?

"No way," I said to the doctor. "Look how happy he is."

She didn't say anything. She looked down at the floor instead.

Then I was in the room with him and as I picked him up, I could feel him go lifeless again. He was looking up at me, trying his best to lick, but whatever energy he had left in his tiny body had been expended when he first saw me.

Still, I wanted to believe he was okay.

"Are you sure?" I asked the doctor.

She nodded. I held him tight against my chest as the tears began to flow from my eyes again. I'd never felt so guilty about anything in my life. Ten weeks ago, Lena and I had rescued Bruno. Now I'd have to be his executioner.

I was hurting in places I didn't know I could hurt. My head was pounding, my chest was empty, my stomach was in cramps, and I could barely breathe from crying so hard.

The doctor gave me a few minutes alone-time with Bruno before she returned to administer the sedative. Then she gave him the Sodium Pentothal. When I felt his breathing stop, I let out a growl from somewhere deep in my soul, a primitive howl of rage.

It was over. Bruno was gone.

There was a brief argument about what to do with his body, but there was no way I wasn't taking him home with me. I wrapped him in his blanket and returned to my car. It was a two-month-old white Cadillac STS with a white-leather interior, but now the dashboard and front seats were stained with Bruno's vomit and blood. I could care less.

We drove straight to the store where Bruno had lived. As I approached the front door and realized he would no longer be wagging his tail on the other side of the glass, that I was carrying his body, another growl erupted from my chest. It took me another few minutes to compose myself, but then I took him into the back of the store and groomed his body.

Bruno had been treated like shit most of his life, abused and abandoned for who knows how long before we found him tied to that parking meter. I had treated him with dignity when he was alive and I would do the same now that he was gone. I was crying the entire time I washed him. Sweat mixed with my stupid hairspray and stung my eyes. Lena and her mother were talking to me, but I couldn't hear them. I was lost in a kind of grief I'd never experienced before.

I dried him with a towel and then wrapped him in his blanket. I can still picture him wrapped in his blanket. It still haunts my dreams.

After I removed his collar and leash, I completely broke down. I had dropped to my knees and was pulling at my hair.

"Why!" I yelled. "What the fuck did he ever do to anybody?"

Lena and her mother tried to console me, but it was no use. I needed to expel my rage. Later Lena would tell me that I growled so loud at one point, she had to take a step back.

Eventually I was composed enough to head outside to the yard behind the store. I searched for a shovel, but there was none to be found. I had to dig Bruno's grave with a stick.

For all he'd been through, I wanted his burial to be more than digging a hole and shoving him inside. This poor dog had brought nothing but joy to my life. I did my best to provide him with an extra dose of dignity and honor. For all his suffering, Bruno deserved a king's burial. I was on my knees sniffling the entire time I dug the hole. I evened out the bottom of his grave with my hands. I even smoothed the sides, wiping the dirt off on my tracksuit pants before picking Bruno up.

Placing his blanket-wrapped body in the grave was pure torture. I must've held onto him a good ten minutes while praying that his next life be a happy one. After I said my last good-bye, I kissed his head one more time, and then set him in his grave.

Still crying, I covered Bruno's remains with the dirt I'd dug up earlier. When the grave was filled, I smoothed out the dirt again with my hands. Then I hung my head and repeated the three prayers my mother had made her kids say every night before bed: a Hail Mary, an Our Father, and an Act of Contrition. It was an odd moment, because my mother had died earlier the same year. She'd lived just sixty-six years, and just like my father, Mom never had the chance to see her son live a sober life.

It would take a few more months before my total transformation took place, but Bruno had touched my heart the way nobody in my life ever could: not my mother, whom I loved with all my heart, nor my father, who had prayed to his dying day for me to stop hurting myself.

That night when I finally made it to bed, Lena was trying her best to console me as I hung Bruno's leash and collar on the wall alongside his "Stud" shirt beside our bed. It's all still there.

Lena hugged me when my body started to heave again. I turned to her, then pointed at the bedroom door.

"What?" she said.

"Get Brock."

And then she was crying, but I knew they were happy tears.

The next few weeks I was numb to everything. I was still hurting. I couldn't stop thinking about Bruno. Working at the store every day made it impossible to get through the day without crying. I was a six-two, 240-pound, ex-con, mush. I was useless.

I knew it was a matter of time before I fell off the wagon, and I was more than willing to use Bruno's death as an excuse to escape reality. It wasn't that I was thinking about getting high or drunk, but I knew they were options. It was the simple street math of any addict's ability to live in denial: get high or drunk and forget all your troubles.

Lena did her best to keep me from losing it. She called me at the store sometimes twenty times a day to make sure I was keeping it together. She went out of her way to spend extra time with me when I was home. She rented a dozen movie videos at a time, and we'd watch two or three in a row, except sometimes I'd cry in the middle of a movie that I didn't have a clue about because I was thinking of Bruno.

On July 9, 2006, Italy won the World Cup, and the neighborhood went crazy. Every Italian was suddenly a super-nationalist. Italian flags flew from stanchions, flagpoles, and some were hung from windows. I was Italian and proud of it, but I could care less about soccer or any other sport. For me, Italy winning the World Cup was just an excuse to party.

If I was alone and could think straight, I thought about Bruno and fell into a funk of depression. If I did a few lines or drank a bottle of vodka, I was oblivious to everything and anything.

So, as the neighborhood celebrated Italy's World Cup championship, I remained in a funk. My Bruno was still dead. There was one more stage to my redemption, but I wasn't ready for it. Not yet. I couldn't get past losing Bruno so soon.

I was about to fall off the wagon. I would fall hard.

Very hard.

Chapter 2

Growing Up James "Head" Guiliani

In 1967, the United States ramped up its war in Vietnam, Muhammad Ali refused military service, Elvis married Priscilla, and on May 20, Maryann and Big Lou Guiliani added a fifth kid to their expanding brood. I was the fourth of five boys, and probably the last of the Guiliani planned pregnancies. Our youngest brother, Thomas, would come along seven years later. He was the kid we joke about being Maryann and Big Lou's love child.

Mom was twenty-nine years old when she had me. Dad was two years older. Once Thomas arrived in 1974, we were an even half dozen; five boys and one girl. Maryann and Big Lou didn't believe in wasting time: Louis was born in 1959, Joseph (Nipper) in 1960, and Anthony in 1961. Our sister, Dorothy, arrived in 1964.

Both my parents were proud second-generation Americans. Mom was of German descent and Dad's family was Italian. The German-Italian mix was sometimes volatile, but each of our parents had a deep respect for the other, and nobody, family or friend, could ever come between them.

Typical of the neighborhood where we lived in Richmond Hill, Queens, New York, we were a blue-collar, Catholic family. Our three-bedroom, one-bath, one-family colonial was my parents' American dream. Our block was made up of detached one- and two-family homes with no more room than a driveway or walking space between them. There were trees scattered around the block, some in front of the homes, others in backyards. The back of Richmond Hill High School was around the corner on 113th

Street, the entrance was on 114th Street. The Holy Child Jesus School, which we all attended, was nearby on Eighty-sixth Avenue.

Richmond Hill was a tough but tight-knit neighborhood. People knew their neighbors and watched out for one another. Families that had carved out their slice of the American pie were protective of their turf and suspicious of strangers. Most of the homes sported laundry lines in backyards, unlocked front and back doors, stoop sitting on hot summer nights, garbage cans that had to be moved to the curb on pick-up days, and American flags that were hung from windows and flagpoles on national holidays.

Also characteristic of the neighborhood were Italian grandmothers, seemingly forever in mourning, dressed in black. Lace mantillas covered their heads while they attended daily mass or waited on line to say confession. What they could possibly confess, nobody knew.

Parish priests were revered as well as feared. Parents were never called by their first names, especially not by kids. They were either Mr. or Mrs. So-and-So, and there was no such thing as backtalk to an adult, not without suffering a consequence.

Our block was a microcosm of our neighborhood. Homes were owned by second- and third-generation working-class Irish and Italian Catholics, and most of those families were large enough to field their own sports teams. We had a Brown family as next-door neighbors, and a Brown family across the street. The kids for both Brown families totaled thirteen. There were also the Mauros and Abbruzzinos, and the Gallahue families. And these were all small armies compared to the national average of 3.28 persons per household back then.

Kids shared beds, and most families, like ours, shared a single bathroom. Grandparents often lived with their kids and grandchildren. Senior citizens in Richmond Hill didn't snowbird down to Florida come winter.

At dinnertime, kids were called in to sit at the table to eat as a family. We ate a lot of macaroni and whatever cheap cut of meat Mom could stretch into a dinner for eight. Money was tight, but we always had enough to survive.

The political turmoil of the late 1960s and early 1970s wasn't a big deal to families living in Richmond Hill. Unless someone's son was drafted into the war, nobody discussed it. People were busy surviving. There was church, the local gossip, and the day-to-day struggle of trying to do the best with what they had.

Our house at 87-87 112th Street was our parents' pride and joy. Big Lou's hard work as a union carpenter, including all the overtime he could work and never taking a sick day, along with Maryann's dogged persistence in maintaining her household, kept us with a roof over our heads and food on our table.

The six of us kids were spread around the house. Louis, Nipper, and Anthony shared the attic. Dorothy had her own bedroom in the basement, and I was in the middle room on the second floor. By the time Thomas needed his own room, Louis had already joined the army, and so we shifted—Thomas got the middle room and I was relocated to the attic in place of Louis. We all shared a single first-floor bathroom with our parents—prime real estate, especially in the morning.

Of course, during the summer months, the living-room became the primary bedroom for everyone in our family, including when friends slept over. It was the only room in our house with an air conditioner.

The rush for the bathroom on school days was always intense. We were lucky our father was out of the house at dawn. Being the only girl in the mix, Dorothy was usually the first to occupy the bathroom. The rest of us suffered the wait for her to finish.

Once Dorothy had finally emerged from the bathroom and was on her way, it became total chaos. There was no real chance of privacy, especially once we were older. Multi-use of the bathroom became a necessity, although it often appeared more like a Ringling Brothers act. More than a few times Louis would be showering while Nipper was on the throne, Anthony was shaving, and I was in line—a step ahead of Thomas, once he was old enough to use the bathroom.

It was outside that same bathroom that our family was devastated on March 11, 1985. Nipper, waiting his turn to use the bathroom, suffered a fatal heart attack. He'd already served his country in the US Army and had been working construction since he returned home. He was twenty-four when he died.

It was a frantic scene at the house. My mother screamed at God to spare her son while my brother Louis tried his best to perform CPR. I ran to the corner and pulled the fire alarm, but by the time the fire department emergency team arrived, Nipper was already dead. It was a tragedy from which our family would never recover. Everyone had witnessed Nipper's death except Anthony, who was in Camp Lejeune with the marines. I was eighteen at the time.

Anthony flew home for the wake and funeral, but I know he never got over being away when Nipper died. Nipper's sudden death devastated both our parents. Mom could barely get herself up in the mornings and began to drink heavily. Dad became a shell of himself and seemed to go through the motions of living from day to day.

Nipper's sudden death also put my father on constant alert. He'd literally practice running out to the car and driving to Jamaica Hospital as fast as he could, timing himself the entire drive, just in case tragedy struck a second time. Big Lou was haunted by Nipper's death. The thought that my brother might've lived had he received the proper treatment sooner than the time it had taken the fire department to get to our house kept him awake nights. Deep down, I think Dad knew it wouldn't have made a difference, but I suspect he lived with a ton of unwarranted guilt over not having been able to help his son.

Nipper's was the first death I'd ever witnessed. He was special to me, and I can still remember lying in bed waiting for him to call me downstairs to watch one of our favorite television shows, *The Honeymooners*. A month after his funeral, I still couldn't believe he was gone. To this day, every time I watch an episode of *The Honeymooners*, I'm reminded of the laughs we all used to share around the television, with all of us saying the lines along with Ralph and Norton. Even Dorothy would occasionally join in and run Alice's lines, along with Audrey Meadows.

My best memories from our shared youth on 112th Street come from a dozen or so years before Nipper's fatal heart attack; when we were playing board games on the floor in front of the television or wrestling in the living room, or when my brothers would pull a sneak attack and try to feed me one of our grandmother's dirty stockings.

Before I learned what was coming, they'd often catch me daydreaming while watching television. I was about eight years old at the time, and the three of them worked as a team. I'd be sitting on the living-room floor staring at the television. Nipper, Anthony, and Louis would be on the couch behind me. I was oblivious as I waited for a particular scene I'd watched a dozen times already, like when Ralph Kramden was about to slap the egg timer and call Alice's mother a blabbermouth. It was my favorite *Honeymooners* episode.

"James, you hungry?" Nipper would ask.

Usually I didn't answer because all my attention was focused on the show.

"Hey, James!" Louis would yell. "Hungry or not?"

"Huh?" I'd finally say.

"You want something to eat?" Anthony would ask.

And then before I could answer, they'd be on top of me, Nipper holding my arms, Anthony holding my legs, and Louis feeding me one of our grandmother's dirty socks.

It would happen again another dozen times before I smartened up and ran up the stairs as soon as anybody but my mother asked if I was hungry. It wasn't that my brothers were into torture, but it was a rite of passage in the Guiliani house. Thomas had arrived the year before, so I was no longer the baby of the family. From the day Thomas turned one year old, it was open season on James.

If eating dirty socks didn't provide enough entertainment, my brothers found other ways to break my chops. I had a big noggin for a kid and my brothers never let me forget it.

"Hey, James, move that planet out of the way, nobody can see the friggin' TV!" one of them would yell.

"How do you hold that thing on your neck?" another would say.

Fortunately, my mother would come to the rescue and reassure me that the rest of me would eventually fill out; that my oversized melon would eventually look normal. Mom was always protective of whoever was catching the shit, but sometimes my father couldn't help laughing at my brothers' comments.

"James, your head is so big you have to step into your clothes in the morning."

"James, your clothes ever get wet when it rains? Your head must be like a friggin' umbrella."

"You must have a strong fuckin' neck to hold that thing up."

"James, you don't have a forehead, you have an eight head."

My father especially enjoyed a comment made after someone praised me for something, like getting a rare good grade from school.

"Hey, James, now don't get a big head about it," one of my brothers would say, sending my father into hysterics.

Eventually the moniker stuck and my nickname became "Head." Although I was still James to my parents and to my teachers at school, on the streets I became Head for the next forty-plus years.

School mornings were always hectic in our house, especially when it was time to get dressed. It was up to Mom to keep the bathroom line moving. If she saw we were running late, out came the thick piece of rubber hose. A swift whack on the backside was a warning. The whacks climbed up our backs pretty fast afterward.

And if it was my turn to catch one while we were in the bathroom, the inevitable wisecrack was uttered.

"James, stick your head in the door and block Mom from coming in."

My mother didn't have it easy. Even while Thomas was young, the rest of us were a lot to handle. Between the energy four young boys could produce, the mayhem that followed, and with Dorothy yelling at all of us to leave her alone, Mom had her hands full. That said, there was never any doubt that Mom was the enforcer during the day, especially while our father was at work. Mom not only carried that thick piece of rubber around, she enforced the religious code in our house with extreme prejudice. We were never to use the Lord's name in vain, not ever. It could be 15° outside, but if one of us was foolish enough to say "Goddamn it" or "Jesus Christ," she'd chase us with that thick piece of rubber and we'd end up out on the street for at least a few hours, sometimes without our coats, unless we could snatch them on the way out the front door.

Mom also made us say three prayers before bed each night: an Our Father, a Hail Mary, and an Act of Contrition. She made sure we were at mass every single day of the week, year-round, all 365 days of the year. And if that wasn't enough, each one of her five sons had to become an altar boy. We had to learn the Latin prayers and serve at mass from the time we reached the fifth grade until we graduated.

James "Head" Guiliani an altar boy? Thirty-eight years down the road, with a history that includes a stint with the notorious Gotti crew, it's still hard to imagine.

When it came to school, all of us boys screwed up from time to time, and there was always a price to pay when we did. Punishment in the Guiliani house, after getting whacked with the thick piece of rubber, meant no television or games, and no going outside. It wasn't exactly a prison sentence, but it was a form of torture for me, a kid with what today I assume they'd label ADHD. Back then I had the attention span of a flea and zero interest in school. I liked goofing off and making people laugh. Whether I was a kid with ADHD or just a class clown, I was definitely in need of discipline.

Enter Big Lou, because it wasn't just my mother who meted out discipline in the Guiliani house. My father was a quiet man, but he could get crazy in a heartbeat if pushed too far. Sometimes his five sons weren't sharp enough to realize when they'd gone too far and poked the bear. Big Lou could make all of us weak at the knees with just a simple angry stare.

My father was a hard worker, and as I said, he took as much overtime as he could find to pay the freight for his family. He went to work every day, healthy or sick, and he never complained about his job or the dull routine that consumed his short life. Taking care of us was his responsibility and he never shied away from it.

Dad's favorite saying, especially after one of us broke something in the house that had to be replaced, was: "You know how many nails I had to hammer today to pay for that lamp?"

Some days it was a lamp. Some days it was a picture frame, a glass, a cup, a dish, or whatever else we broke horsing around and wrestling with each other. Each of us caught one of Dad's favorite lines sooner or later. "You half-wit, pea brain. You donkey crumb."

Probably his most uttered line when we were making a racket upstairs was the ominous, "Don't make me come up there."

Usually once we heard that threat, we quieted down.

Dad had another side to him that had to do with getting things done. He'd always been a pragmatic person. "Do what you gotta do, even if it's wrong," he'd sometimes say. It wasn't that he was promoting criminal activity, but it did have to do with not letting people take advantage of us. People who grew up in different environments than ours might not understand the advice, but ours was a competitive blue-collar neighborhood that often required aggressiveness. And let's face it, some kids take parental advice differently from others. All four of my older brothers sowed some wild oats, but however wild they were through their teen years, they each joined and served in the military. I was the black sheep, the one who never adjusted to a legitimate life. I was the one who stayed with street gangs and worked for the mob. I was the one who turned to drugs and alcohol, things Big Lou Guiliani never approved of.

I was twenty-three years old when my father died in 1990. I'd already been involved with two different gangs, the Gambino-Gotti crew and our 112 Nutso Park street gang. I was also a drug addict and well on my way toward my advanced degree in alcoholism. By the end of the same year my father died, I'd be arrested on gun charges, sentenced to prison, and later divorced while I was inside. It remains a continual source of pain for me that my father died long before I straightened out my life.

All the Guiliani kids attended the Holy Child Jesus School in Richmond Hill. My mother insisted on us receiving a Catholic-school education. It was an expensive proposition that required our father to put in all those extra hours at work. Nothing was to be taken for granted growing up, yet I seemed to go out of my way to do so.

My older brothers weren't angels, but none of them caused our mother half as much grief and aggravation as I did. Probably from the day I started school until the day she passed away, my mother was worried about what would eventually happen to me.

My best friend going back to forever was Ralph Salzano. I've known Ralph since kindergarten, when we officially met the first day of class at Public School 90. The school had been robbed the night before, so there were police cars all over the place. While most of the kids waited for instructions in the school yard about what to do next, I snuck into the building and grabbed all our kindergarten snacks, then climbed out onto the short roof so we'd have them at recess. Ralph thought it was cool that I'd saved our snacks, and we became best friends that day.

Over the next few years, Ralph and I became the nucleus of what the school labeled "The Troublemakers." There was me, Ralph, Mike Murphy, and Kevin Rooney. Ralph had the brains. I had the muscle. Murphy was a goofball who would laugh at anything we did. Kevin was okay with whatever we did and was a loyal follower. If there was an organizational chart like the ones the FBI uses to identify the leadership of organized crime families today, ours would've looked like this:

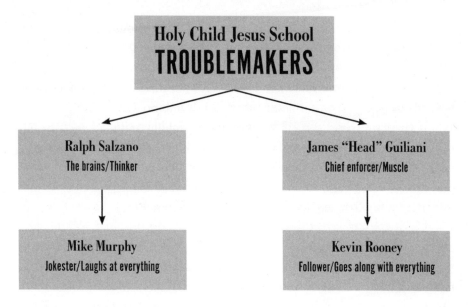

The guys in our tiny crew were best friends and partners in all forms of petty crimes and general school mischief. Over time, the four of us built a reputation as an unholy quartet at the Holy Child Jesus School. We were always getting into trouble and were watched everywhere we went. No matter what was going on in school, there was always an extra set of eyes spying Guiliani, Salzano, Murphy, and Rooney. I can remember feeling their gaze when we walked into the school, all during recess and lunch, and then again when we left the building after school ended. And if the four of us happened to turn a corner in the hallway and walk into one of our teachers, the first words out of that teacher would be, "And what are you four up to now?"

We could've been on our way to confession and they would've asked us the same thing.

"What are you four up to now?"

There were a few teachers at the Holy Child Jesus School who seemed to go out of their way to screw with us. This was a time when nuns were becoming scarce as teachers, so we mostly had lay teachers. Ms. O'Toole, Ms. Hamill, Ms. Bartoldus, and Ms. Spiro seemed to take the most joy in our punishment, and the most popular form of punishment at the Holy Child Jesus School was having students stand under the clock in the main hallway. It was the most boring and embarrassing thing in the world. Instead of detentions where you could sit in a classroom, we were put on display under the clock for hours on end. Sometimes we'd have to keep our hands raised over our heads or out to the sides. If what we did pissed off the wrong teacher, we'd have to hold books in our hands.

If there's a world record for standing under that clock, I own it, but Ralph, Mike, and Kevin were close seconds. If I wasn't standing under the clock, I was visiting Mother Superior in her office. There I might catch anywhere from five to ten whacks across the knuckles with a ruler before earning some extra smacks from my mother if she was called to pick me up.

Usually it was at recess where we found the most mischief. While most of the other guys played sports of some kind—baseball, football, or basketball—the four of us would do our best to impress the girls in our class. Smoking was one way to look and act cool, but smoking anywhere near the school was dangerous, especially for us. Sneaking them into school was also dangerous, but lighting up at recess with teachers patrolling the school yard was the ultimate challenge.

If the slightest whiff of cigarette smoke hit the school yard, and it inevitably did because all four of us used to sneak smokes all the time, we four were taken out of line and strip-searched to the point of taking off our pants. It wasn't anything like sexual abuse, but it was something we learned to prepare for once we were caught stuffing cigarettes down our pants a few times.

Sometimes when we were caught smoking, we were suspended or had to serve time under the clock. The beatings we took at home were twice as bad, but mostly because our parents were embarrassed.

Eventually, between not showing up on time for mass, or not showing up for meetings, and/or getting caught a few too many times smoking in the school yard, I was kicked out of the altar boys. I wasn't heartbroken over the punishment, trust me, but my mother was disgraced.

The one thing we had going for us at the Holy Child Jesus School was a street code that extended throughout our neighborhood. Most kids didn't snitch. It was a matter of honor to keep things to ourselves. The few snitches who were around were immediately ostracized by the rest of us, usually after a beating.

How we eventually got around the strip searches was by asking one of the girls who enjoyed our special brand of classroom entertainment to hide our cigarettes for us. From that day on, we had smokes whenever we wanted them.

And the look on Ms. Spiro's face every time she didn't find anything after a strip search was priceless.

"What, did you eat them?" she said to me one day.

Although all four of us would fight anyone who challenged us, we weren't bullies. In fact, there was one kid who was deemed an outcast by the rest of the school, a nerdish but artistic kid we were all sure would make it big someday. Joe Valli was short and quiet, and he usually kept to himself because most of the other kids wanted nothing to do with him. Sometimes kids a grade ahead of us would pick on Joe in the school yard or in the hallways, bumping into him and knocking him down, or just peppering him with spitballs.

The teachers could call us whatever they wanted, but it was our unholy quartet of troublemakers that protected Joe Valli a lot more than the teachers ever did. Once we set an example and beat the shit out of two bullies from the eighth grade when we caught them pushing Joe in the school yard. From that day forward, if anyone picked on Joe Valli, they had to deal with us.

The day Ms. O'Toole picked on Joe in class, I went out of my way to crack jokes and make her crazy. She'd been extra mean to Joe that day, calling him a little jerk. The poor kid seemed to shrink a size smaller behind his desk. I wanted to make fun of her the same way, by picking on her shape.

Ms. O'Toole was not an attractive woman. In certain clothes, she could pass for a small refrigerator. The day she picked on Joe, every time she turned her back to the class to write something on the blackboard, I stood up, puffed out my cheeks, and did an exaggerated walk, as if I were a refrigerator with legs. I took just a few steps toward the front, then backed up quick and sat again as soon as the class started laughing, a moment before Ms. O'Toole turned around.

Of course her eyes went to me first, then Mike Murphy because he couldn't stop laughing. Then she'd look to Ralph, who was probably still smirking, and finally at Kevin, because he was probably smiling ear to ear. I did my impersonation once, twice, three times, and eventually I was caught when Ms. O'Toole turned her back, started to write, and then quickly spun around just as I was putting my arms out to my sides and puffing my cheeks.

Needless to say she went crazy.

"You may think you're being cute, Mr. Guiliani," she yelled, "but what you are is a selfish little brat. You're taking time away from your classmates who are here to learn. I'm getting pretty sick and tired of your antics, you and your gang of four. I don't know what your parents think of you, but you make every teacher here sick to their stomachs. If you can't control yourself, maybe another day under the clock is what you need."

Bringing my parents into it embarrassed me pretty bad. It was the first time I didn't have a comeback. I asked if I could be excused and she went off again.

"Good God, you're impossible," she yelled. "Did your mother drop you on your head when you were a baby? Fine, go to the bathroom. You're excused. It's not as if you're going to learn anything anyway. Your mother knew what she was doing when she sent you here for us to babysit her little brat."

Once again her mentioning my mother embarrassed me. I wound up running to the bathroom to hide my shame. I was too embarrassed to return to class from fear of what she'd say next, so I hunkered down in one of the stalls and figured I'd wait until class was over. About fifteen minutes passed and then Ralph came into the bathroom looking for me. He could see I was still upset. He had this big smile on his face and said, "I'll handle this."

A few minutes later, I could hear Ms. O'Toole outside the boys' room completely frantic. "Oh, my God!" she kept saying. "Oh, my God!"

When I stepped out of the room, she looked like she'd faint. "You were in there?" she yelled.

For whatever reason, I couldn't resist the obvious comeback. "When you gotta go, you gotta go," I said.

I thought she was going to kill me. By the time she calmed down, she'd already marched Ralph and me to Mother Superior's office by our ears. We spent the rest of the day in the main hallway under the clock. On the way, I asked Ralph why the hell she was so crazy.

"I went back inside the class and sniffled," he said. "I told her I think she pushed you too far this time. The bathroom window was open and I thought you jumped."

Of course I couldn't stop laughing after he told me, which was almost a capital offense when you're standing under the clock, but the two of us had to suppress our giggles for almost three hours before school finally ended.

It was not just Ms. O'Toole who suffered my discretions. A few days later, we were learning about various rock formations and minerals in Ms. Bartoldus's class. The only rocks I knew about were the ones we'd pick up outside and throw at each other. Our assignment was to go home and dig up the rarest rock we could find, and then bring it back to class the next day. This was Richmond Hill where we lived, not some archeology dig in Montana someplace. I thought it was about the dumbest thing in the world to go look for rare rocks, so instead of digging for rocks that afternoon, I tagged along after my brother Anthony and his friends. They hung out in Forest Park and had already graffiti-tagged the handball and basketball courts. I wanted to be with them, not shoveling up rocks in our backyard.

The next morning, Ralph saw me outside Marty and Loretta's candy store on Jamaica Avenue, and he asked me if I remembered to bring a rock to class.

"I'm getting it now," I said, then proceeded to go inside the candy store and buy a few green Jolly Rancher candies.

Ms. Bartoldus wasn't much impressed when I stood up and told her it was a fine piece of quartz that I'd found. She told me to sit down and be quiet, but I received a pretty good laugh from the class. The laugh was a lot louder a few minutes later when she turned her back to us to write something on the blackboard and a piece of mostly chewed, green Jolly Rancher candy stuck to the back of her sweater.

Ralph was the only one of our junior crew who played any kind of organized sport. He joined up in the Little League every year. I tried to do the same, but every year I was rejected. I guess I wasn't an athlete. I had neither the ability nor the desire to be coached. I enjoyed goofing off way too much to get serious about anything other than becoming a member of my brother's street gang, called "112."

There's no doubt in my mind that some of the trouble I got myself into had a lot to do with the age disparities between me and my older brothers. Teachers who had dealt with Louis, Nipper, and Anthony were probably at the end of their Valium prescriptions by the time I came along. Another Guiliani boy had to be the last thing they wanted to see. Like I said, back then my attention deficit disorder was more likely labeled being a wiseass. All I knew was I hated school and loved to goof off. The class would be reading from a book and I would stare out the windows daydreaming about what to do after the final bell.

And God forbid I was asked a question.

"Mr. Guiliani, can you tell us anything about Lincoln's Gettysburg Address?"

"No," I'd say, and the class would roar.

I loved getting a laugh, and sometimes, no matter what the subject, I couldn't resist going for one. One day while we were preparing for a religious instructions final, Sister Mary Frances asked the class what were Jesus's final words on the cross. There was a handout she gave us with the first two words: "Eli Eli ___ ___." We were supposed to fill in the blanks, then read our answers aloud. The correct answer was—"Eli Eli lama sabachthani?" (My God, my God, why have you forsaken me?)

This was too much of a softball to let go, so when it was my turn, I stood up and sang (to the tune of "Old MacDonald"): "Eli Eli Ohhhhh-hhhhhh, with a Roman here and a Roman there, here a Roman, there a Roman, look at poor Jesus on a Cross, Eli Eli Ohhhhhhh!"

The shellacking I took in the class wasn't close to the one I caught later at home from my mother, not to mention that I had to stand under the clock holding two Bibles for the rest of the school day.

"What's wrong with you?" my mother yelled. "How could you make fun of something like that?"

Had she been one of my teachers, I probably would've gone for another laugh and said, "It was easy," but knowing I'd shamed her, and that there was still a tiny chance she wouldn't tell Big Lou, I apologized and kept my tail between my legs.

Toward the end of seventh grade, a kid named Andrew Benson and I pulled the dumbest stunt of our Catholic-school careers. We decided to adorn our school with our special brand of graffiti one afternoon. We waited until school was over, then hid in a closet. Nobody knew where we were or what we were up to, but we must've sat in that closet a good hour before we felt it was safe to get out. When we finally did step outside the closet, we grabbed whatever magic markers we could find and spent the next four hours writing our graffiti tags, "Head" and "Hypo," all over the classroom and hallway walls. We also carved our tags into desktops and bulletin-board frames, giving ourselves up without any need for an investigation.

We thought we were being clowns, but the next day when we showed up to school there were police cars outside the building just like the time Ralph Salzano and I first met back in kindergarten. An investigation was conducted, but it didn't take long before they singled out Andrew and me. It was a sure sign I wouldn't be a very good criminal down the road, an omen of bad things to come, no doubt.

We were suspended for an entire month, during which our parents still had to pay our tuition. That was one that didn't get by Big Lou, and the beating I took for that one still hurts. It was one thing to be a clown, it was another enchilada when your parents have to pay for your performance with hard-earned cash. That graffiti escapade cost Mary and Big Lou money they had struggled to earn.

The humiliation my school graffiti cost my mother when I was suspended wasn't to be forgotten anytime soon. Mom made me attend church every morning during my suspension, and some days she'd wait for me to come out of church just so she could beat me with that thick piece of rubber all the way home. She'd start with a few quick shots to the back of my head and finish it with one hard one on my tailbone that hurt a lot more than all the head shots combined.

Not that the thick piece of rubber taught me anything, because by the eighth grade, I was pretty much a lost cause. Ralph, Mike, Kevin, and I had graduated to petty crimes like stealing candy, cigarettes, and anything else we could stash under our clothes. When we heard about a stash of soda, beer, and snacks that was locked up in the school cafeteria, it was too tempting a score for us to ignore. The goods were used for church bingo nights. I was working as a busboy at the Four Star Diner on Jamaica Avenue after school and on weekends. We decided to steal the stuff they were using for bingo and sell what we could to the diner. We'd keep the beer and snacks for ourselves, but the soda would earn us a small profit.

It was during a basketball game in a snowstorm when we made our move. A long brick hall ran between the gym and the cafeteria. Mike stood by the gym end of the hall and I stood by the cafeteria end. There was no way for us to get all the booty out of the school to somewhere safe without being seen carrying it in the streets, so Ralph and Kevin removed the goods and stashed them in the snow outside the cafeteria door in the school yard. Thank God it was deep snow. Nobody thought to look there.

The thing of it is, Kevin had a bright red Afro, but he wore a black ski cap to keep it down. It was one of the funniest things we'd ever seen, as if nobody would know who it was if he were spotted. His red hair was jutting out all over the place.

Later the same night, we went back to the school and hid the soda, beer, and snacks in a dropped ceiling inside the cafeteria. Kevin was the only one tall enough to reach up into the ceiling while standing on a desk. I can still see him with that black ski cap and his thick red Afro sticking out all around the cap.

We eventually sold the soda as planned, split the money, and kept the beer and snacks for ourselves. It was one of the few petty crimes we got away with, and it also must've registered somewhere in my oversized melon that at least sometimes crime pays.

I suspect the school couldn't wait for us to graduate or leave, but there was no way we were going out without a few more bangs. On our way to watch a basketball game at another school, we stopped to get ice cream cones. We were close to the school yard when I spotted Ms. O'Toole's small white two-door car. We decorated the windshield with our cones, making a smiley face: two eyes, a nose and a smiling mouth with the last cone, dragging it across the bottom and then turning the corners up to form the smile. Of course, the next day everyone wanted to know if we were anywhere near the scene of the crime. Ralph and Mike said they didn't know anything about it, but in my infinite wisdom, I said, "I have no idea who made the face with the vanilla cones on your windshield."

We all spent another day under the clock, and letters were sent home to our parents.

And then a few weeks before graduation, my brother Anthony and a few of his friends conned me and Ralph into making complete fools of ourselves.

"There's a way into the teachers' faculty room where they keep all the tests they're gonna give," Anthony told us. "The midterms and finals."

"You serious?" I said.

"How do you think we passed?" he said.

"How do we get in the faculty room?"

"Underneath the stage in the auditorium there's a set of tunnels. You gotta pull off one of the screens on either end of the stage, climb the ladders next to them, and then crawl inside. Just follow where they lead and you'll see where you can get inside the teachers' faculty room. Then you just go through the desks until you find the tests you want."

Suckers and cheaters that we were, first chance we had, we pulled off the gratings on the end of the stage and crawled inside. We must've spent half an hour crawling all over the place, but little did we know, we were crawling around the air ducts gathering all the dust and dirt inside them onto our school uniforms. We finally gave up when we realized we'd been set up, but neither of us thought to run home and change our clothes before the morning roll call. Everybody in the school yard was laughing at us because our clothes and hands were black from the dust and dirt. Ms. McNally, our gym teacher, thought she saw a pair of ghosts. I can still see the expression on her face when she saw us; her eyes opened wide, her eyebrows somewhere high up on her forehead. Then she started to yell at us, but it came out funny.

"What? . . . How? . . . What the hell did you two do now?" she finally said.

There was no way we could tell how or why we looked like chimney sweeps, so that day we spent the next half hour in the bathroom cleaning up, and the rest of the day under the clock.

Most eighth graders couldn't wait to graduate and move on with their lives. Me, I couldn't wait until school was over so I could chase after my brother Anthony. To prepare me for becoming one of his 112 gang, he put me through a few challenges to test my stones. I'd already learned how to rip off meat from Key Food for the 112 pit barbecues in Forest Park. Those were relatively easy because we knew which girls working the registers were girlfriends of the guys in 112. We'd go to their registers, pay for a six-pack of soda and a large bag of pretzels, then walk out with two packs of franks, two packs of hamburgers, and the buns to go with them. The girls never rang up the expensive stuff, just the cheapest items. They'd simply make it look as though they were ringing everything and bag the expensive stuff without touching the register. We'd hand them a $5 bill for $20 worth of groceries, and we'd still get some change. Big grocery chains wrote those losses into their markup, so it wasn't like we were robbing a bank. At least that's how we justified the petty thefts.

A new challenge Anthony had for me was the simple solo act of stealing a magazine from a local stationery store that refused to donate to the local Little League. Stealing something had nothing to do with teaching me to be a thief and everything to do with seeing if I had what it took to follow through with the challenge. The fact that the guy who owned the store was a cheap fuck didn't help his cause.

The day of the test, Anthony stood outside the store and watched me slip a magazine down my pants while the guy behind the register was distracted ringing up sales. I was a nervous wreck, but I couldn't show it. I grabbed a magazine without looking, stuffed it down my pants, and then waited until we were safely down the block before I pulled the thing out of my pants and handed it to my brother. When I saw Anthony's face twist with disgust, I said, "What?"

"You donkey crumb," he said. "The fuck you take this for?"

"You said get a magazine, right?"

"Yeah, a *Playboy* or *Hustler*, or something we could sell to somebody. You took *Home-and-Fucking-Garden*."

Ralph, Mike, and Kevin were with us and they couldn't stop laughing, but Anthony was pissed off. I felt like a moron, yet there was no way I could admit to being too nervous to see what I was taking. It was getting a magazine out of the place without having to pay for it that mattered to me, taking one more step toward becoming a member of 112.

A few days later, I began my own graffiti campaign in the neighborhood. I started using a variation of what I'd used in the Holy Child Jesus School. I was looking to make my mark in the neighborhood, which to me was the world. I had no idea how small that world would become over time. I spray painted "Head" or "Headbird" on everything from the Jamaica Avenue El columns to stop signs. I tagged the walls along Forest Park and the sides of storefronts that bordered parking lots. I tagged commercial vans and box trucks, industrial garage doors, and the school yard of the Holy Child Jesus School.

Unfortunately, like usual, I never considered the consequences. It was only a matter of time before my mother recognized my tag, and it was one more time I'd shame her in front of the entire neighborhood. Once more she had to answer for that wild Guiliani kid, James.

When it finally came time to graduate from the Holy Child Jesus School, guess who wasn't invited to the ceremony? Frankly, I couldn't blame them. I'd caused enough grief to be put into a juvenile detention home. The cost of my education to my parents would've been better spent about two miles away at Aqueduct Racetrack. At least there they might've gotten a return on their investment.

In any event, I received my diploma in the mail about a week after the rest of the school graduated. For whatever it was worth, I had graduated and would be attending high school in the fall.

There are two forms of education in blue-collar neighborhoods like Richmond Hill—formal and street. The first is the most common; a kid goes to school, pays attention, does well, and maybe moves on to college and/or beyond toward a profession. It's a nice, clean, legitimate way to go. Naturally, most parents push their kids toward a formal education.

My parents tried, but I opted for a street education that began early on and would last the rest of my life.

The streets are hard and unforgiving, and there are good and bad lessons to be learned on them, but they also provide a wisdom unattainable in books. How one chooses to use that wisdom is another story altogether. Early on, because my father and older brothers were in construction unions, I knew I'd follow their lead. There was no point in worrying about a professional career, not for me.

So, who needed school? It used to be a blue-collar mentality that probably still exists today; the idea that a child's career is predetermined by what his or her parents' did to earn a living.

It isn't necessarily a bad choice to go into construction or any other trade, especially those protected by unions. My brothers certainly did fine living normal blue-collar lives. The problem for me, of course, had to do with the crazy detours I'd take along the way. I wasn't looking for a degree, and I knew I'd have a union card in just a few more years.

In the meantime I worked on my street degree. It started with a class I call Street 101. Our Richmond Hill neighborhood, the high school, and Forest Park—those were my classrooms.

The early 1970s saw a tremendous surge in spray-painted graffiti in and around all five boroughs of New York City. It was about the time my brother Anthony became the official gang leader of 112, as well as the number-one graffiti artist in Queens. He used the tagline "Sike 112." Taglines were signatures for individual graffiti artists. "Sike" was popular street slang meaning "psyched out" and 112 was his gang name. The Jamaica Avenue elevated line ran through the heart of Richmond Hill, and Anthony spray painted his tag inside and outside of every Jamaica Avenue train on the line. Back then, if you rode the J train, you couldn't avoid seeing "Sike 112" spelled out in a variety of designs and colors.

Anthony was also a bodybuilder and one of the toughest kids in the neighborhood. His street reputation was solid, even before he left Richmond Hill High School and served in the marines, but he was never a bully.

Contrary to the stereotype portrayed in movies like *West Side Story*, most street gangs didn't pick on civilians. Street gangs protected their turf, usually from other street gangs, and it was rarely with weapons. Sure there were the occasional two-by-fours, baseball bats, homemade brass knuckles, and/or pocket knives brought to a gang fight, but for the most part it was skin on skin. Anthony took pride in fighting that way, bare fisted, one on one.

And more than a few times I was the direct beneficiary of his street-fighting reputation. Just having him as a brother kept me from getting picked on by older, tougher kids.

"Hey, don't fuck with Head, he's Sike's (Anthony Guiliani's) brother."

I'd heard that at least a dozen times from members of other street gangs in Richmond Hill. Nobody wanted to risk having to fuck with Anthony, not even when I did something deserving of catching a beating or two, like writing my own graffiti tags, "Head" or "Headbird," over other street-gang tags—something definitely worth a beating in Richmond Hill back when we were kids.

In time, I'd follow Anthony's lead, but only up to a point. As much of a gangster as Anthony might have been, when it was time to straighten out, he joined the US Marines and served his country. I never even thought about the military. By the time I was of age, I'd already pledged my allegiance to being a dumbski, a street guy with no future.

Before I even started high school, I wanted nothing more than to pursue being a street-gang member. Once I was out of the Holy Child Jesus School, my baby pranks were over, and it was time to prove my stones.

It was time to grow up, street style.

I began shadowing my brother and his gang as often as Anthony would let me. Some days he'd allow me to tag along without a hassle, but most times I had to contribute to the parties they held in the pit in Forest Park, a big hole they'd dug to use as an open barbecue. If I could steal enough frankfurters, hamburgers, and buns from Key Food, they'd let me hang out with them.

Of course I could smoke there without concern, but then there was the added thrill of drinking beers or the Strawberry Hill assortment of flavored wines that were popular back in the day. The girls that hung out with my brother wanted nothing to do with a kid my age, but it was still pretty cool to know their names and get acknowledged by them on the streets. At least the other kids in the neighborhood thought I was extra special when sixteen- and seventeen-year-old girls would say, "Hey, Head," when they saw me.

Less impressive acknowledgments occurred whenever a local scumbag cop raided our 112 pit parties in Forest Park. This cop seemed to enjoy slamming his nightstick on my oversized noggin, but he'd also nailed my brother Anthony on the head a few times long before I came along. This particular cop was the scourge of all the street gangs in Richmond Hill, whether we were involved in fighting one another or just smoking and drinking. He was the guy responsible for my very first arrest, a disorderly conduct charge he handed me after he split my head open with his nightstick. That day I received fourteen stitches, one for each year I'd been alive.

That same cop used to beat on what he determined were unruly kids all the time. Today he'd be behind bars for anything near the same abuse, but back then it was excused and ignored. The prick also had a reputation as a shakedown artist, getting everything from his morning coffees to his lunches and bar drinks on the arm. If a deli owner was dumb enough to charge him for a coffee, the prick would write tickets for anything from unsanitary garbage disposal to disturbing the peace for playing a radio too loud (even if the radio wasn't on).

This cop hated me the same way some of my teachers seemed to hate me, except he had a badge and that fuckin' nightstick. I was a kid he caught smoking a cigarette, or maybe I was drinking a beer, and he went to town on me almost every time he pulled one of his Forest Park surprise attacks.

I hated that guy back, so it was an extra-special treat for me almost twenty years later when he was accused of being a dirty cop.

I had my first serious fight, one where Anthony's name couldn't count for anything, in high school. The only problem for me was fighting a guy who took a cheap shot rather than squaring off like a man. He was two years older than me and one of the school's tough guys, but when he challenged me, I dropped my hands in anticipation of him doing the same. To my naïve ass, I thought we'd set a time and place and start from scratch, but this punk took the first swing and caught me flush when I wasn't ready.

Round one to him.

A couple of days later, I found him in the school yard and challenged him again, this time with my hands up and ready to throw. I was still sporting the shiner he gave me, but it was a fair fight he wasn't ready for. I kicked his ass pretty good, but then the fight turned into a total gang brawl between friends of his and mine. By the time it was broken up, my street cred was established. Word spread fast throughout the school that James "Head" Guiliani could fight.

Ultimately, it was in Richmond Hill High School where my life would take a turn toward more serious crimes. I was no less a goofball than I was in Catholic grammar school, except my parents didn't have to pay for me to attend a public school. It was a class-cutting paradise for those of us who had no intention of going to college. The high school was where we made our street bones, so to speak; proving our toughness with fistfights rather than cheap talk.

There were two entrances to our high school, the main one on 114th Street, and the back entrance on 113th Street. As racial tensions racked New York City, there was a ripple effect felt in Richmond Hill. I learned very quickly which entrance to the school I was allowed to use; 114th was reserved for the black and Hispanic kids, and 113th was for the white kids.

We weren't racists by any measure. Hell, I'd marry a Colombian girl six years later, but we didn't take shit from anybody. Sometimes the fights were between black and white gangs, but they were always portrayed in the news as race riots. They weren't, not really. They were gang fights—nothing more, nothing less.

I was in a few gang fights my freshman year at Richmond Hill, but then my high school life was cut short when I met the guy who would introduce me to John Gotti Jr.'s crew. It would be the end of one education and the start of another, a premature graduation that would lead to some good times but a lot more suffering, especially for those who loved me.

My life would be anything but normal over the next thirty-plus years.

Chapter 3

First Rescues

In 2006, the Italians won the World Cup, my Brooklyn neighborhood celebrated, and I went on a forty-eight-hour bender. Cocaine and booze were my weapons of choice, and they nearly cost me Lena.

The day of the World Cup Championship, I woke up to find Lena sitting at the dining-room table in tears. With all the attention focused on my grieving for Bruno, Lena had grieved in solitude. When I asked Lena's mother what was wrong, she whispered one word to me: "Bruno."

"Fuck," I said. "I know what to do. Come with me."

I told Lena that her mom and I were going for bagels, but what we did was go to a local pet store where I picked out a purebred shih tzu. The dog cost me just over a grand, but I was still flush with cash from dealing cocaine. I'd been dealing since I moved in with Lena, using the cash to help carry my end of the store. Lena knew I'd been a gangster, so she didn't ask or want to know what I did with some of the people I used to be around. Her biggest concern for me was that I stay clean, especially since Bruno died.

The Diamond Collar was doing okay, but we were still a new operation and had to establish credibility for word to spread around the neighborhood. I'd been out of construction for just over a year, the result of a back injury lifting weights high on cocaine while juiced on steroids. Hustling was the only other way I knew to earn. I sold blow to users and steroids to bodybuilders.

The key was keeping the blow out of my own nose. I'd been tempted to snort a few times since Bruno died, but I managed to stay clean. Maybe it was common street sense finally getting through my thick noggin—the idea that dealing drugs was a lot more profitable than doing them.

The shih tzu I bought for Lena was tiny, just eight weeks old. He was the only male in a litter of three. I knew as soon as Lena saw him, she'd become that dog's mother the way she'd been a mother to all her animals. The new pup would get her mind off Bruno, at least while she helped nurse him to adulthood.

That day I had just enough time to stop for bagels, deliver the pup, and then get over to see a couple of friends at a coffee shop on Thirteenth Avenue, Cafe Isabella. My friends Danny and Sal had somebody looking to score some blow. I had established a good clientele in the area over a short period of time, but I was always on the hunt for new blood. It was simple math: a new customer meant more money, and I was always more comfortable dealing to friends of friends rather than dealing with strangers.

After picking up a dozen bagels and some cream cheese, I stopped to pick up Lena's mom. I couldn't help but notice all the Italian flags. They were everywhere I looked. "Look, Ma," I said. "You didn't know better, you'd think it was Columbus Day."

"This neighborhood is going to be crazy if Italy wins that soccer game," she said. "The kids are going to be scared from all the noise."

By kids, she meant Lena's cats and her pug, Brock.

"We'll keep the air conditioners running," I said. "That'll keep some of the noise out."

"I hope so," she said, "but they cry from fireworks. That's why Lena doesn't like the Fourth of July."

"We'll be okay," I said.

I parked in front of the house. Lena's mom took the bagels and I grabbed the pup. I followed her inside so Lena couldn't see him until the last second. Then I set the pup on the table right in front of her and said, "You wanna take care of this thing before it pisses all over me?"

Lena might've been tearful before, but once she saw the pup her eyes became waterfalls.

"Oh, my God!" she said. "James, what did you do?"

"It's time to get over Bruno," I said.

"What a little Gizmo," she said. "He's adorable."

The dog was licking Lena's face like it was an ice cream cone.

"That's a good name," I said. "I like it. Gizmo."

"He's adorable. Where'd you get him?"

"A pet store, and don't break my balls about the cost."

"A pet store? Okay, but we need to take him to a vet. Pet stores don't take care of their animals, James. I'll have him checked out. He's probably got kennel cough or something."

"He was just born eight weeks ago, Lena. How could he be sick?"

"Because the stores don't care about the dogs they sell. Trust me on this. They put sick dogs with healthy ones all the time. Even when they're on display, they don't separate sick dogs from healthy ones. Don't worry. I'll take him to the vet today. You do what you have to do and I'll meet you later. Pick me up after I close the store. Ma can stay here with the kids."

"Alright," I said, "but I have to see Danny and Sal over at Isabella in half an hour. Then I have to see somebody in Bay Ridge. I'll pick you up tonight."

I was talking, but Lena wasn't hearing. She had Gizmo up close to her face and was smothering the pup with kisses. My enormous head could've been on fire and I don't think she would've noticed.

I left the house a few minutes later to meet the potential new customer. It was the last time I'd see Lena for another two days.

The hookup through my friend wound up being a beautiful thing. The new guy took what I had on me, five $100 bags. Afterward, Danny and I hung around bullshitting while a steady crowd started to gather in the streets. Italy was scheduled to play France for the World Cup, but the game was being played in Berlin, Germany. In anticipation of a possible victory, the entire neighborhood was preparing to party.

I ate biscotti and had a few espressos while we watched the crowd. It was crazy the way people were getting pumped up. Somebody smart enough to foresee the score was selling little Italian flags on the corner. He must've gone through two hundred flags in fifteen minutes. Parents were buying them for their kids. Everywhere you looked, somebody was waving an Italian flag.

"What the fuck happens if they lose?" I said.

"Bite your tongue!" Danny said.

We had a good laugh.

By noon, traffic was halted on the avenue, and people spilled off the sidewalks into the street. There were people everywhere you looked.

It was a hot, hot day; July 9, 2006. Some of the food stores started hawking cold soda and water in front of their storefronts. Stores that didn't sell food closed early. It was feast or famine for the businesses on the avenue, but it was a blast to sit and watch from our table outside Isabella, especially after we switched from hot to iced espressos.

At one point, Danny headed to the bathroom and Sal was shooting the shit with a woman wearing an Italian flag halter and matching hot pants. She wasn't beautiful or anything, but she had an incredible body and wasn't shy showing it off. I could tell Sal was about to take her someplace when all of a sudden a very loud roar erupted from the street. A chant began: "I-tal-ia, I-tal-ia!, I-tal-ia!"

Italy had won the World Cup. Everybody in the street was going crazy.

"Holy shit, bro!" I said. "What, they have money on the game?"

People were waving flags, hugging and kissing one another, and hugging and kissing strangers. I turned to Sal and he and hot pants looked like they were about to screw right on top of one of the tables. Their mouths were locked tight together, their arms wrapped around each other like it was their honeymoon.

I turned back toward the street and shook my head. There were two teenagers pounding their chests as if they were auditioning for roles as King Kong. *Assholes,* I thought. Then I had to laugh. I would've bet everything I had that more than half of the people going crazy in the street had never watched, never mind played, a soccer game in their lives. It was that crowd craziness that too often permits people to get out of control. Maybe it was from my Richmond Hill memories of 112 brawls with other street gangs. I kept thinking that sooner or later there'd be a single fight between two guys that would quickly turn into a riot.

Fortunately, I was wrong. The celebration, although loud, remained peaceful. Hey, I'm Italian, too, but I didn't kid myself about the World Cup. I didn't know a thing about it or any other sport. I'm glad Italy won, don't get me wrong, but the truth of the matter is I would've been happier if America had won.

In the meantime, the celebration inside Isabella included bottles of amaretto, sambuca, and scotch. Danny was back from his bathroom break, except this time he was holding a bottle of Johnny Walker Blue in one hand and a pair of glasses in the other. He handed me the glasses and poured.

"James, you can't just drink coffee now," he said. "It's time to celebrate, *fratello* (brother)."

I took a few sips of the scotch and passed it along, but that's all it took. I felt an all-too-familiar rush from the booze and then headed home to grab whatever leftover blow I had in a Tupperware container I kept hidden behind a wall in the kitchen closet. I diluted the cocaine with inositol from a container I kept in the same hiding spot. Lena knew I was still involved in a street life, but she never questioned me about how I earned my money. I know she would've been upset knowing I was selling drugs, so there was no way I could tell her. So long as she remained focused on keeping me away from my addictions, the other stuff I did, illegal or not, was another fight for another day.

Half an hour after I diluted my stash of cocaine, I was at Isabella doing lines between shots of Johnny Walker Blue with people I'd never met before. Before I knew it, the cocaine had seduced me one more time, and I was partying like the drug addict I'd been in the past.

Of course I didn't notice the time, nor did I pick up Lena at the store. I didn't even leave her a note. I was off and running as if I didn't have a care in the world. I was back to being James "Head" Guiliani, all-star drug addict and alcoholic.

I know I started at The Wicked Monk, a bar on Third Avenue, but I was so wasted so fast, the next forty-eight hours became a total blank. A cocaine and booze binge will fry a brain faster than a microwave. I remembered very little of what happened, but there were a few clues about my actions: my brand-new Cadillac looked as though it had gone through a demolition derby, and so did I. I was sporting a black eye and a bruised jaw.

I was broke, I didn't have any cocaine left, and all my clothes were strewn on the front stoop outside Lena's house. A week later, I was told to avoid a certain bar in Richmond Hill because it had been robbed during my two-day binge.

The last time I'd been on a bender and was gone for more than a day, Lena broke my jaw with a lucky punch. It was a few months into our relationship and I was fucking up big time. I'd go out for days at a time, then come home drunk or high, incoherent, and usually unable to speak. Back then Lena was trying her best to deal with my addictions, but when I disappeared one too many times, I'd pushed her too far. She'd had enough of my bullshit and wasn't willing to listen to any more of my *fugazi* (fake) apologies. The night she broke my jaw, I walked in the house, apologized, and got caught flush on the tip of my chin with a right cross that would've decked a horse. I didn't go down, but I knew my jaw was broken because I'd heard it crack and I could feel the pain on the left side of my mouth.

"Fuhhh you do thah for?" I'd moaned.

"Because I'm sick of your shit," Lena had said. "And the next time I'll use a baseball bat."

It had been a long time since I screwed up as bad. Although I was using before Bruno came along, I wasn't disappearing like the old days. While caring for Bruno, I had virtually stopped using drugs and booze. Of course I wanted to believe that Bruno had cured me of my addictions, but I obviously wasn't cured of anything.

I'd pulled the typical bullshit that addicts do to justify getting high. I'd used Bruno's death as an excuse to grieve with my two old friends, cocaine and booze. This time, after two days of bingeing, I was careful not to try to bullshit Lena.

As I approached the stoop, I could see that she'd cut up a few of my favorite tracksuits.

"Fuck me," I said.

Then when I tried the door, I discovered the locks had been changed. I went around to the back of the house, but she'd had those locks changed as well.

Then my ability to be stubborn as a mule kicked in. I pounded on the door with one hand and rang the bell with the other hand. I pressed the doorbell and kept pressing it until she finally gave in and answered the door.

"I'm through with it, James," she said. "I've had it."

I wasn't going to apologize because I knew she wouldn't buy it. I was wrong and I knew it, but the realization that she was serious scared the shit out of me. It was one thing to kid myself about how much bullshit she'd put up with, but this time she meant it.

"I'm not leaving," I said.

"Oh, no?" she said.

"No."

"Well, you're not coming inside."

"Then I'll sit in the backyard."

"Knock yourself out, asshole."

"I love you."

"You love your drugs and booze."

I was about to say something else when Lena slammed the door in my face. It made me more obstinate. I walked to the back of the house and plopped down in a lounge chair in the backyard. It was morning and I had a hangover and I felt like shit, but I wasn't leaving. I knew I'd screwed up, but I also knew that if Lena threw me out, I'd be lost all over again. I didn't realize how much I missed her until she stood in front of me and told me to fuck off.

Thinking I'd finally gone too far and that Lena, the best thing that had ever happened to me, no longer wanted me, scared me shitless. I choked down my emotion and became a fighter again. I wasn't going to allow myself to give in this time.

I could hear Lena and her mother arguing through the kitchen window, but I couldn't make out what they were saying. I knew she had to open the store in a few hours, so I'd either be left alone in the yard all day or she'd let me inside to shower and sleep.

Once again, I started to feel sorry for myself, a typical defense mechanism for addicts and drunks alike. Here I had a woman who had done nothing but love and care for me, and I was ignoring her for the sake of my self-destruction. I had to remind myself that what I was doing, feeling sorry for myself, was what I'd always done—look for any excuse to use or drink again.

I fought the urge and remained in the chair. I must've fallen asleep at some point because it was the heat from the sun that woke me again. I was stiff from being in the chair all that time. I stretched and yawned and finally managed to stand, but I was sore and aching. I made it to the back door and could see my reflection. The bruises on my face had started to change color and my eye was still puffy.

I stood there like a moron, but then the door opened and there was Lena holding the pup I'd given her two days ago. She didn't say a word. She held Gizmo out to me through the bars on the door.

"Here," she finally said. "This is why you can't drink and get high anymore. Just like Bruno, Gizmo depends on you."

I held Gizmo in my hands and brought him up to my face. Just like Bruno, he was licking me. It was his natural reaction, to show love and affection. He had no idea what I'd done over the last two days. He had no idea that I was a junkie, an alcoholic, and an ex-convict. He was voiceless to express it, so he did what came naturally. He showed me love.

Lena had always been my rock, but I never realized how much so until that moment. I knew she loved me and I knew that I loved her, but at that moment, holding Gizmo up to my face so he could lick my grille, I was overwhelmed. Lena had provided all the rehab in the world I'd ever need with that one sentence.

"This is why you can't drink and get high anymore. Just like Bruno, Gizmo depends on you."

Tears flowed from my eyes. Just like Bruno, this puppy shih tzu we'd named Gizmo loved me unconditionally. How could I not love him back? How could I not protect him?

Like any infant, Gizmo was totally dependent on us. Lena was right, the puppy needed us to survive. Like any parent, we wanted to raise him to be a happy, healthy dog. Like any parent, we wanted to protect him.

Just like that, Lena's lifelong love of animals had won me over. I finally understood how much love, all of it unconditional, animals give. I also realized how much they desire our love in return. It's really all they ask for, to be loved. The animal boutique that was Lena's idea would provide me with a venue to treat and care for animals. The same boutique I'd once scoffed at had become a place where I'd be around animals all day. The Diamond Collar would become my refuge, while Lena, Bruno, and Gizmo became my saviors. My life would finally have a purpose other than selfishness and self-destruction.

My sobriety began that very day in our backyard. Holding Gizmo up to my face, crying while he licked my face, I swore off my demons and have remained sober ever since.

A few days later, while working at the store, a series of walk-in rescue situations would convince me that I'd made the right choice in becoming a Dogfella.

You say "animal rescue" and people assume it has to do with running into a building to save a dog or a cat from fire. Sometimes it may, but the most common form of rescue has to do with saving animals from being brought to a shelter that performs animal euthanasia after a prescribed amount of time. Unfortunately, far too many of the people who purchase or adopt animals are unaware of all the work required to raise them.

Training is probably the most common reason owners abandon their pets. It takes a lot of work to train a dog. It requires patience, persistence, and love. New pet owners are often frustrated at their inability to achieve the results they want with minimal effort. A lifestyle change is another reason owners give up a pet. Whether it's a divorce or having a child, owners will sometimes return an animal they recently adopted or purchased to offset a change in their household environment. Cost is another factor. Pets get sick, hurt, or sometimes come with genetic diseases that require expensive medical attention. Aggressive behavior is also a reason new owners return pets. A house with too many pets can also lead to the latest adoption/purchase being returned. Last but not least, sometimes new owners aren't aware of allergies they or someone in their family may have, and a new pet is either returned or dropped off at a shelter.

The bottom line is that once a pet is rejected, it is most often brought to a shelter, and most shelters have limits on how many animals they can accommodate and/or how long they can do so before they put an animal down. Too many shelters keep a dog for no more than seventy-two hours and will keep a very aggressive dog no more than twenty-four hours.

It makes me sick that so many pets are euthanized each year. The Humane Society estimates that animal shelters receive and care for 6–8 million dogs and cats every year in the United States, of which approximately 3–4 million are euthanized. It is a terrible reality that I once knew nothing about.

Until I was confronted with Lena's love, finding Bruno, then losing him so quickly to cancer, and then having Lena place Gizmo in my hands after my last bender, I was a man determined to self-destruct. If for no other reason than to care for those who can't protect themselves, I became an animal advocate in more than name only. I became a true Dogfella, and The Diamond Collar became my headquarters.

Four days into the sobriety I have maintained to this day, four days after Lena handed me Gizmo, a woman came into The Diamond Collar with a pit-bull–labrador mix. She and her boyfriend had broken up and she could no longer care for the dog. The dog's name was Lacey, and she said she was going to bring it to an adoption shelter where they put dogs down after thirty days. She'd decided to come in to The Diamond Collar to see if we'd take it first. Thank God she took the time to ask.

"We have to find it a home," Lena said.

"How?" I said.

"We'll make calls," she said.

"To who?"

"Family first, then friends."

I thought it was wishful thinking until she had her uncle Paul from Pennsylvania on the phone. As it turned out, Uncle Paul wanted a dog for his farm. "Anything but a pit bull," he told Lena. He'd believed the negative stereotype that pit bulls were cursed with from the exposure of dogfighting rings. I got on the phone and told him that the dog we had wasn't a pit bull, it just looked like one. Uncle Paul said he was coming to New York and he'd take the dog, but it better not be a pit bull.

Once he was in Brooklyn, I had to resort to my very best street-hustle bullshit to convince Uncle Paul that the dog was actually a labrador-terrier mix.

"Forget what it looks like, Paul," I told him. "It's half lab, half terrier. You ever see the movie *Patton*? His dog in the movie, that looked like a pit bull, too, right? But it wasn't. It was a terrier."

"What movie?" Uncle Paul said.

"*Patton*, you know. The one about the army general. He was a big animal lover. He had a terrier that everybody thought was a pit bull, but it wasn't."

Uncle Paul eventually took the dog back to Pennsylvania with him, but a week later he brought the dog to a vet and was told, "What a fine-looking pit bull."

Uncle Paul called me up to yell about the bullshit I'd fed him, but I wouldn't budge. I told him the vet was crazy. Uncle Paul said he was bringing the dog back the next chance he had, but fortunately for Lacey, Uncle Paul was too busy to make the trip anytime soon. In the interim, he learned that no dog is born vicious, that it's what their owners do to them that ultimately determines their behavior. Uncle Paul fell in love with his pit-bull–labrador mix, and Lacey's still with him.

My very next rescue had to do with a purebred bulldog named Buster. A woman claimed she'd been phoning different pet stores and animal boutiques to find one that would take a purebred puppy to resell or keep. We were the second Brooklyn store she called. She told Lena that she lived on Staten Island and that she was concerned about the new puppy she'd bought. She claimed she already had two mature bulldogs who weren't taking to Buster. Lena put me on the phone and the woman begged me to help her.

"Of course I will," I told her.

I drove to Staten Island and pulled up in front of her house. I didn't even have a chance to get out of my car when a woman came running out of her house with a bulldog puppy in her hands and a manila envelope tucked under her chin. My windows were down, and before I could say anything, she literally tossed the dog inside my car.

"Hey!" I yelled.

She took the envelope from under her chin and dropped it inside the window. "Those are his papers," she said, then ran back inside the house.

"What the fuck?" I said.

How could someone be so cold, I was thinking. Then I looked at the puppy and could see it was petrified. It was trying to climb up the passenger door to get out of the window. I put up the windows and headed back to Brooklyn thinking Buster would probably have to stay with us for a while. On the way home I thought to give my brother Anthony a call. I figured it was a perfect match, a tough marine and a bulldog. Sure enough, Anthony came to the store that night and has had Buster ever since, except he changed the dog's name to Bubba.

Watching these two together is a genuine treat for anyone who sees them. Anthony is a powerhouse of an ex-marine. He continues to body-build and is one tough dude. He and Bubba are naturals together. I've seen people smile from ear to ear when Anthony takes Bubba for a walk.

I was two-for-two rescuing dogs, but let's face it, I would run out of family and friends a lot sooner than I'd run out of animals to rescue. I talked to Lena about it, and she was all for continuing to do what we could to save animals from euthanasia. Her house had been filled with cats since she was fifteen years old, and we'd already added two dogs to our clan—Brock and Gizmo. Brock surprised us both when he accepted Gizmo.

A few days after my brother took the bulldog, Dr. Salvatore Pernice called me from his office at the Brooklyn Veterinary Group to tell me about a kitten with a neurological disorder called cerebellar hypoplasia. The kitten's disease had probably come from a virus. He was permanently disabled without coordination but was otherwise okay. The problem had to do with adoption. Lena and I had run out of family and friends to take another pet. Chances were, nobody would want a cat that couldn't walk straight and that always lost his balance. Dr. Pernice offered his skills as a veterinarian if I offered to take the kitten. Maybe he was testing me, I honestly don't know, but I couldn't resist the offer. I picked up the kitten and put a ton of love and effort into nursing him. I bathed him daily because he would often fall into his own feces and urine in the litter box. It was tough to watch him suffer, but I refused to give up on the little guy. Making him feel secure was my number-one priority over the next several months. I named him Spaz and he's been with me at the house ever since.

My next rescue remains one of the toughest. An abused female Pomeranian was brought to Dr. Pernice. She was small, maybe seven pounds, with a dirty blonde coat. She had become violent, a result of the abuse she had suffered. Once again, here was an animal most vets would put down without a second thought. Dr. Pernice called me and I went to see the dog. He was busy with an emergency operation, so one of the technicians there brought me to her cage. I was warned to be careful because she'd already tried to bite them when she was dropped off. I crouched down and shook my head at the poor thing. She looked as if she'd been left in some cellar for weeks.

Then I went to pet her head through the cage bars and she bit me. She would bite me at least another hundred times by the end of our first year together. The technicians at the BVG put her in a portable cage, and I brought her to The Diamond Collar to groom. I used thick gloves to remove her from the cage and after a few more bites, she was calm enough to let me shave her back. What I saw when I did so, I couldn't believe. Some piece of shit had put industrial staples all along her back. There had to be twenty or more staples from the back of her neck to her tail. There was swelling around each and every staple. How could anyone do that?

No wonder she was biting anyone who went near her.

I brought her back to the BVG, where Dr. Pernice removed the staples. He gave her antibiotics and something to calm her nerves, all free of charge. I asked him if he'd ever seen that kind of thing before and Dr. Pernice told me, "Some people are just cruel bastards, James."

When I mentioned the staples to a friend of mine from the club, he put it all in perspective for me.

"You ever hear of Michael Vick?" he said.

Point made, although at least Vick served some time. Most animal abusers are never caught.

When I brought the dog home, Lena immediately became the next bite victim, but it only made both of us more determined to help her recover. We had to keep her separated from our other animals from fear she'd attack them, so she spent the next three months underneath our couch in the front room of our house. Hiding was her way to protect herself, an obvious defense mechanism against the abuse she'd suffered.

A doorway separates the front room from the living room and the rest of the house. We put food out in the morning and again at night. We put down wee-wee pads for her to use in between our visits to feed her. Sometimes she used the pads and sometimes she didn't, but whenever we checked, her food was gone and she was back under the couch hiding. I tried a few different trainers to work with her, but all of them suggested putting her down.

"No fucking way," I said.

Eventually, I'd had enough and I started taking her with me wherever I went. I used a training loop leash to walk her, but she refused to let me put a collar on her. For whatever reason, it made her growl just to see me approach her with one.

Of course she bit me the first dozen or so times I took her, but eventually she remained calm and went with me. She'd growl if someone came near, but I was careful to warn people not to try and pet her. A few months into our new routine, her back wounds from the staples had healed, and it was time to groom her again. By then she was familiar with our groomers at the store, so I decided to let them do the haircut. Our grooming was done in the basement at the time, so I was upstairs behind the counter.

After a few minutes, one of the groomers ran upstairs to tell me there had been an accident. I could hear a dog crying while I followed him down the stairs, but I wasn't sure which dog it was. We had several being groomed, some awaiting their turn in cages, and some already on grooming tables. I stepped inside and one of the other groomers was pointing under an equipment table.

"What happened?" I said.

None of the groomers could look me in the eye, so I asked again. "What the fuck happened?"

"She fell off the table," one of them said.

I knew it was bullshit, but I was more concerned about the dog than listening to their lies. I went down on all fours and tried to coax her out. She bit me, then bit me again. I wrapped my hands with towels and made a few more attempts to get her out. When I finally managed to pull her out from under the equipment table, I could see something was wrong with one of her back legs. She yelped when I touched it. I knew then she hadn't fallen off any table. I asked who was working on her. It was the groomer who'd come up to tell me there was an accident. I figured the dog had bitten him and he'd slapped or punched her off the table, but I honestly can't say for sure. I would fire him over the phone later that same night, but first I had to get the dog to the BVG and have her back leg examined.

Dr. Pernice accepted her as an emergency and immediately found the dog's kneecap had been dislocated. He told me that it required surgery from a specialist and that it would be expensive.

"How much?" I asked.

"Thirty-five hundred," he said.

"Whatever it takes," I said.

Dr. Pernice asked me if I was sure.

"Yes, Sal, please," I said.

He called a specialist, Dr. Fuerst, and the operation was performed within a few hours. In the meantime, I ran home and grabbed all the cash I had, just over $3,000. I put it in an envelope and when the operation was over, I handed it to Dr. Pernice.

He shook his head. "I can't take that," he said.

"Why not?" I said.

"We talked it over and decided we can't," he said. "Anyone willing to do what you just did, with that dog's history, is a true animal lover. Most people would've put her down, James. I appreciate what you're doing for this dog. We're not charging you."

It was at that moment that I realized just how compassionate Salvatore Pernice is about the animals he treats. He is a true healer, one who has devoted his heart and soul to caring for animals. I couldn't thank him enough. I still can't.

I brought the dog back home to her foyer residence, still keeping her separated from our other animals, but I was determined to help her socialize. I felt that so long as I let her hide under the couch, she'd remain afraid and violent.

I began to take her with me again when I left the house. She continued to bite, but not as often as in the past, at least not with me. She eventually grew used to being my companion and we became a team. After another month of her socialization training, I was able to adopt her out to a policeman named Felix. He named her Princess at the store before he brought her home. They seemed fine when they left The Diamond Collar, but then the dog attacked Felix and his wife as soon as they got home. The deal I made back then, and I continue to make to this day with people who adopt one of my rescues, is this: no matter what the reason, if they find they can't handle the rescue, they must bring the animal back to me and no one else. I will never abandon an animal I have rescued and/or adopted out.

Felix called me the next morning. Princess was hiding in one of their closets and they were afraid to try and get her out. I went to the house and brought Princess home. Another long and painful training period began that same day, except this time I knew Princess couldn't be adopted. She'd have to stay at the house with us. Then one day she managed to slip out of the foyer into the house itself, and Princess attacked Brock. Lena was all for keeping her, but she insisted that I take her with me to work.

Thus began a beautiful and sometimes funny relationship.

Princess favored my left side when I carried her with one hand. Until I got her used to a training leash, it was the only way I could carry her—snug against my left rib cage. What can I say, we were a cute couple.

I took her everywhere with me, to work at a pornography store I'd bought into with an old street connection, on deliveries we made to various strip clubs on Long Island and in the city, and to my weekly card games.

Princess and I became attached at the hip, but nothing short of a miracle happened when I delivered outfits to the strippers at the clubs.

The porn shop was located in Hempstead, Long Island. It was a good business. Aside from the various sex toys we sold over the counter, we also carried the more kinky paraphernalia and exotic dancewear some strippers used on stage.

When I first walked Princess into one of the clubs I was delivering outfits to for the dancers, the looks I got were priceless. Picture a tall and beefy guy, his exposed skin covered in tattoos, wearing a mobster tracksuit, walking a tiny Pomeranian on a training leash into a strip club like Goldfingers in Queens or Scores in Manhattan. The guys paying for the strippers had a good laugh, but it was the strippers themselves who had the most fun.

"Look, James the white knight and his little pooch!" one of them would yell whenever she saw me.

It had to be comical to see us together, but Princess ate up the attention. She let the girls pet her, feed her, sing to her, dress her, and some would buy Princess outfits on their own. Eventually, some of the women picked Princess up and held her. It was a miracle by my standards, that's for sure. Here was a dog that had bitten me for months and months suddenly trusting people she'd met just a dozen times or so.

I was shocked by the turnaround, but taking Princess on those strip-club deliveries did more for her socialization than I ever could. She took to the attention the strippers gave her and became the socialized dog we'd prayed for.

Sometimes I'd dress Princess in the little outfits the strippers had bought for her and we'd get standing ovations from both the dancers and their customers when we showed up to the clubs to make deliveries.

I left the porn-shop business after six months, after which Princess was fine with Brock, Gizmo, and all of our cats. Another miracle, there was peace among the Guiliani kids again.

Although Princess became part of our expanding family, she still wouldn't let us collar her. I suspect the collar had something to do with the abuse she'd once suffered. In any event, she did fine without her collar and continued to travel with me as my new best friend and companion. She was with me at The Diamond Collar, at my weekly card games, and whenever I had to hit the road, whether to rescue another animal or pick up a container of milk. Princess lived with Lena and me for eight years before she passed from cancer. I still miss her, especially the way she'd let me carry her against my left side. I have a huge tattoo of her in the exact spot where I used to carry her against my left rib cage.

A few months into my sobriety, I was returning to the store with an espresso when I saw a Maserati pull up to the curb and park. It was an impressive-looking car, probably worth a hundred grand or more. A guy with a cane stepped out of the car and walked around to the other side. He opened the door, leaned in, and then seemed to yank or pull on something. There was an immediate yelp, and then the guy was pulling a shih tzu out of the car by its leash and dragging it toward the store's front door. The dog had obviously been abused. Its hair was matted and filthy. It cowered as it was pulled.

I wanted to push this guy's head through a window.

"Oh!" I said. "Go easy there."

"What?" he said.

I pointed to the dog. "Go easy. You're hurting your dog."

The guy shrugged. I shook my head and let him inside the store. I walked to the back where I could take possession of the dog for whatever grooming was to be done, but what I wanted to do was smack this guy off the head and maybe wake him up.

"What do you need?" I asked.

He spoke with a Russian accent. "She wants haircut, short. How long?"

He was a regular conversationalist.

"Two hours," I said. "Phone number?"

"I don't give number. I come back in two hour."

"What's your name?"

"Dog's name is Oreo."

"So, what? I should call him when he's ready?"

He didn't get my sarcasm.

"I need your phone number," I said.

He reluctantly gave it to me.

"I come back," he said. "How much is haircut."

Normally I charged $45 for a shih tzu cut, but not this jerkoff.

"One-forty," I said.

"You're focking kidding," he said.

"One-forty."

"Focking dogs," he said. "Fine. I come back."

I called him a jerkoff through a phony cough as he left.

I had the dog groomed first, then I brought Oreo to the BVG for an evaluation. Dr. Pernice said the dog was undernourished and that his ears were swollen from a lack of circulation. I'd already made up my mind to try and hold him for a few days, at least until he was healthy again, but when I returned to the store the guy who'd dropped Oreo off was waiting for me.

He pointed at his watch and said, "How come you doesn't call?"

"I did call," I lied. "You gave me a wrong number."

"What you are talking about?"

"Forget it," I said, "but we have a problem."

"What is problem?"

"Your dog is being abused," I said. "Maybe you don't understand how to train them, but you can't pull on them when you take them out of a car. And you have to keep them clean. You have to make sure they get enough to eat and that they have some exercise."

"Is my friend's wife. Dog belong to her. I just bring him for haircut."

"Where does she keep him?"

"With her when she's home. Always with her."

"And nights? What about when she's not home?"

"In cage," he said, then held his hands about two feet apart. "Small cage."

I rolled my eyes. "When does she feed him? How often?"

"Sometimes she goes Atlantic City, she leave food in cage."

I couldn't believe what this guy was saying. Maybe it was a cultural thing. I had no idea, but I tried my best to understand.

"Does she leave him in a cage when she's away?"

"Sure, of course."

Like it was nothing. What a moron.

"That's abuse," I said.

This time he held two fingers about an inch apart and smiled. "Maybe little," he said.

I really wanted to clock this asshole, but I bit my tongue. "No," I said. "You can't do that to a dog. Not any pet."

He shrugged.

"What? That's it?" I said. "So what?"

"I know, is hard for dog sometimes. He cry in cage."

The moron knew the dog was being abused, but at least he wasn't fighting me about it.

"Look," I said. "Let me keep the dog. Tell her it got lost or something. If she doesn't understand how to treat it, the dog is better off with somebody else."

His thick brow furrowed. "What?" he said. "She go crazy I lose dog. Her husband shoots me."

"Tell her it jumped out of the car window or something."

"I can't do this."

"Then tell her I'm keeping Oreo for a few days just to nurse him back to health."

"I'm saying to you, she goes crazy."

"Just for a few days. Then when she comes in, I'll explain how to treat the dog in the future. Come on, man, you know it ain't right what she's doing to that dog."

He shrugged again and said, "Okay, I tell her you hold it. Then is your headache."

He finally left, but just before we closed, another exotic car pulled up in front of the store, a red Porsche with black racing stripes. It was Oreo's owner, an attractive middle-aged woman with sharp features and about ten grand in jewelry around her neck. Five years earlier, I would've snatched her jewelry and her car.

Needless to say, she was livid. She pointed an accusing finger at me and started cursing in English, but with a Russian accent.

"Give my focking dog back, you thief! My husband shoot you! Give back Oreo. Where is dog?"

I did my best to explain why I wasn't giving the dog back, but she wasn't hearing me.

"My husband shoot you!" she yelled.

There were a few other customers in the store. I tried to calm the crazed Russian lady, but she wasn't having it.

"Listen to me," I said. "You have to treat the dog better. You can't leave Oreo in a tight space the way you did. No more cage. He was covered in his own urine."

"The fock you talking about? Give me dog!"

"No, not if you don't know how to treat it."

"I want dog! I focking shoot you myself." She made a motion like she was going in her purse for a gun, but I knew she was full of shit. I smiled and folded my arms across my chest.

"What?" I said.

Then she stopped what she was doing.

"Give back dog!" she yelled one more time.

"Not until you hear what I have to say," I told her.

She pointed at me, snarled something in her own language, and finally left the store.

An old woman buying dog food had witnessed the argument. She was also Russian. She said she'd take the dog home and care for it if I didn't mind. I thought it was a good idea to let her hold the dog.

The next afternoon the old woman returned to the store. She was nervous because she'd learned something about Oreo's owners. The husband was a Russian mobster from Brighton Beach. The old woman said she wasn't comfortable holding their dog. I asked her to wait for my phone call. I would pick up Oreo from her house at the end of the day.

It was right before closing again when a convoy of exotic cars pulled up in front of the store. The red Porsche was back. So was a brand-new black Audi, a blue BMW, the silver Maserati, and a pair of light-blue Jaguars. A line of bulky dudes dressed in gray sports coats stood in front of the store and stared me down as I stepped outside. The woman was standing near her Porsche, but it didn't look as though any of the men there were her husband. She'd brought his muscle instead.

"We talk?" one of the bulky guys said.

I motioned for him to step inside the store. "Just him," I told the rest of them.

His name was Yuri. He was somebody associated with the woman's husband. I could tell because he never mentioned the woman's husband or his boss. He was there to negotiate, not intimidate me.

"What's happened with dog?" he asked.

I explained to him how I found the dog when it was brought in, and how I brought it to my veterinarian because it looked abused. I told him what Dr. Pernice told me; that the dog must've been confined to a tight space because its hair was covered in urine and feces. I told Yuri about the swollen ears and lack of circulation the dog was getting. I told him that I tried to explain that to the woman, but that she was too upset and wasn't listening to what I was saying.

"So, we have doggie sit-down instead," he said.

When the mob holds a sit-down, wiseguys (mobsters) representing opposing sides in a dispute meet to discuss a settlement. It's like having arbitrators for criminal activity. I don't know for sure, but I assume the Russians do something similar.

Yuri and I shared a laugh. Then he pointed to my spiderweb elbow tattoo. "That is prison tattoo, no?" he said.

I nodded.

"I don't ask why," he said. "Woman is okay, a little spoiled from husband, but she doesn't understand how to listen when others speak. I tell her about dog and space it need. She can have dog back?"

"If you promise to bring it back here when it needs grooming the next time," I said. "Just so I can see for myself she's taking care of the dog."

Yuri shrugged. "Fair enough," he said.

We shook hands.

I called the old woman and told her to bring the dog back to the store. Now, Oreo comes regularly to The Diamond Collar for grooming and is a healthy, happy shih tzu.

It was 2008 or so when I spotted an Amish dude selling mastiff puppies out of the back of his pickup. He'd parked in front of our store and was doing business right there on the street. *Where's a cop when you need one?* I thought.

I had business to take care of inside the store, but as soon as I had the chance, I stepped outside and asked him what he thought he was doing.

"I own a farm in Pennsylvania," he said. "I raise mastiffs and sell them. I was in Brooklyn today delivering one and I saw your store. I had five pups and now there's just one left. Do you want it?"

I was curious. "How much?" I asked.

"For you, two hundred," he said. "Because of your store."

"What, it was good publicity for you?"

"Two people bought dogs on the way out of your store. It's a natural spot."

"Let me talk it over with my partner and I'll get back to you," I told him. "Wait here."

I went inside and called three friends from the social club where we played cards. I told them I needed some help and to hurry to the store. All three were banged-out weight lifters. None of them required a detailed explanation of their roles.

I went back outside and stalled the Amish dude with bullshit about future dealings. He thought he'd made a score. Then my friends arrived and I told him to let me hold the puppy. He handed it to me and I said, "Thanks. Now get the fuck out of this neighborhood and don't ever let me catch you here again."

"But you didn't pay me," he said.

I pointed to my friends. "Talk to them about payment."

The Amish dude saw my three friends and was immediately intimidated. At least he seemed to get it. "Fine," he said. "I don't come back."

I took the mastiff to the BVG for evaluation and a policeman adopted the mastiff the very next day.

Lena and I already had more than a dozen cats and three dogs (Brock, Gizmo, and Princess) living with us when we learned of another guy selling dogs out of his car. I knew the guy by face, but knowing what was likely to happen to the dogs if they weren't sold, we couldn't resist saving them. We bought both shih tzus. Lena named them Cucuzza and Cappuccino. We hustled them to the BVG to make sure they were healthy. When the dogs received a clean bill of health, our family had grown by two, but it was more than obvious that we were running out of space. There was no way we could keep up what we'd been doing. We didn't have enough room at the house for more animals or money in the bank to support them. At some point, we'd have to say no to animals that needed a home. Just the thought made us both sick.

I can't say enough about Dr. Salvatore Pernice. There isn't a price tag you can put on his contribution to animal rescue in general. Since the first day we met, when he explained how I couldn't sell puppies out of my store, Dr. Pernice has always been there for me and my rescues. A selfless humanitarian, he's answered rescue calls from me at all hours of the day and night. He's provided medical evaluations and treatments. He's the man who explained to me that for the sake of the other resident animals, rescued animals should always visit a veterinarian before being brought into a home or shelter. Dr. Pernice also took in rescues when I ran out of room in our house and store. He sheltered them for as long as it took for someone to adopt them out of the BVG office.

As kind as he was to me and my rescues, Dr. Pernice was nobody's fool. He'd seen a lot of wannabe animal advocates come and go. He'd often say, "A lot of people have best intentions and they say they want to help animals, but there's a big difference between saying and doing."

It took some time, but eventually Dr. Sal saw that I wasn't some fly-by-night animal rescuer, that saving animals was my vocation. Once he was confident in my conviction, he pushed me toward starting an animal-rescue shelter. As my individual rescues continued and I ran out of both house and store space to keep the dogs or cats, I started bringing Dr. Pernice a cat or dog every month or so, but when it picked up and I started bring him more and more rescues, Sal would give me a speech about how he didn't have the room to handle any more. He'd give me the speech, and it always sounded convincing, but then he'd relent and make room at the BVG. No matter how much of an inconvenience it was to him and his staff, Sal Pernice never failed to help me save animals.

It would be several years before I opened a rescue shelter. The cost alone can be prohibitive. The time and effort to run a shelter can be overwhelming. Still, with the support of Lena and Dr. Pernice, there was no way it wasn't going to happen. Some of the other rescue shelters I'd dealt with set rules too absurd for me to comprehend. I wanted to set my own rules for adoption. I wanted people who adopted a rescue from me to promise to bring the rescue back if for whatever reason, they couldn't handle it. I wanted a cageless environment, rather than keeping animals locked up the way I had been locked in a cell. I didn't want to charge people for adoptions. To my mind, there's no difference in telling someone a particular dog is a $200 donation rather than a $200 sale. People should give what they can afford, end of story.

Lena and I opened Keno's Animal Rescue in June 2013. It is located directly across from the Brooklyn Veterinary Group on Seventy-seventh Street near New Utrecht Avenue.

Back in 2007, however, with the selfless assistance of Dr. Pernice and his amazing skills, I was rescuing animals one at a time.

Chapter 4

The Gotti Years

Although we would remain lifetime friends, when our unholy quartet graduated from the Holy Child Jesus School, each of us headed in different directions. Ralph Salzano had the brains, and he attended the prestigious Aviation High School. Mike Murphy and Kevin Rooney also attended private high schools. They were looking toward their future. My future would remain whatever happened in the next five minutes.

I was fifteen years old in 1972 when I attended Richmond Hill High School, but I was doing it without my boys. I had other friends from the neighborhood attending the same school, but by then my loyalty was to our street gang, 112 Nutso Park. Forest Park was where we'd hang out after school and on weekends, and oftentimes instead of going to school. Most of us were destined to be dropouts sooner or later. School wasn't for us. It certainly wasn't for me. I was more interested in trailing after my brother Anthony and 112 than paying attention to anything going on inside the walls of Richmond Hill High School.

When I did show up for classes, I was either clowning around or clock watching. I had zero interest in anything the teachers had to say. I was simply taking up space and waiting for the next bell. Sometimes I'd sit through a full day of classes and be bored out of my mind, but most times I'd cut one or two classes and wind up in the school yard, Forest Park, or somewhere on Jamaica Avenue hanging out with the other kids destined to drop out. I wasn't worried about a job or my future. I knew I'd wind up with a construction job because of my father. Being in high school was like being a jet stuck in a holding pattern while waiting to land. I could do whatever

I wanted because it wasn't going to make a difference anyway. When I was old enough to get a union card, I'd land.

With that kind of *capa fresca* (clear head) guiding my actions, I decided to have some fun while biding my high school time. So at age sixteen or so, I had my first taste of cocaine at one of the local bars in Richmond Hill. At the time, cocaine was way out of my reach financially, so I couldn't become addicted right away. I depended on the kindness of strangers, so to speak— there was always somebody passing it around at the bar. It quickly became a treat I never had to pay for, and I loved the immediate adrenalin rush that white powder provided. Even when I'd go weeks without another taste, I was anxious for more, but unless it was a freebee, who could afford it?

What was supposed to be my sophomore year, I returned to my job busing tables at a local diner. Suddenly I had money to buy my own cocaine and I no longer had to wait for freebees passed around in bars. It was something I had to hide from Anthony, so until he joined the marines, my adventures with drugs remained a secret in our house.

I'd been drinking beers at the park since I was thirteen, but it was never anything serious. We were boys being boys, hanging out in Forest Park with a few six-packs, and cooking franks at the pit. We were dumb kids practicing to be bums. Once in a while we'd share a bottle of hard liquor, but alcohol was never part of our daily diet. Like a baseball player going through the minor leagues to make it in the majors, I nurtured my alcoholism over time. I graduated from beer to vodka and scotch, and eventually anything that contained alcohol, but not for another few years.

By my junior year in high school, although I was still officially a student at Richmond Hill, I was basically a no-show. Then, a few months before I became an official dropout, I met a kid named Fat George DiBello. A few months later, I'd meet the Gotti crew.

I was in the school yard having a smoke after a fight with a kid from Ozone Park. The fight didn't last long because the kid couldn't take a punch to the gut. He went down fast and waved at me to stop. Fair enough. I wasn't into beating on anybody for the sake of getting my rocks off. We'd fought and he lost and that was it. We actually become friendly a few days later.

While I was smoking, a heavyset kid approached me to bum a cigarette.

"Sure," I said. "Here." I handed him the pack.

"You're good with your hands," he said.

"I'm okay," I said.

He introduced himself. "I'm George DiBello," he said. "Everybody calls me Fat George." I told him my name and he did a double take. "What, like the prosecutor Giuliani?"

"Fuck no," I said. "Sounds the same, but it isn't. No relation."

"Good. You with anybody?"

"What do you mean?"

"You around anybody? You know, a wiseguy?"

I was embarrassed. I knew about wiseguys, but mostly through my father. His best friend was a mobster, but I didn't know any wiseguys personally. I also didn't know if this kid was showing off or just bullshitting. "No," I said. "I'm with One-Twelve. We're a street gang from around the corner."

Fat George chuckled.

"What's funny?" I said.

"Nothing, man. Forget it. I was just curious."

My father was tight with one of the Vario brothers affiliated with the Luchese crime family. They'd known each other through the carpenters' union, but I wasn't about to name-drop, especially to somebody I knew less than five minutes. I was uncomfortable talking about people I didn't know personally. Fat George and I hung out that day, but I still thought the guy had been showing off. He'd mentioned a few heavy hitters, scary names I'd read about in the newspapers, so it made me think. Why would anyone bullshit about a name like Gotti?

I saw him at school a few more times on days when we both attended, but we didn't hang out again for more than a few minutes. He had his crew of friends, and I had 112.

The week of Nipper's funeral was a shitty time for our family. My brother Anthony was back from Camp Lejeune, but it wasn't to party with 112. He was already a marine by then and had straightened out his life.

The day of the funeral, close to a thousand people showed up to pay their respects. All of 112 was there, past and present, along with all our neighbors and family friends. I was standing near Anthony when he tapped me on the arm and pointed to Fat George. "Who's that guy?" he asked.

Fat George was looking my way at the time. We exchanged nods. He'd done the right thing by coming, something I'd never forget.

"A friend," I told Anthony. "He's good people."

"Introduce me," Anthony said.

Fat George and I started to hang out after he showed up at my brother's funeral. It was a genuine sign of respect and I appreciated it. We became tight, especially after we both dropped out of high school. Shortly after I turned eighteen, Fat George gave me an address to meet him at on 101st Avenue. He said to call a phone number from the corner and to wait there for him. He also told me to make sure I came alone.

I didn't know why I had to go alone, but I wasn't about to show fear and bring somebody once I'd been told not to do so. I did what he asked and waited for him on the corner of 101st Avenue and Ninety-ninth Street. I stood at the pay phone and waited until I heard footsteps. When I turned toward them, Fat George was smiling ear to ear. We shook hands and he said, "Let's take a walk."

We crossed the street and walked past a brick storefront with a sign in the window, "Members Only."

"That's John's place," Fat George said. "Gotti."

I swallowed hard. Then he explained to me where we were going and who I might see. I have to admit I became pretty nervous. He told me the two social clubs were around the corner from each other. They'd been passed on from former wiseguys to current ones. Then, as we turned the corner to walk around the block, Fat George said, "The one we passed with the sign in the window? That's belongs to members of the most powerful crime family in New York."

Over time, both clubs would become a part of New York mob history, the Bergin Hunt and Fish Club, where John Gotti Sr.'s Bergin crew hung out while in Queens, and the Our Friends Social Club, which had become John Gotti Jr.'s club. The difference between the clubs was what went on inside. The Bergin club was more business oriented, while Our Friends was where the guys went to relax.

At the end of our walk around the block, Fat George told me to keep quiet and to let him do the introductions. "Don't expect anything warm from these guys until they're comfortable around you," he said. "More than likely, they'll give you some shit about your last name."

Of course they would. Rudy Giuliani was the guy trying to put the mob away in New York. The difference was he spelled his name Giuliani—G-I-U. We spelled our name Guiliani—G-U-I. The former federal prosecutor and mayor of New York was hated by street guys.

"Alright," I said. "I'll be cool."

Fat George wasn't kidding about the guys inside Our Friends being a little cold. Fuckin' frozen was more like it. I was lucky to get a nod as an acknowledgment. I was never good with names, so when I tried to remember a name after Fat George introduced somebody, I forgot one guy's name by the time he introduced the next guy.

Fat George was clearly at ease in the club. I wanted to be just as comfortable, but I knew it would take time. I'd have to prove myself with those guys and I'd have to be cool while doing it. I'm glad I didn't get to meet John Jr. that day, because I probably would've been overwhelmed. I did meet most of his alleged crew: the younger Gotti kids, Mike McLaughlin, Joey D'Angelo, Frank Lividisi, John Alite, Steve and Jeff Dobies. Of course I couldn't remember their names that day, but I would over the next few weeks.

I kept to myself and let Fat George lead the way, but I was both intimidated and in awe of the place and what it represented. John Fuckin' Gotti was hanging out right around the corner. I wouldn't get to meet him until I was accepted in his brother's place, but going home that day, just like most kids enamored with gangsters, my head was in the clouds. Seriously, to a kid like I was at that time in my life, to know I'd been within a hundred feet of a street legend was like some Little Leaguer being within ten feet of Mickey Mantle.

I would meet John Jr. in another week as he walked a dog up 101st Avenue. It was a big beautiful German shepherd and I could tell John Jr. was an animal lover just from the way he talked to the dog. At the time, I couldn't have cared less about dogs or any other animals, but Fat George warned me to never say a bad thing to or about dogs in front of John Jr. It was confirmed a few days later, when Fat George took me on a hunt to find some guy who'd beaten his dog in public outside The Big Bow Wow on Cross Bay Boulevard. Thirty years later, at least I can say the first punch I threw for the Gotti crew was at an animal abuser.

I became a part of the Our Friends Social Club over the next several months. It was a drastic change from life as a 112 gang member. There were rules to follow and a dress code. The first time I saw John Gotti Jr.

inside the club, he pointed at my mustache and told me to shave it. "Rats and cops have mustaches," he said.

It was old mob folklore having to do with rat's whiskers. Needless to say, I went home and shaved.

There were other similar rules: no earrings, never discuss anything that goes on in the club outside of the club, never talk about anything regarding business on the phone inside the club. Never even mention the word *drugs* inside the club, on the phone or not, not even if you were discussing a prescription.

The zero tolerance on drugs wasn't a rule I was as anxious to follow. By that point in my life I'd been snorting cocaine for two years. I'd never let anyone from the club see me do drugs, but if you think it's a small world in general, try existing in a world of organized crime. Everybody knows everybody else's business, and if they don't know it, somebody always wants to know it. Like every social setting, there are always those who can't wait to talk about it.

There was also a rule about smirking or rolling your eyes while someone was getting reprimanded by John Jr., or anybody else with authority. Make that mistake and you'd catch a beating, the first punch thrown would be from the guy who was catching the lecture. I saw it happen more than once and made damn sure I never made the same mistake. When somebody was catching a verbal beat-down, I looked down at the table until I knew it was over.

The "must attend" night came on Thursday, and nobody could miss without an authorized excuse. If you didn't show up, you caught a lecture or you became an immediate outcast.

My father had secured me an apprentice job with the Laborers' Union, so my days were occupied. So long as we worked, nobody asked questions at home and I never discussed what I was doing at Our Friends on Thursday nights. I kept my family in the dark about what I was doing. There was no point in giving them something else to worry about.

I also remained as low key as possible at Our Friends, never asking for favors and always following orders. If I had to go out with someone to collect, or bust up a slow pay or someone who disrespected somebody connected, I did what I was told. And make no mistake, it wasn't all breaking legs and making threats. A lot of what crews do, especially the newest members, is nothing more than serving as a gopher.

"Hey, Head, go pick up this thing here on Long Island."

"George, I need two of these things for the yard. Go to the hardware store for me."

"Joey, make a run to the laundry for my wife. She's breaking my balls."

"Head, take a ride to Chinatown and pick up some Chinese from 69 Bayard."

The restaurant called 69 Bayard served the best Chinese food in the city. It was also a hangout for wiseguys from every crew in the city as well as cops from the Fifth Precinct house on Elizabeth Street. It was the weirdest thing in the world to me the first few times I went in there. Cops and wiseguys eating right alongside each other, neither one bothering the other.

Maybe Chinese food from 69 Bayard could solve the world's problems.

One of the more anxious moments for me at the club was having to park John Jr.'s brand-new Lexus. At best, John Jr. was five-ten, maybe five-eleven. I'm six-two, so when John pulled up to the curb and told me to park his car, I almost had an anxiety attack. I'd already known from a past incident that there couldn't be a seat or mirror or steering wheel or any other kind of adjustment to what John had preprogrammed for himself. Everything in his car was set exactly the way he wanted, and nobody was permitted to adjust anything for themselves. The last time somebody adjusted a seat position, they'd caught a verbal beating.

Needless to say, I went through all sorts of contortions to fit behind the steering wheel of his new car. In the end, I drove it like a cripple; hunched forward and stiff as a board. When I got out of the car, I had muscle spasms up and down my back and legs.

To be fair, John Jr. wasn't a prima donna. Some Thursday nights after our show of colors at Our Friends Social Club, we went bowling at the Americana Lanes on Rockaway Boulevard. One night John Jr. set a new rule. "First gutter ball has to put out a cigar on his hand," he said.

Holy shit, I was thinking. I couldn't bowl to save my life. Most of the guys there weren't bowlers. Some, like me, were horrible bowlers. Most of the balls we threw in the past wound up in the gutter, after which we'd catch a ton of ball breaking. Mostly it was fun giving each other a hard time for being lousy bowlers, but that night it was getting serious. I mean, putting out a fucking cigar on your hand?

As it turned out, John Jr. picked up the first ball, set himself at the line, started forward and released a ball that traveled maybe ten feet before it wound up in a gutter.

"Fuck me," he yelled.

And just like when there was a reprimand at the social club, nobody said a word about his new gutter-ball rule. To his credit, he stood there until we all looked up. Then he said, "What, you think I won't follow my own rules?"

He took the cigar he'd brought inside the alley, lit it, and then gritted his teeth as he put it out on his hand. We were all stunned. Not so much because he'd followed through on his own rule, but because it was fucking crazy. The bottom line was, it worked. John had established a level of respect, crazy as his methodology was, by following through on his own rule. Nobody could cry about having to follow his lead after that night.

In any event, running errands was part of mob protocol that could get boring fast. It could also make a guy feel like a moron, but everybody had to do it. Taking the next step, becoming an associate, was another story. Associates are earners, the guys kicking up a weekly percentage to whichever wiseguy or crime family they work under. Some associates own legitimate businesses that serve as fronts for hiding wiseguy money. Other associates, like bookmakers and loan sharks, are simply operating under the protection of a crime family through a wiseguy. Associates were responsible for kicking up and therefore had to be in control of themselves when it came to handling money. I never kidded myself about trying to earn for other people. I was happy being in on scores at the airport or shaking down drug dealers and bars. Collecting for bookmakers and loan sharks didn't require me to kick upstairs. I knew I couldn't trust myself with money, so it was safer to do the dirty work.

The cream years for the crew started in December 1985, when John Gotti Sr. became boss of the Gambino family. For the next five years, we were untouchable. I was no longer an apprentice and had my union card with Local 46 by age eighteen. I worked construction during the weekdays and squandered my nights either partying in Richmond Hill or showing colors (showing up) at Our Friends Social Club in Ozone Park. The money flowed like from a waterfall, but for me, when money was readily available, so were drugs. I'd go on a shakedown run on a Saturday afternoon, deliver the money to the club by Saturday night, and then party back in Richmond

Hill through to Sunday morning. I was leading two lives, one as a mob enforcer for the Gotti crew, and the other as a drug addict with my old gang, 112.

One day when I showed up to the club with Fat George after a night of partying, John Jr. had a stray dog he'd found walking the streets. He handed me the leash and said, "Take care of this guy until tomorrow. I'll pick him up back here."

I looked at Fat George after John Jr. left and shrugged. We were stuck with the dog for the next twenty-four hours, but there was no way we could party if we had to babysit the dog. Of course we screwed up and tied the thing to a fence near the Harbor Club in Queens, but when we came back out, we saw the dog was gone.

"What the fuck?" Fat George said.

"Shit," I said. "Maybe we can go buy one from somebody. Something that looks like the same dog. You think John would notice?"

"Notice? He'll fuckin' kill the both of us."

I don't know how or why, but we avoided seeing him over the next few weeks and somehow he'd forgotten about the dog. Fat George and I lived those next few weeks in total terror.

A similar near-calamity, all my fault, happened when a few of us went out to a club and met up with some girls. I had a substantial drug habit by then and I'd already spent my construction paycheck and was broke at the time. We were all sitting at a table together having drinks, but when the girls went to use the bathroom together, I carefully went through their bags and lifted their wallets. I excused myself before they came back, ran to the men's room, and removed the cash. Then I returned the wallets to the bags before the girls got back. It wasn't a setup, nobody knew what I was doing, but a week or so later, John Alite grabbed me on the side and said, "You better never let John know what you did to those girls or he'll kill you."

Either Alite knew or he'd figured it out after the girls bitched about being robbed, but that's the way I was back then. I didn't think more than a few minutes ahead of my actions. I never considered the consequences of what I was doing to feed my habit.

Being an accepted member at Our Friends, I decided I wanted a gun I could carry. I made a connection with a guy nicknamed Big Lou. We were to meet at a 7-Eleven on Woodhaven Boulevard, but I'd lost my license and needed a lift. So without a second thought, I asked my mother to drive me. Had she known what I was going to buy, she never would've taken me, but it was easy to leave out the details and play on her sympathy. Once we were there, she asked me to get her a cup of coffee.

"Of course," I said. "No problem."

I went into the store, found Big Lou, and we made the exchange. Seventy-five bucks for a Raven MP-25, also known as a Saturday night special.

I grabbed a coffee for my mom and headed back out with the gun in a paper bag.

"Thanks," Mom said when I handed her the coffee. "Didn't you get anything for yourself?"

I whipped the gun out of the bag and smiled. "I got a gun!" I said.

My mother was no wallflower. She didn't want to know what I was doing hanging out with gangsters, but she also knew there was nothing she could do about it. She looked at me and shook her head.

"Just don't get yourself in trouble with that thing," she said.

The Raven MP-25, a .25-caliber semiautomatic handgun, was very popular on the streets back in the day, but you'd have to be standing really close to somebody to do any damage with one. It came in handy shaking down drug dealers from my old neighborhood because most people, especially drug dealers, as soon as they saw a gun, they panicked themselves into paralysis. The gun helped me make scores I couldn't share with the guys from Our Friends, scores that kept me high on cocaine.

Like most gun stories, there's usually something dumb that happens, and one night while I was heading to a bar with Mike Murphy, he decided to play with the thing, racking the slide and waving it at my head while he made gunshot sounds, "Pewsh, pewsh, pewsh."

I was trying to make him point it away because I always kept a round in the chamber, but he wasn't hearing me over his sound effects. Fortunately, he had it pointed straight ahead when the thing fired. Mike had put a small hole in my windshield, directly across from where he was sitting. All I could remember was the ringing in my ears and the smell of cordite. Mike sat there with a big dumb grin on his face.

"Ooops," he said.

The hole was visible enough to cause problems if it was spotted, but I came up with the idea of caulking the hole like it was a window frame.

It was a hectic life, working my union job during the day and splitting my nights between hanging with my old 112 friends on Jamaica Avenue and putting in my time at Our Friends. I had money coming out of my ears, but it didn't take long for me to send it up my nose. I bought myself a new 1984 Cadillac and several dozen Michael Jordan tracksuits. Thirty years later, the Cadillac is long gone, but the tracksuits remain my wardrobe every day of the week.

My addictions continued to worsen. I was a full-blown cocaine addict and a raging alcoholic. I was still working days, but they were mostly tit jobs. My father's association with the Vario family kept me employed doing the easiest work. Still, come night I was a mess. Thursday nights I showed up to Our Friends as straight as I'd gone to work the same day, but once I left the club, I was at one of the Richmond Hill bars drinking vodka and snorting lines of cocaine with my friends from 112.

There were nights when I was caught doing drugs by other members of the Gotti crew, but usually they were doing the same thing. John Jr. was probably the only one in the crew to abide by the no-drugs rule, but the more drugs and alcohol I used, the more difficult they became to hide. I managed to continue wearing two hats, three if you counted my legitimate job as a union laborer, but it was only a matter of time before I hit rock bottom from my addictions.

In 1989, my father's smoking habit came back to haunt him in the form of lung cancer. He suffered a full year before he died in 1990. It was devastating for all of us, but especially my mother. My father had worked hard his entire life. Big Lou had done a good job raising his family. He'd provided for six kids and had done his best to raise us to be hard workers. All of his sons except me had joined the military and lived good, decent lives. Our sister, Dorothy, had been a loner as a kid, but she grew out of it, married, and raised three beautiful sons. It still remains a regret of mine that my father never had the chance to see me become a sober adult.

In August that year, just six weeks after Big Lou died, I married a woman I'd dated since high school. Because I promised I would never involve her in my life after our divorce, all I can say about my short marriage is that I obviously wasn't ready for any kind of commitment. The marriage ended two years later while I was in prison, but who could blame her for divorcing me? I will always regret the way I treated her.

The party with the Gotti crew officially ended in December 1990, when John Sr. was arrested, along with Salvatore "Sammy" Gravano and Frank Locascio at the Ravenite Social Club on Mulberry Street in Manhattan. It would take two more years before Gotti was convicted, but without a powerful boss, the high times were over.

The Our Friends crew attended all of John Sr.'s court appearances. We stood outside the courthouse wearing "Free John Gotti" hats and shirts and chanting the same to stir up a crowd. The day he was convicted was no exception. We were there in our shirts and hats, chanting through bullhorns, but it eventually got out of hand and a car or two got overturned. Some of us were arrested. I was lucky and escaped with a few other guys.

The bottom line was, the government had finally won. The authorities were willing to deal away the nineteen murders Salvatore Gravano had admitted to committing in order to convict John Gotti. Our mob lives would never be the same, not for "made guys" (mob-member inductees), associates, or enforcers—not for anybody around the life. The string of mob defections that has followed since Gravano would eventually include the boss and underboss of another crime family. Fathers would rat out sons. Sons would rat out fathers. Nobody was immune from a government deal, not cousins, best friends—nobody.

Not long after John Gotti Sr. was convicted and sent away for life, a pair of murders cleared my head of any thoughts about remaining connected to the mob. Not that I was much concerned about my future, because I can't make that claim, not while I was doing drugs and robbing drug dealers to support my habit. But when two guys I respected were killed, reality set in. Catching a pinch was one thing. You did your time and were back out. Getting killed was something else. It was over—bang, you're dead.

In April 1991, John Gotti Jr.'s bodyguard and chauffer, Bobby Boriello, was killed outside his home in Brooklyn. Whatever his mob past might've included, Bobby was a beautiful person. One thing I came to understand over the years was something reiterated by John Gotti Jr. during a CBS *60 Minutes* interview he did with Steve Croft. People in the life understood the choices they'd made. Murders were part of the life, and very rarely, usually by mistake, did they involve innocent civilians. When Bobby Boriello was killed, whatever the reasoning behind the murder allegedly attributed to Anthony "Gaspipe" Casso (another tough guy turned rat), it was something everybody in the life had to expect.

Still, Bobby's murder rattled me. I knew him. I knew what a decent guy he was to people inside and outside the life. It made me sick that he'd been killed.

Two years later, in October 1993, another guy I knew and admired was killed. Joe Scopo was with the Colombo crime family, but he was also a union official with Local 6A of the Cement and Concrete Workers. He was killed outside his home after being ambushed, along with his future son-in-law and nephew. He tried to flee the scene but was killed a few doors from where he lived. His wife and kids were in the house when it happened.

I was in prison at the time or I might've been hanging out at Our Friends Social Club just nine blocks away. Joe's murder had something to do with an ongoing war between the Persico and Orena factions of the Colombo crime family. All I know is that I admired Joe big-time, and I'd just lost another good friend.

The murder of two friends was sobering, at least when it came to thoughts of remaining in a knock-around life. The fact I couldn't follow mob rules that required I stay away from drugs made it an even easier choice to eventually walk away. If I continued to hang around the mob, it would only be a matter of time before my addictions would get me in the kind of trouble that ultimately led to a premature burial.

It was after John Gotti Sr. was convicted on April 2, 1992, after only fourteen hours of jury deliberation, that I started to do my own thing with a little more urgency. If you made a score, whether it was robbing a truck, a store, or some drug dealer, it was supposed to be shared with the people you were around. For me that meant the wiseguys at Our Friends, but hitting on local drug dealers without letting anyone from the club know about it was one way to earn some of the money that had dried up after Gotti's conviction. I was a full-blown junkie and a drunk at the time, and I needed cash to feed my habits. There was no way I could share everything I came across without coming up short to feed my addictions.

If I couldn't rob drug dealers of their cash, I took their drugs, whatever they had on them. I started to spend less and less time around the social club and more time doing drugs and drinking. There was no way I could walk into the club high without catching a beating, so I stayed away.

I became a little more reckless than usual when I was one of a dozen grooms for a Gotti wedding at Russo's On The Bay. The night before the wedding, I wound up wasted on drugs and booze. Ralph Salzano was with me in a bar—God knows where—from midnight through to the morning. All I could remember was him screaming at me to take a shower and go to sleep.

"They'll fuckin' kill you if you screw this up!" he yelled.

"I'll be okay," I kept saying (or trying to say) before I took another drink. I'm sure I was slurring every attempt at speech.

Come morning, I could barely stand. Ralph helped me get to the church on time, literally pulling me out of the car and standing me up. He kept telling me, "You have to pull this off or you'll wind up in a dumpster, James."

Somehow I did pull it off, but there was no way people didn't notice how James had fucked up once again. The Gotti family was pissed off. Word came back that somebody wanted to kill James (me). It was probably just a rumor, but the truth was nobody could've been surprised. Everyone knew that I'd become a drug addict and they let it go, but not with any kind of a blessing.

The following week when I showed up to the club, I was ignored. It was awkward and it pissed me off, but by then I didn't even want to be there. It wasn't like we were earning the way we had before 1990. It wasn't as if we were feeling untouchable anymore.

The funny thing was, I'd always felt that wiseguys had an invisible Rolodex in their heads loaded with information about the guys they kept around them. My card no doubt had more bad things on it than good. Showing up to a Gotti wedding stoned probably topped the list.

So when an opportunity for a big score came my way, I kept it to myself and took a giant step out on my own, a step that led me straight into prison.

I went from James Headbird to James the Jailbird.

The day I committed the crime that would send me to the Riverhead Correctional Facility, I was coked-up for a hijacking on the far end of Long Island. I was doing the driving. Sean Fitzpatrick and Angelo Sforza were in the backseat. We each had a gun, and all the guns were loaded, which made absolutely no fuckin' sense, because the hijacking was supposed to be an inside job. I had a guy who was setting the thing up for an equal cut of the take. We would be moving a truckload of very popular Gameboys, a huge score if everything went as planned.

It was close to midnight, but I was so high on cocaine I never noticed the lack of traffic heading west on the Long Island Expressway. Once we passed Exit 50 for Smithtown, the eastbound traffic lightened up enough to make some time, except we weren't in a rush. We were doing 70, then 80, 90, 100 and finally 110 miles per hour heading farther east. In fact, until I noticed the lights from a helicopter flying pretty low ahead of us, I assumed there had been some monstrous accident up ahead.

We were supposed to get off at Exit 72. The truck was supposed to be at a loading dock in a nearby warehouse. A mile or so after the Smithtown exit, I saw a police car up ahead. I immediately slowed down. Probably from criminal instinct, I told Sean and Angelo to pop the clips from their guns. Then, as I came to a stop, two cars without their lights on raced up ahead of us and blocked our path. The next thing I knew, Suffolk County policemen had surrounded our car and were pointing shotguns at our heads.

"Freeze, motherfuckers, or we'll blow your heads off!"

It was simple math we'd never bothered to check on before making the drive, an important detail I'd ignored. Our inside guy for the hijacking had been caught a few weeks earlier in a drug bust and had offered us up on a silver platter for his own deal. It would've been easy enough to check on the rat, but the thought had never crossed my mind.

The fact that I was high as a kite meant so little to the law that my driving under the influence was ignored. It was a "kidnapping kit" that did me in: a bag with gloves, tape, ski masks, plastic cuffs and handcuffs, along with burglary tools and the guns we were carrying. When all was said and done, the charges included conspiracy to commit burglary, kidnapping, and murder.

Because of the charges, the FBI was brought into the case. I was still being interrogated when an agent walked into the room holding my .25 Raven with a pencil through the trigger guard.

"Hey, asshole," he said to me. "Look what we found."

What could I say?

Exactly, so I said nothing. It was mine. I'd forgotten I had hidden it under the front seat of my car.

Of course that dopey little bullet hole that Mike Murphy had made playing with my Raven a year or so earlier, the bullet hole I'd never bothered to have fixed in a windshield I'd never bothered to replace, was what the police claimed they used as an excuse to pull us over so their rat wouldn't have to appear in court to testify if we'd gone to trial. It was a crock of shit. The police couldn't have seen the bullet hole in the dark, but there was nothing we could do about it. In the end, they didn't need to expose their snitch, which meant he could go on to snitch again another day.

We spent a total of twelve hours being interrogated, then another thirty-two hours in custody at the Fourth Precinct in Smithtown. After we were finally processed through the Suffolk County Court, my bail was set at $500,000.

"What the fuck?" I said to my court-appointed attorney. "Where the hell am I gonna get a half a million dollars?"

"You got family, kid?"

"Yeah, but they're not rich."

"They own a home?"

Before Mom could come to my rescue with bail money from remortgaging the house, I spent the next fifty days in jail. Frankly, it was a relief not to have to face the guys from Our Friends. When Angelo was bailed out, he caught a beating and had his jaw broken for disrespecting the crew at Our Friends. He got word back to me that I was dead for pulling a job on my own, a big time no-no. It was bad enough they were still pissed off from my attending a wedding all fucked up on booze and drugs.

If they broke Angelo's jaw, they'd do worse to me. I'd been the ringleader. I could deal with the fifty days inside a lot easier than having to show my face at Our Friends. I figured the first fifty days inside were a bargain.

Of course I felt like shit when my mother showed up to bail me out. I told her there was no way I was going to trial so some lawyer could rape her for the mortgage money. If I had to go away, so be it. I knew I'd screwed up worse than ever before, but this time it was a direct hit on my mother. She wasn't the junkie. She wasn't the fool hanging around wiseguys and street gangs. This one I'd have to take on the chin, but I wasn't about to leave my house or go anywhere near Our Friends. I stayed home and remained MIA (missing in action).

Two weeks of genuine tension followed. The unwritten law was that a prosecutor would make three offers before going to trial. The first offer was for a seventeen-year plea deal. I'd be forty when I got out. A second plea deal never came, but that was because there had been a series of 7-Eleven robberies on Long Island and the prosecutor believed we were responsible for them. Apparently we fit the description. I was screwed everywhere I turned.

The attorney my mother hired told me he could stall the actual sentencing a good two years, but I wasn't interested in having that over my oversized head. As it turned out, they only wanted two of us, so we let Angelo walk away because he had a wife and kids. Sean opted for the long stall and wound up going in a month or so after I came out some eighteen months later. I told my attorney to get me the best deal he could, but without wasting another dime of my mother's money. Between the jails being overcrowded and whatever magic he worked, I was offered back-to-back bullets—two years straight time without parole.

I remaindered myself to Riverhead at the end of the two weeks.

One of the first things you learn when your time is up inside prison is to never look back. If you do, you'll be back. If you don't, you'll stand a chance of staying out.

It was the last thing the guard who walked me out of Riverhead said to me. "Don't look back."

I didn't, but long before I caught that advice, I had a lot of jail time to serve in one of the most abusive prison environments in the state. Riverhead Correctional Facility is still one of the most feared prisons for the conditions that continue to exist behind its walls. Back in 1993, when I had the pleasure of vacationing in that shithole, the first night inside was one that could make or break fresh fish—the new kids on the block.

We had seventy-two hours of lockdown before we were sent to the tiers; three days of absolute boredom that could make you crazy thinking about your overall sentence. To make things worse, I had a junkie in a neighboring cell crying the entire time. He wanted his methadone.

"Please, give me my methadone! Please, I can't take it. I need my methadone. I need a fix!"

After a few hours of listening to him piss and moan, all I wanted to do was fix his head through a wall. Every hour he was awake, he was crying for his fix. For me it was a total reality check. I was also detoxing, but it was nothing like the guy in the next cell. I wanted to get high, too, but I understood the situation I was in. I was stuck in a cage like an animal. My freedom was gone. There'd be no more booze or drugs for at least two years.

The next step was a move into the tiers, where we had to wait until we were officially sentenced. One man to a cell. One more reality check. Inmate counts three times a day, surprise cell tossing (searches) where the storm troopers (guards) had their fun fucking with us. Lining up for meals like zombies.

I had a plea deal, the back-to-back bullets, but until it was stated in court, I was in limbo. It took a month before I was sentenced and finally moved down to one of the dorms.

Living in a dorm might sound like college life, but it's far from it. Dorms were the most dangerous environment because there was nothing separating inmates. There were anywhere from sixty to eighty beds to a dorm, leaving a lot of open space for trouble. Everything from stealing to midnight attacks occurred because the rooms were wide open. By the time correction officers even attempted to stop something, a lot of damage could be done.

Once I was moved down to the dorms, my first fight was with a black kid nicknamed "Jackal." He was also a new inmate and probably overanxious to show his stones. I was given the job of handing out meal trays in our dorm. One night Jackal accused me of stealing one of his fish sticks. Jackal started cursing me. I told him to go fuck himself and he called me out. He told me to "strap up." He had a crowd behind him, including the biggest dude in the entire facility, a weight lifter doing life named Melvin. Once the COs saw there was trouble, they jumped out of their bubble and separated everyone.

On the street, when you were told to "strap up," it meant bring a gun. I was new to prison and didn't understand what Jackal had meant. A Latin King explained that it meant wearing your work boots for a fight, rather than prison issued flip-flops. The same kid also told me that once I hit Jackal, the other blacks would jump me, including the beast, Melvin. Melvin was a lifer from somewhere upstate awaiting trial at Riverhead. He benched five hundred pounds and could break a neck like snapping a twig.

I was nervous waiting for the fight, but then I noticed how Jackal didn't go out into the yard the next few days. He stayed inside reading a book instead. At the end of the week, I waited until everyone went outside and we were alone in the dorm. Then I yelled at Jackal across the room, "Okay, motherfucker, *now* let's strap up."

I was taking a risk, but I was sick and tired of waiting for the fight. What happened next was Jackal changed his tune.

"Hey, bro, I was only messing with you," he said. "I don't want no trouble."

The next day I heard that Melvin gave Jackal a slap-down for being a bitch. All I know is Melvin nodded hello to me and that was the end of that situation. I'd earned my space and never had to throw a punch or use my work boots. There were other fights later on, but they were nothing more than quick scraps with a few punches thrown before they were broken up.

Maybe because he respected me, but one day Melvin approached me about smuggling in some heroin his girlfriend was bringing on a visit. I had a cleanup assignment at the time, sweeping and mopping different areas of the facility. That day I was working the visiting room. Melvin said his girlfriend would leave a can of Nestlé's Quik on the floor for me to grab. In it would be six bags of heroin. I was scared shitless the entire time, but there was no way I could punk out. If I was caught smuggling heroin inside Riverhead, I'd be heading upstate for ten or more years. What I did was ass-rack (body-conceal) the heroin bags, and I delivered them to Melvin later the same day.

In retrospect, it was some dumb shit I did, but from that point on, nobody could fuck with me while Melvin was at Riverhead. As it turned out, he was there until a few months before I got out.

Once my stones were established, and probably because I'd remained a bit of a clown, I became an accepted member of the club—not any particular club like the Latin Kings, Bloods, Crips, or Skinheads, but the general population. Although my hijacking debacle and drug and alcohol addictions had strained my affiliation with the Gotti crew, if push came to shove, I could still reach out to them. In that way they were like the marines about not abandoning their own. The problem with reaching out, however, was the lack of connected guys doing time at Riverhead. Wiseguys and their associates tended to head upstate or to Pennsylvania, with the occasional brief layover on Riker's Island or in the Tombs in downtown Manhattan. I was pretty much on my own in Riverhead.

One thing I liked about the dorms was the way they were divided. Blacks had cordoned off an area they named Martin Luther King Avenue. The Latin Kings had San Juan Plaza. A few Mexican inmates had their strip named by the rest of the dorm. It was called Skid Row. Over time I bonded with the other four white guys in my dorm—we were the minority, make no mistake—and we moved to a corner we named John Gotti Boulevard.

Prison is a bad place, but it isn't nearly as bad as it was depicted on the HBO show, *Oz*. Inmates aren't raped or killed every day, the way some of the episodes in the show portrayed. Riverhead was a bad place and you had to show your stones to survive, but once the initial bullshit was over, it was a matter of staying away from trouble you could avoid. You see a fight, look the other way. A correction officer asks you for information, you don't know anything. Somebody looks to confide in you, tell them you're not interested.

And then sometimes there was trouble you couldn't avoid. Direct confrontations, whether you were being tested or not, had to be met head on and without hesitation.

And sometimes something really shitty went down right in front of you and you had to step back and ignore it. For me it was watching a black kid get his face cut open from one corner of his mouth up to his ear.

I was playing cards with a Latin King named Perricho. We were playing against two black guys with the Bloods. The protocol for cards inside Riverhead was simple. You brought whatever you were playing with (betting) to the table, no exceptions. If it was a game being played for smokes, you didn't leave your cigarettes back in your cell hidden under your mattress. You brought them to the game and you put them on the table.

That day we won the game. One of the black guys had his cigarettes. The other didn't. The guy who didn't have any went back to his cell to make a peanut butter sandwich. I knew it was bad when Perricho followed him. I saw the guy take a bite of the sandwich and then Perricho struck. It was the weirdest thing I'd ever seen. The guy's mouth opened from one corner up to his ear, but there was hardly any blood. All you could see was this chuck of peanut butter sandwich falling out the side of his mouth.

Of course the guards wanted to know what the hell had happened, but there was no way anyone was going to talk.

I was inside just about four months when the chaplain sent for me. In the mob when you're sent for, it usually isn't good. It isn't much better when the chaplain inside a prison wants to see you. The first thing I assumed was my mother had passed. Then I wondered if it was another of my brothers, or maybe my sister. Prison can give a person a ton of time to think the worst thoughts. The time between being summoned to the chaplain and actually speaking to him was one of total anxiety for me.

I nodded at the chaplain and saw he was holding a folder with papers inside. I assumed it was somebody's death certificate. It wasn't. They were divorce papers.

"Your wife is serving you," he said.

The few years we were married, I'd made her miserable. Going into year three, I was in the joint. Like I said, who could blame her?

Not everything about jail was horrible. Sometimes some funny shit went down. One time somebody snuck a tattoo machine into the dorms and it made the COs crazy. Every other day somebody sported a new tat, sometimes way too visible not to notice. Suddenly there were surprise searches every other day. Cells would be tossed and then retossed, but the tattoo machine was passed from one dorm to another without being discovered. At one point the warden must've been so frustrated, he had the guards put a mole into circulation. He was a guy who claimed to have already done a year upstate and was waiting for trial. He might've gotten away with it if he didn't have to shower, because as soon as he was naked, we all noticed his perfect tan lines. The guy was full of shit. When nobody would talk to him, he suddenly disappeared from circulation.

Another time I was told by one of the COs that I was being allowed outside to wash out the laundry bins. It was a big deal because normally I wasn't allowed outside to the loading dock, or anywhere else considered outside the main building, because of my violence charges. I'd always been assigned the shit jobs like sweeping the recreation areas and cleaning the bathrooms. That August day it was blistering hot outside and twice as bad inside. The CO was giving me a break by letting me wash out the laundry bins on the loading dock. I appreciated it, probably too much, because as soon as I had the laundry bins cleaned, I filled one with water and took a dive off the dock into the bin to cool off.

The CO didn't appreciate it, especially since he'd done me a favor. The warden had a good sense of humor about it, but I still had to be punished. I was being led down to the hole when the warden's voice could be heard over the facility loudspeaker: "Today history was made at Riverhead. Mr. Guiliani from North Four has performed the very first dive off one of our loading docks. He received a 9.2 for his dive, along with a week in the hole. Congratulations to him."

Although most of the COs were pricks, not all of them were. One particular CO was a good guy. At least, most of us liked CO Rivera. He got himself in a jam one day when he forgot his keys on his desk. I saw the keys were still there after his shift ended, and I immediately put them inside one of the drawers. Another CO was on duty when Rivera came back to the facility in a panic about his keys. He couldn't mention it to the other CO, so he ran from place to place looking for them. Apparently he could've been fired for losing them. As soon as I caught his attention, I told him where I put the keys. He was very grateful. The next day he brought me and a few of my friends a box filled with Burger King Whoppers, fries, and Cokes.

Incarceration did two things for me. First, it dried me out. Not that I'd remain that way once I was released, but during the eighteen months I spent in Riverhead, I remained sober. Second, it kept me off the streets and away from the bad shit that was going down in the two worlds I inhabited—the mob world and the drug world. All of the legal troubles I'd ever found for myself revolved around drugs and/or alcohol.

It wasn't a tough decision to walk away from the Gotti crew. Both John Sr. and John Jr. had no use for drug addicts. Aside from the impairment in judgment that drugs cause, the feeling on the street was that anyone dealing in drugs could be expected to cut a deal and turn rat to protect themselves and their habit. Snitches were what kept most mob bosses up nights.

Today you can read about the overall effect the government snitch program has had on the mob almost daily. The mob has a much closer-to-home problem these days. When underbosses get to trade nineteen murders for a new life in the desert, or when mob bosses get to avoid the death penalty by snitching on their former crime family, it doesn't take a degree in physics to see the glory days are over.

I was playing in-house prison card tournaments the last six months of my sentence. In fact, the day I was released, I was scheduled to play in the final tournament. Truth be told, I would've waited another day, but it wasn't an option. I was officially released from prison on Halloween weekend in 1995. I was clean and I couldn't wait to return to my work as a laborer. Unfortunately, I wouldn't be out of the joint five minutes before I was back to using cocaine and alcohol.

Chapter 5

Lena and Our Diamond Collar Store

The year 2001 ended on a shitty note. My brother Thomas, the baby of the Guiliani brood, felt some pain in his pelvic area and discovered there was a lump. He went to a doctor who told him it was a harmless cyst and prescribed antibiotics. Thomas took them for a few weeks, but the pain didn't go away. He was keeping the pain and his situation secret from the family, except for my mother. She made him see another doctor, a specialist, and he ordered tests. The harmless cyst turned out to be testicular cancer, and it had already started to spread.

The pain in Thomas's groin eventually reached his lower back. He went through a few surgeries, but the cancer always returned. Eventually the cancer was too advanced to remove surgically and had spread to his lymph nodes. Thomas was administered chemotherapy, but the treatments weren't going well. The doctors told my mother what was happening, and she kept what they'd said from her son. When she told the rest of her kids what was going on, we were all devastated. She kept the darkest news from Thomas until he was rushed to a hospital one day. The doctors told my mother there was nothing more that could be done and that she should make him comfortable. Thomas was brought up to our aunt's house in Saratoga Springs. While he was there, he suffered a brain aneurism and was rushed to a hospital in nearby Albany. Mom called us and said that Thomas had fallen while he was upstate and that he was being brought back to our aunt's house in Saratoga. She didn't tell us how severe the situation was. Instead, she asked us to come upstate to try and cheer Thomas up.

We knew he'd been sick, but we had no idea how advanced his cancer had become, so when Anthony and I drove up to Saratoga, it was with plans to break our brother's balls. We even joked about what we'd say.

"Get up, you lazy bastard," I said.

"Enough with the jerking off in bed," Anthony said. "At least use the bathroom."

It's what we used to do to each other as kids, break balls, but when we walked into the hospital room and saw Thomas, there was no joking. We realized our brother didn't have long to live.

Thomas was in a coma. He looked tiny in the hospital bed they'd rented for him. His skin had turned a horrible shade of gray that I'll never be able to forget. My mother told us that the doctor had said Thomas was brain dead. It was just a matter of time before he passed. None of us wanted to see him like that, least of all my mother.

We all stayed with Thomas until my mother made the decision to take him off life support. We crowded around his bed, said our good-byes, prayed, and cried.

I couldn't believe the strength my mother exhibited. As bad as it was for her children, it was the second time in her life that Mom would have to bury one of her kids. It was also the second time her children would have to say good-bye to one of their siblings. It was a somber and painful day.

Thomas was twenty-seven when he died.

The irony, of course, was what we learned afterward; that testicular cancer is one of the most curable forms of cancer. The first doctor who'd prescribed antibiotics for a harmless cyst had fucked up.

Needless to say, I had a brand-new reason to continue my downward spiral with drugs and booze. I still had my job working as a construction laborer, but that was because friends in the union continued to look after me. Most guys showing up to work high or forgetting to show up at all would've been canned, but some gangster connections still embedded in the construction trades were like guardian angels for me.

I was living with my brother Anthony in Richmond Hill, occasionally working out with him at the Olympia gym on Fresh Pond Road in Ridgewood, Queens. Anthony had already sculpted his body with weight lifting and could've competed if he wanted. He worked out religiously, while I showed up sporadically; one week on, two weeks off, and so on. Occasionally I'd have a good month or two when I'd work out several weeks in a row, but it never lasted. I'd get myself buff and look healthy, but my body was loaded with steroids. Eventually, I'd fall into a funk and wind up in some local bar drinking vodka and snorting cocaine.

I still couldn't save a penny. My paychecks were spent as soon as I could cash them. Dealing drugs and steroids was a way to support my own habits and had nothing to do with saving coin. All I had in my life was a good job, thanks to some old mob connections, and a place to sleep, because no matter how bad I fucked up, my brother wouldn't turn me out.

Sometimes the realization of what I'd done with my life caught up to me, and my funks would turn into depressions so severe I couldn't look at myself. It's not an easy thing to wake up one day and realize your entire life has been nothing more than getting over and never taking responsibility for anything. At thirty-five years old, I had nothing to show for my time on this planet except heartache for those who loved me, prison tattoos, and a conviction record.

Sometimes we don't think about our future until it's staring us in the face. What the hell was I going to do in another ten, fifteen years? What was my future going to be if I ever lost my protection with union connections? What the hell kind of work could I do besides lifting and carrying heavy shit on a construction site? Who the hell would hire me with my past?

My brother Anthony was helping me survive by sharing his apartment and keeping an eye on me, but I was facing middle age. I didn't have a steady woman friend or anybody else I could depend on outside of family. It was a lonely time in my life, and my future wasn't exactly bright.

I'd severely handcuffed my options by making bad choices all my life. When I thought about what the future might bring, I was overwhelmed with depression. I'd known way too many toothless barflies, men and women in their sixties and seventies, who lived from drink to drink. Was that what I was staring at?

The reality was: yeah, no doubt. I was never meant to be a rocket scientist, but I knew that if I continued the shit I was doing to myself, eventually I'd overdose and drop dead, which would be merciful compared to the alternative—winding up a bum on Jamaica Avenue, Richmond Hill's skid row. Thoughts about my future only deepened the depression I began to experience. Some days I couldn't get out of bed and missed work because of it. Some nights I drank just to put myself under. I began to experience more and more blackouts from booze and cocaine frenzies. It became a vicious and destructive cycle; the worse I felt about myself, the more drugs and drinking I did.

Add a heavy dose of guilt to my two addictions and I had a trifecta. Whenever I thought about all the shit I'd put my mother through, the wife I'd completely neglected, my felony record that had left me with nothing more than prison stories and tattoos, I wanted to crawl into a hole and die. The more I thought about it, the more depressed I became. I was a grown man with no money, no self-esteem, no girlfriend, and no future. At that point in my life, what woman in her right mind would go near me? When I wanted sex, I paid for it, but not through some escort agency or uptown call girl. I went with unattractive street hookers, the kind that would scare a normal man into celibacy.

Frankly, I thought I was a piece of shit. I felt comfortable around those who felt the same way about themselves; skank streetwalkers, barflies, cokeheads, crackheads, you name it. Those were the only people I wasn't embarrassed to be around. I used to think, "If the Gotti crew could see me now."

One day I made a small score ripping off a drug dealer on Atlantic Avenue. Whenever I was broke or needed drugs, I'd watch a dealer operate, sometimes for hours on end, then follow him to his stash and wait for the right moment to grab the drugs and run. Being a sneak thief became my specialty. That day I found about a grand's worth of the dealer's drug stash, and I went on a bender that would leave me on a beach with a gun and a plan to kill myself.

It was in the early afternoon on a steaming hot August day when I walked into Doyle's on Lefferts Boulevard and Jamaica Avenue. Chrissy, a friend from back in the day, was working the bar. First thing she did when I sat at the hook of the bar was point a finger and say, "No credit today, James. You don't have any cash, no drinks."

I looked at her dumbfounded. I'd just ripped off a dealer. I had several bags of cocaine and more than $300. I was loaded, and I was there to party.

I pulled out the cash, waved it alongside my head like I was flaunting $100 bills, and said, "Start pouring, honey. Pour yourself one while you're at it. Then we'll do a line together."

"Fuck you, James," Chrissy said. "You know I don't do blow."

"Fair enough," I said. "I'll do your line."

She shook her head at me and poured me a drink. I did one line, then two, then another couple of lines. Before I knew it, between the booze and the cocaine, I shared some of my loot with a few other cokeheads and depleted my supplies of cash and drugs.

It was dark outside when I finally stumbled out of Doyle's. I was wasted to the point where I couldn't speak without slurring. Tripping around a fire hydrant and then bouncing off a Jamaica Avenue El column, I somehow made it to the driver's side of my car. The miracle continued when I drove the five blocks to The Little Brown Jug without crashing.

I stepped inside the bar and saw my friend Tommy was working. He saw the mess I was and helped me to a table where I must've blacked out, because when I was conscious again, Tommy was closing the place.

"James, come on, brother, time to go," he said.

"What's up?" I said.

"You. Let's go, its three o'clock in the morning. I'm closing up. You gotta go."

I twisted and stretched my aching body where I sat, and then Tommy brought over a cup of black coffee and set it on the table.

"Here," he said. "Drink this and wake up. Use the bathroom. You got ten minutes."

I never drank a cup of American coffee in my life. I almost threw up looking at it. I excused myself and stepped inside the bathroom. What I did in there, I have no idea, because fifteen minutes later Tommy found me crawling around the floor. I'd had a mini-blackout, something that had become more and more prevalent of late.

"James, what the fuck?" he said. "Come on, man, I have to close."

I used the toilet and washed my face enough to see straight, and then I remembered that I was broke.

I said, "Tommy, I need a few bucks to get home, bro."

Tommy went to the register, grabbed a twenty, and set it on the bar. "There," he said. "But leave your car. You're still too fucked up to drive. Drink the coffee I poured you and let's go. I want to get home already."

"Not the coffee again," I said. "You got espresso?"

Tommy laughed. "What the fuck is this, *Young Frankenstein*? Espresso?"

I waved him off. "I can't drink American coffee," I said.

"That's too bad, Head," Tommy said, "but you gotta go."

I thanked him profusely, the way drunks often do when they're especially sloppy, and then I stepped out onto the avenue. I made it to my car, sat behind the wheel, and started the engine. If I had thought about going home at all after Tommy mentioned it, I forgot about it as soon as I remembered I had a fresh twenty on me. I drove up and down the avenue looking for a bar that was still open, or at least one where I knew the bartender would be having a few drinks at the end of a long day.

I tried Pete's on 114th and Jamaica, but he'd already closed. I backtracked a few blocks to My Place/Your Place on 111th. Jimmy Wells, somebody I called Uncle Jimmy, was just ushering out the leftover drunks. Jimmy saw me and smiled.

"Head, again?"

"Uncle Jimmy!" I yelled.

"You ever get tired of it?" he said.

"Only when I run out of coke."

He shook his head.

"You know a place I can take a piss and maybe have a drink?"

We exchanged a hug and went inside. Jimmy closed and locked the door behind him. He didn't do blow, but he knew plenty of people who did. He put out a call before breaking open a fresh bottle of Absolut. He half filled a pair of highball glasses and we toasted the old neighborhood.

"To the hill," Jimmy said.

"To One-Twelve," I said.

"Forever," we both said.

We touched glasses and we each downed our drinks. Jimmy immediately poured another two shots. I don't know what we talked about or what we did besides drinking, but by the time the blow arrived, the sun was coming up. I needed the cocaine to offset the booze, because I'd already started to slur again.

I did two lines and felt like new. At least I thought I did. I started pounding the vodka again, this time skipping the glass and drinking straight from the bottle. Uncle Jimmy had started to yawn and wanted to get home. He told me he'd let me sleep in the back if I wanted, or he'd give me a few bucks for a cab home.

I reminded him I had my car.

"You drive like that, you'll wind up dead," he said. "Sleep it off or let me get you a cab so you can get home. I'll call a cab and you can leave me your car keys. I'll hold them for you."

There it was again, people looking out for me, but his mentioning home didn't register. I took another hit off the bottle, did one last line, and accepted his offer for money.

When he asked me for my car keys, I told him I was fine.

"You're fucked up, Head. Cops pull you over like that, you'll have a headache."

"I'll be okay," I said.

Jimmy knew he wasn't going to get me into a cab. He closed up the place and headed upstairs to his apartment. Once back on the street, I backtracked to Pete's on 114th Street. Of course it was still dark inside the bar. If it was closed before, why wouldn't it be now, a couple hours later? It probably wouldn't open for another four or five hours.

I don't know why, but I took a shot and pulled on the door. Miracle of miracles, it was unlocked. It wasn't unheard of on Jamaica Avenue. There were a few dumps like Pete's that stayed open after hours because the late-night bartender was too drunk to notice the time or because he'd passed out after drinking himself unconscious. Whoever had closed Pete's for the night had either done exactly that, or he'd forgotten to lock the door. Or maybe he'd gone to pick up something for breakfast and would return any minute. Who cared? Not me. All I knew was that I had access to more booze, and if I was lucky, an unlocked cash register.

As it turned out, nobody was inside the bar. I started by going through the cash register and tip jars, taking in about sixty bucks in small bills, probably what the bartender had left for change the next day. Then I picked a bottle of Stolichnaya off the second shelf, removed the cap, and drank deep. Then I drank again, and again.

At some point I blacked out, but this time it was a long one. When I woke up, the lights in the bar were all on, and I was spewing everything inside me onto the floor near the men's room.

I felt a pain in the middle of my stomach. Then I heard cursing. Loud cursing.

"Motherfucker! God damn it, James!"

"Don't take the Lord's name in vain," I mumbled.

The next kick caught me in the side of the face and rolled me into my vomit. It isn't a pretty picture, but it's one I'd grown accustomed to during my worst days as a junkie-alcoholic—waking up in puddles of vomit and urine.

I must've been pretty stunned because when I was able to clear my head again, I was outside on the sidewalk under a very hot sun. Between the heat, the sunshine, the kick in the stomach that had started my spewing, the kick to my face, and the sound of the J train rumbling overhead on the El, I thought my head would explode. I crawled my way to the curb and used one of the El's columns to stand. There was a ticket on the windshield of my car. I tossed it.

I saw myself in the reflection of the bar window and cringed. My tracksuit was filthy from dust and vomit. The smell made me sick. I removed the jacket and tossed it in a garbage pail. I spotted a sprinkler in a yard across 114th Street and headed for it. I unhooked the hose from the sprinkler and gave myself a shower.

I was at it for a few minutes before I heard someone yell, "What the fuck?"

I turned around and saw a middle-aged bald guy on his stoop.

"Sorry, man," I said as I doused my head with more water.

He waited for me to finish before saying, "Done now?"

"Yeah, I think so."

"You think you can hook it back up to the sprinkler?"

I didn't know what he was talking about until he pointed at the sprinkler. I hooked it back up, thanked him, and then headed back to my car on Jamaica Avenue.

I was under the El at 109th Street. The bar there, Finally Al's, wasn't open yet. I needed a pack of cigarettes. I crossed the avenue and walked inside a deli. I stuck my hand inside my pocket for what I thought were small bills and pulled out a roll of twenties. It was like Christmas. I had no idea how I got my hands on it until I remembered taking money from the register, something like sixty bucks.

"Fuck me," I said.

"Excuse me?" the Indian behind the counter said.

I looked up and saw he was staring at me.

"What else you need?" he said with an accent. He set my cigarettes on the counter.

I must've been nervous from my newfound score, because I said, "Oh, a sandwich. Ham and Swiss with mayo and a coffee. Two coffees."

What the fuck? With all the cocaine and booze in my system, I couldn't eat with a gun to my head. And coffee? Really? Two of them?

He watched me as he made the sandwich, probably because I was standing there soaking wet in sweat suit pants and a wife-beater T-shirt. I tossed the sandwich and coffees in a dumpster outside the deli. I found shade under the El and stood there smoking a cigarette. I saw people heading up the stairs to the 111th Street station, normal people, probably on their way to work, but none of them made direct eye contact with me. One woman, an attractive lady, looked at me with pure disgust. How could I blame her? My face was bruised where I'd been kicked. I was still soaking wet. My tracksuit pants were filthy dirty and my wife-beater T-shirt exposed my tattoos. I probably looked like what she'd seen in her worst nightmares.

When she was gone, it hit me: it was a Monday morning. I was supposed to be on my way to work. I was supposed to be normal, too, except I wasn't. I was a mess. I looked like an escaped convict.

What I was was a bum.

When I finally made it home, I called in to work and told them I'd be out for a few days. The image of that one woman looking at me with disgust haunted me. I kept seeing the normal people climbing the stairs. I kept seeing that woman's face and I fell into a funk of depression. I crashed in bed and couldn't get myself out of the apartment for three days in a row. My brother Anthony would ask me if I wanted to go to the gym, or grab dinner someplace, but I couldn't make myself do it. All I wanted was to stay in bed or watch television without really watching it. I couldn't eat and I didn't want to drink or do drugs. By the weekend, it became obvious to me what I wanted was out.

So on a hot August afternoon in 2002, I drove to Rockaway Beach in Queens with another cheap .25 Raven I kept under my bed. It was about six-thirty when I sat near the rocks of a jetty and stared out at the ocean. My plan was to wait for sunset before wasting myself, another two hours or so. It had to do with my delusion about God not seeing what I was doing if I waited until it was dark.

I was staring straight out to sea, amazed at an ocean I'd never taken the time to observe before. The waves and their sounds had a calming effect, but all I could think about was the darkness beneath the sea I'd seen on documentaries about the deep. There was all that life out there beneath the surface, and all the killing as well: big fish eating smaller fish, sharks ripping apart their prey with vicious and relentless shakes of their heads. I closed my eyes and saw myself in the darkest depths of the ocean. I saw my soul floating into an abyss of darkness. All I needed to do was set the barrel of the gun against one of my temples and pull the trigger. One shot and it would be over, all the pain I'd caused those who loved me, all the guilt from all the trouble I'd caused would be gone.

The crowds on the beach had already started to disperse. There were a few small clusters of people left, but all of them far enough from the water so I wouldn't have to worry about them when I put the gun to my head. I kept it in my right tracksuit pocket in the meantime, a round waiting in the chamber.

I kept my eyes closed and said the prayers my mother used to make us repeat at bedtime: an Our Father, a Hail Mary, and an Act of Contrition. The prayers brought back memories of my mother and how much more disappointed she'd be if I took my own life. She was a religious Catholic and the church frowned on suicide, but what was one more disappointment? Going to hell certainly didn't bother me. The way I felt about myself, I belonged there.

I whispered the prayers over and over, trying my best to say penance for the one last crime I intended to commit, my own murder. I was deep in prayer when I heard giggling behind me. I stopped praying and turned to see a group of four girls, all somewhere in their late teens to early twenties, all of them dressed in tight cutoff jeans and halters.

"Hi," one of them said.

I nodded a hello.

"Whatcha doin'?"

"Nothing."

The girl who'd said hello extended her hand. I shook it.

"I'm Kristina. Kristina Piazza."

"James Guiliani."

She introduced her girlfriends. "Sally, Terri, and Jennifer."

"Hi," they said.

"Nice to meet youse," I said.

"Want to party?" Kristina said.

"I'm a little too tired tonight."

"You sure? We have something that'll pick you up."

Great, I thought. The last thing in the world I needed right then was one more line of cocaine.

"No thanks," I said. "I'm trying to quit."

Kristina winked, then proceeded to give me a giant flirtatious smile. "Well, would you help us get some beer?"

"Excuse me?"

"Can you get us some beer?"

"You trying to tell me you'll get carded?"

"Just in case," Kristina said. "Please."

I had to laugh. These girls knew how to operate. I glanced at my watch again, saw I had time, and tried to stand up. I didn't realize how long I'd been sitting there. My legs had fallen asleep. I must've looked like I was stoned as I stumbled. Kristina locked an arm under one of my arms to steady me.

"You okay?" she said.

"Yeah, give me a minute. I was sitting there a long time."

She helped me walk until the circulation returned to my legs. I led them to my car. Kristina sat up front with me. The other girls sat in the back. I searched for a delicatessen near the address where they were going to party. I found one after fifteen minutes or so. I parked out front and the girls all jumped out of the car ahead of me. I went inside and grabbed a case of beer from one of the refrigerators in the back. The girls were buying cigarettes at the counter. I paid for the beer and brought it back out to the car, but then I had to wait for two of the girls who were still inside the deli. They came out a few minutes later with fresh packs of cigarettes, one of them my brand. They gave it to me as a gift, they said, for doing them the favor.

A few minutes later I dropped them off at the party. I carried the beer into the house for them, but then I got out of there before I was tempted to do something that would lead to another bender. Kristina followed me outside. She leaned in the open passenger window when I sat behind the wheel. She wanted to know why I wouldn't stay.

"I have to get back to the beach," I said.

"What?" she said.

"I have to take care of something."

"Back at the beach? What for?"

"I have something to do," I said.

She smirked, then opened the door and sat in the car with me. "Alone at the beach? Like what?"

I wanted to tell her to fuck off, but I shook my head instead.

She asked me for a cigarette. I gave her one and then lit it for her. She took a drag and smiled at me.

"What?" I said.

"Why are you going back to the beach alone?" she said.

I noticed the time and saw I had less than an hour before sunset. I shook my head again.

"I think you need to talk it out," she said.

"You a psychiatrist?"

"No, but I can tell you're in a bad way."

I smiled from embarrassment. "Oh, yeah? How's that?"

She pointed to my right tracksuit pocket. "That, for one thing. I saw the outline when you picked up the beer. It's a gun, isn't it?"

I didn't answer.

"You looked depressed on the beach and now you're trying to hide it," she said.

I was getting pissed off, but I didn't want to take it out on her. I took a long drag on my cigarette while she stared at me. She was waiting for me to say something, but I couldn't. I finally looked at her and shrugged.

"Come back inside with me," she said. "Please."

"I can't," I said.

"Then I'll stay here and we'll talk."

I looked at my watch again. "I can't. I have to go."

She stared at me until I could feel it. It was uncomfortable. I didn't like it that she'd figured me out. I also didn't appreciate her being so pushy. I was about to tell her to get the fuck out of my car when she pulled out a pen and piece of paper.

"What's that for?" I said.

"I want you to talk to somebody," she said. "Not me, don't worry. A friend of mine. Let me have your phone number."

I rolled my eyes.

"What harm will it do? She'll give you a call and you can talk to her. We work together at a diner in Brooklyn."

At that point I was thinking I'd be dead anyway, so what was the harm in giving her my number?

"And promise me something," she said.

"What?"

"You'll go home instead of back to the beach."

"You're kidding, right?"

"No, I mean it. I want you to promise me."

"Promise you what? I have to do something tonight."

"Do something like what? You have to go home and wait for a phone call."

I looked at my watch again. "Come on, give me a break."

"No, no breaks. Promise you'll go home and wait for my friend's call. You can't break a promise to a woman."

"Look, honey, I really have to go."

"Then promise me. Or I won't get out of the car."

She wasn't kidding. There was no way this girl was getting out of the car unless I promised. I glanced at my watch again. It was already seven-forty-five. I was at least fifteen minutes from the beach where I wanted to take care of business. I sighed, exaggerating it to let her know I wanted to leave.

"Promise," she said.

"Alright, I promise," I said.

"You can't break it."

"I won't."

"Now promise you won't break it."

"What?"

"You heard me. A double promise. You break that and you'll have nothing but bad luck."

I pointed at the door for her to get out.

"Promise," she said.

"I promise. I promise. I promise. Okay?"

She winked at me.

I had to laugh. This girl had balls. Wherever she was from, she had the kind of moxie I had to admire.

"Okay," I said, then crossed my heart. "Hope to die."

She leaned in close and pecked me on the cheek. I watched her get out of the car and walk up the porch steps to the front door. She turned around to wave. I waved back but then waited for her to go inside. It was an old habit.

Once she was inside, I didn't even think about heading back to the beach. I'd never make it in time and I'd sworn I'd do it at night. I headed back to Richmond Hill instead. The gun remained in my right tracksuit pocket. It would be one less disappointment for my mother, at least for one more day.

I had regrets about not getting the job done as soon as I settled in at home. I realized that nothing had changed. It was the weekend and whatever cash was left in my wallet wasn't enough for groceries, never mind paying my half of the rent. Unless I robbed someone or pulled another sneak thief attack on some drug dealer's stash, I'd have to wait until the end of the next workweek for money.

If I still had a job.

If I could stay clean for a week.

Thinking about work brought back the image of that woman's look of disgust while she climbed the stairs at the train station on Jamaica Avenue. I felt trapped all over again. I couldn't whack myself in the apartment because I couldn't do that to Anthony, let him find my body. I wanted to kill myself right then and there, but it would have to wait. I pulled the Raven from my pocket and looked at it a long moment before setting it down on my dresser. I stared at it until I began to reach for it again, but then the phone rang.

"Hello?" I answered.

"James?"

"Yeah, this is James."

"Hi, this is Lena Perrelli. My friend Kristina gave me your number and said I should call you tonight."

I'd completely forgotten about Kristina and giving her my phone number. I had to smile.

"Right," I said. "She made me promise to come home and wait for your call."

"She told me. She's crazy, that kid."

I told her about buying her the beer and dropping them off at the party.

"She works with me at the Kings Plaza Diner on Flatbush Avenue," Lena said.

I couldn't begin to cover what we discussed over the next six hours, but we talked and talked and then talked some more. Music, television, movies, family, friends, everything you could think about, we covered, and not once did my situation at the beach come up. I was never comfortable opening up to strangers, but something about Lena made it easy. I wasn't trying to con her. I wasn't looking to bullshit her about anything. I just told her some of what my past life had been like, and she told me about herself and her past, and we hit it off. I know we stayed on the line until we were both yawning and our arms had cramped.

Lena lived in Dyker Heights, Brooklyn. We set up a dinner date for the following weekend, when I'd at least be able to pay for dinner again. I never realized it at the time, but just arranging that date had at least temporarily erased any plans to commit suicide in the next week.

I met her at her house after I finished working my construction job in the city and took a shower at home. When I saw what she was wearing, I felt as if I'd drawn a straight flush. I already knew Lena was special from our phone conversations, but seeing her step outside her house in the outfit she had on—that turned me on big-time. I had a nice Italian hottie and I wasn't about to let her go.

We ate dinner at Vesuvio's on 3rd Avenue and 73rd Street in Brooklyn. I was looking to impress her, but that wasn't going to happen. Everybody in Brooklyn knew somebody connected. I was just another connected guy to Lena. Big deal.

But we hit it off and wound up back at her place. At first I was a little put off by all the cats she had living with her, too many to count.

"*Madonna mia*," I said. "Whatta'you got here, a zoo?"

"Be nice," Lena said. "Those are my babies."

We watched a movie and wound up wrestling in bed. I spent the night with her. The next day I was anxious to see her again, so I stopped by her job to pick her up after her shift, except I was really there early to check things out. I was the jealous type, make no mistake. I knew I'd met somebody special and I wasn't about to share her with anybody. Like I said, Lena was a hottie and there was no way guys weren't hitting on her at the diner. Hell, I used to hit on waitresses all the time. She also liked to dress like a hottie and that drove me crazy. I loved it when we were together, but I didn't like the idea that other guys were looking at her the same way when I wasn't around.

We had another great night together, but I had to leave early the next morning to get to work. We spoke every night on the phone, but I couldn't wait to see her again. The following Friday I took off from work early with some bullshit story about having a doctor's appointment. I parked outside the diner and watched while I waited. I was getting possessive and it was obvious. That night Lena told me she saw me parked outside the diner.

"Yeah, so, I got off early," I told her.

"So, you were out there for more than an hour."

"I had nothing to do."

"So you watch me?"

"I watch out for you. There's a difference."

She rolled her eyes and we both let it go.

We had another great weekend together. We ate lunches and dinners out, rented a few movies, wrestled in bed a few more times, and then I moved in. It wasn't like I forced my way into her life, but I wasn't the shy type once I saw something I wanted. Once I had her, I wanted to protect her. I knew what went on in the minds of men when they spotted a babe like Lena, and that waitress routine was bugging me big-time.

We had an adjustment period living together. I wasn't used to sharing a bathroom with a woman, even though Lena complained I spent more time fixing my hair than she did. I also started going through her closets and pulling out the hot outfits I didn't want her wearing when I wasn't around.

To make sure she listened to me, I'd wait until she wore one on a date with me and then I'd tear it when we got home. Lena knew what I was up to. I told her to wear more conservative outfits because it was making me crazy thinking guys were ogling her. She called me *pazzo*—"crazy," in Italian—but I knew she liked the attention.

Dealing with the cats was another issue. She had the one dog at the time, Brock, her pug, but at least he adapted to sleeping on the floor. The cats wanted on the bed. It was something I wasn't used to. I wasn't an animal lover yet, but Lena claimed I would become one over time.

"Fine," I told her. "Until then, let them sleep on the floor."

She didn't bug me about the cats or her dog, but I used to joke with her whenever she told me I'd become an animal lover one day.

"Sure," I used to tell Lena, and I'd launch into my routine: "I will hug it and pet it and squeeze it and love it and call it Bruno."

It made Lena laugh, so I used it whenever I needed to get her out of a bad mood as well as when she told me how I'd come to love animals.

We spent the rest of our summer weekends at Rockaway Beach. We'd pick up something from the deli, put it in a cooler, and bring it to the beach. We'd stay from morning until night, then come home and watch movies we rented from the local Blockbuster. We spent a lot of time in the sack, like two teenagers in heat, but our conversations always flowed, both before and after sex.

We became comfortable enough to break one another's balls like we'd known each other all our lives. We were a natural fit and I knew early on that I'd fallen in love. I was still an addict and alcoholic, as well as a steroid abuser, and there would come a time when my addictions would interrupt our lives, so I did my best to warn her.

"Sometimes it's a single beer after work that'll lead to two nights of bingeing," I told her. "Sometimes it'll be a line I'll do at lunch while I'm at work, something I'll chase after work and wind up staying out for two days. It can get ugly."

"We'll deal with it," Lena told me. "I'll never encourage it, make no mistake, but we'll deal with it. Over time you'll come around."

"Or I'll chase you," I said.

"Or you'll chase me," she said.

Fortunately for me, Lena was a natural nurturer who didn't give up so easily. She had a son from a previous relationship, and she treated her cats and dog like they were her other children. She was a mother to all of them.

We gradually learned more and more about each other, and the more she told me, the more impressed I became. Lena had taken in her first stray, a dog, when she was just five years old. She'd gotten into fights over stray cats when she saw cruel kids tossing stones at one in a school yard. She and a former boyfriend even kidnapped a dog when they saw it was being abused by its owner.

She'd grown up wanting to nurture and protect animals all her life, so when she bought her house and noticed a litter of kittens in her yard, she started bringing them food. She took the kittens to a vet for a checkup, then returned them to the yard once she was sure they were okay. Soon afterward, other stray cats started showing up and she left food for them as well. Before she realized it, Lena had started her own cat sanctuary.

She was soon feeding more than two dozen cats in her backyard. She'd even started giving the cats names and bathing them so she could examine them for ticks and fleas. She'd already become very attached to them when one day she noticed that fewer cats had come for their food. A week later, a few more were missing. A week after that, even more were missing. Lena grew frantic until she learned what had happened.

Unfortunately, one of her neighbors from around the corner was an animal hater and the rumor quickly spread that he'd bragged about killing Lena's cats.

Lena immediately took the rest of the cats inside her house for their own safety. She reported the allegations she'd heard to the police, but there was never any arrest made. Needless to say, she'd never take the chance of leaving her cats outside again.

After a few months of living together, we reached a level of trust that couples wish for, a level of comfort that is sometimes more revealing than is comfortable. For instance, one day during a Q&A we gave each other, Lena claimed she was turned off the first time she saw me.

I could feel my eyebrows pull together. "The fuck you talkin' about?" I said.

"You were handsome, don't get me wrong," she told me, "but you looked more Irish than Italian. I'm used to Italian-looking men."

"What makes you say I look Irish?"

"Blond hair and you're not very dark," she said.

"There something wrong with blond hair?"

"No, but I'm not used to seeing many blond Italians."

"You starting a fight? Some of my best friends are Irish."

"I don't have anything against the Irish," Lena said. Then she shot me a devious smile and said, "Unless they sweat like you."

"And what's wrong with my sweat?"

"You do it profusely. It was tough getting past the sweat."

I put it on a little, exaggerating my response. "Really? Imagine fuckin' that? So, is that why you didn't come to watch me at *my* job?"

She laughed.

Then she told me that seeing me wearing what was considered a mob uniform back in the day, a tracksuit, made her think, "Oh, boy, here we go. Another *cugino*."

It was Italian for "cousin," but on the streets it meant a *guido*, definitely an insult.

I told her if I was a *cugino*, then she was a *cugette*.

"Guilty as charged," she said as she laughed. "Big hair and all."

We both chuckled after that.

The first few times I binged and disappeared for a few days at a time, Lena wasn't a happy camper. She'd be cold to me when I finally came home. Sometimes I'd find all my clothes on the front stoop. Sometimes she changed the locks. I was always persistent about getting back in. I wouldn't go away.

One time when she locked me out and I came home while she was at work, I removed one of barred gates over a living-room window. I pried it off and climbed up inside. When she came home and found me asleep on the couch, she poured a pitcher of water on my head and cursed better than most of the guys I used to hang with at Our Friends Social Club.

Another time I broke in through the side door while she was at work. When she came home and found I'd ordered Chinese for our dinner, she stood in the kitchen doorway shaking her head.

"You're like a fuckin' cockroach, James, I swear it," she told me.

"Because I'm ugly?" I said, attempting some humor.

"No, because no matter what I do, I find you back here."

"Do I still look more Irish than Italian?"

She rolled her eyes at me and cursed again, but then she smiled and eventually laughed, and all was forgiven. We lived like that for the next few months, but my charm began to wear thin when I went on another bender and Lena lost it on me. It was around the holidays when I'd called from work to tell her I'd be home at five-thirty. She'd put up the pasta, the only meal I ate, at five o'clock, but then the hours rolled by and I never came home for dinner.

The next morning, maybe five or six o'clock, I staggered up the front-porch steps and there were my clothes again.

"Oh, shit," I said.

Clothes on the front porch usually meant a long period of me trying to get back in Lena's good graces. She was a nurturer, but nobody's fool. I saw the clothes and tried the door. She'd had the locks changed again. The last time I'd pried the bars off one of the windows to climb inside, but this time I wasn't in any condition to do anything outside of begging.

"Lena!" I yelled.

No answer.

"Fuck me!" I said.

"Yeah, fuck you, James," Lena said. She was standing behind the front door.

"Let me in."

"Yeah, right."

"Lena, come on, let me in."

"Fuck yourself, James."

"Come on. I got a tan. I don't look Irish anymore."

No response.

"Lena, please. I will hug you and squeeze you and love—"

She opened the door and I thought all was forgiven, except this time she wasn't smiling. I stepped inside the house and crack, like I said before, that was the time she nailed me with an overhand right off the tip of my chin, breaking my jaw.

The next few years could've been video replays of our first two years together. I was good, I was bad, I binged, I found my clothes on the front stoop, I laughed, I cried, and I eventually conned my way back into Lena's heart with a dumb joke or six, but only when she was ready to forgive me.

Standing alongside my tag—112. 112 was our street gang. I tagged it everywhere I went. This was the gang I was with before, during, and after my days with the Gotti crew. I still stay in touch with my 112 brothers.

Me and my baby brother, Thomas, playing pool in a local bar in our neighborhood. This was deep into my gangster days with the Gotti crew.

Me and my boy, Fat George DiBello. We jumped on Santa's lap for fun. George introduced me to the Gotti club.

Me and the crew at Carmine's, an after-hours joint in Jamaica, Queens. We were there every night. It was a members-only tough-guy joint.

My beloved Bruno, the dog who saved me.

Here's a dog I rescued from a bad situation in a Brooklyn project. They didn't want to give him up, but I made them an offer they couldn't refuse.

Breakfast (espresso) at Panino Rustico. Nothing happens in Dogfella world until I down at least four espressos. "NO DOGS ALLOWED" doesn't apply to the Dogfella.

My biggest rescue (by size), a 160-pound Cane Corso named Primo. He was a tough dog to handle when I first rescued him, but now he's a gentle giant. Primo is now the star of our operation. He's a Brooklyn big shot.

Dr. Salvatore Pernice, Lena, myself, and my crew at a fundraiser for my rescue shelter—gangster-style.

Ten years ago, I would've been wearing handcuffs in this picture. Today, I work with the police to stop animal abuse. This picture was taken after the police and I chased a loose dog for miles.

Hurricane Sandy kept me, Dr. Pernice, and a whole crew busy. The freezing conditions and contaminated water were deadly for the animals. We rescued a lot of animals from certain disaster. Photo by Rachel McKay

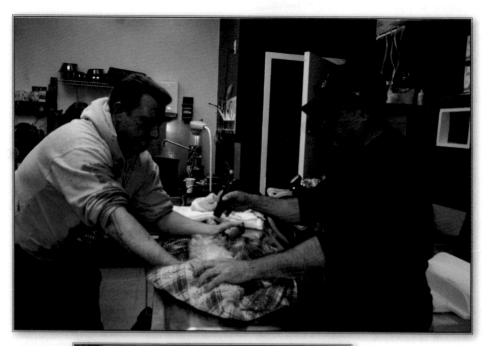

Dr. Pernice and myself working on a rescue the day after Hurricane Sandy. We pulled one cat from six feet of water. He had a ruptured eye. I kept him with us at our home. His name is Pirate. Photos by Rachel McKay

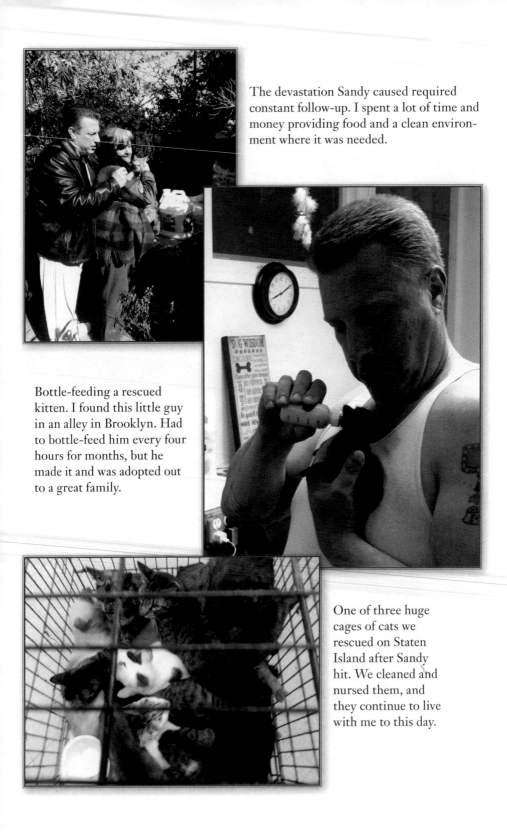

The devastation Sandy caused required constant follow-up. I spent a lot of time and money providing food and a clean environment where it was needed.

Bottle-feeding a rescued kitten. I found this little guy in an alley in Brooklyn. Had to bottle-feed him every four hours for months, but he made it and was adopted out to a great family.

One of three huge cages of cats we rescued on Staten Island after Sandy hit. We cleaned and nursed them, and they continue to live with me to this day.

Me and Lena and a rescue named Buddy. His owner surrendered him to us because she had a medical condition. When she was cured, she asked for him back. We cried returning him, but it was a great ending. Buddy was reunited with his mom, and we couldn't be happier for them both.

Yes, I rescue pigs, too! This guy was supposed to be a fifteen-pounder but grew to ninety. His name is Curtis, and he now lives in a sanctuary in Pennsylvania. His former owner still writes letters checking up on him.

I used to carry a gun. Now I carry kittens. One of six I rescued with their mother from a Brooklyn backyard. I relocated the entire family to loving homes.

My toughest rescue to date, Evil Eva. She growls and she bites, and I have the scars to prove it. Photo by Joanne Schulter/Portraits by Joanne

This picture was a gift for my forty-fifth birthday from Lena. Our kids didn't make it easy, but it eventually worked out. Photo by Joanne Schulter/Portraits by Joanne

I continued to sell drugs, both cocaine and steroids, but outside of Lena's view. Whenever I needed extra cash, I did what I had to do, what I knew best how to do, which was hustle drugs. I'd returned to the gym and put myself back together, lifting myself into what Lena once called, "One buff motherfucker," but I was still using some of the steroids and snorting some of the cocaine I was selling on the side.

My construction job became even more of a tit situation once they made me a foreman. All I had to do was show up and supervise a crew, but I still found my way into trouble from time to time at bars in the city after work. My act was getting old, even for me, but with no reason to put the brakes on, I continued burning the candle at both ends. The day it caught up to me, I was lifting weights after taking steroids and doing a few lines of blow. I was doing a behind-the-neck military press with two-hundred and fifty pounds of free weight when I wrenched my back. Basically, I was a cripple for the next few weeks. The construction company had to replace me with another supervisor. I went on workman's comp for a few more months, but when I came back, I was useless. I could barely walk, never mind lift anything.

My back continues to give me problems to this day, but back in 2005, I couldn't lift a garbage pail to take out to the curb.

The more pain I experienced, the more entitled I felt I was to self-medicate. Today, medical experts claim that self-medication is a prime starting point for drug addiction and alcoholism. For me it was just another excuse to get high. My bingeing returned with a vengeance, but Lena was finally getting fed up with it. After three years of putting up with me and my bad routines, she wanted something in return. My selfish act had run its course.

She'd always wanted to own and operate an animal sanctuary someday. Although I'd made progress and was able to coexist with all the cats in the house, I wasn't thrilled at the idea of being surrounded by animals. We'd talk about it from time to time, but my heart wasn't in it. An animal shelter was Lena's dream. I was still living day to day.

In early 2006, Lena decided to leave her job and open a pet boutique. At first she offered me a partnership, but I wasn't ready for it. Frankly, I didn't even know what a pet boutique was.

"Pet boutique? The fuck is that?" I said.

"Where we sell animal supplies and specialty foods and so on. Eventually grooming, too. People pay a lot to groom their pets. We could carry high-quality products. This is still a good neighborhood, Dyker Heights. People here take care of their pets. They treat them good."

"Animal supplies."

"Yes. High-quality products. Everything from leashes to foods to outfits and bedding. Things people buy for their pets."

"I'd rather open a bar," I said. "A gay bar. Someplace in Manhattan. Those people treat themselves good. They spend money, too."

"I swear you're fucking crazy," Lena said. "A bar, James? Seriously?"

"I still have enough connections, Lena. I could make it fly."

"Yeah, right. Until they find you dead from an overdose or alcohol poisoning."

"I won't drink. I promise. I know better than that."

"You don't know shit, James. You're a fucking addict. You're an alcoholic. If you don't drop dead from one or the other, you'll wind up busted again for getting into a fight or some shit."

We'd have the same argument a few more times over the next few months. I waved her off. "You don't know what you're talking about," I said.

"Look, you've been like a stray dog to me, James. I haven't been able to turn you away, but it's getting old. I'm going to open a business and I won't have time to babysit you anymore. I'll need you there for me."

"Fine," I said. "Open a pet boutique. I'm sure I'll love it and hug it and squeeze it and—"

"Shut the fuck up, James. No more jokes. I mean it. This is for real. No fucking up. Not anymore."

Lena and I opened the first Diamond Collar on Thirteenth Avenue on May 20, 2006.

I was a good boy and stayed out of Lena's way once we opened the boutique. My bad back had officially killed my construction career six months earlier, so I hung around the store and helped out where I could. I even sat behind the counter whenever she needed me. I was making relative progress for a junkie-alcoholic. For all the dumb shit I'd done to myself, Lena had always been there to help me recover. It was high time I returned the favor.

My bingeing was slowing down enough to keep Lena close, but when my mom was diagnosed with pancreatic cancer, all the guilt I'd felt during my darkest times returned. Mom had always been there for me, long before Lena. She'd already gone through a ton of the worst life could toss at someone. Losing one son right in front of her from a sudden heart attack (Nipper), losing her husband to lung cancer, watching another son (me) ruin his life with a prison sentence, drugs, and alcohol, and then losing yet another child (Thomas) to another form of cancer. Suddenly it was clear to me that time was running out on any chance I had to make her happy by getting sober.

My mother suffered terribly during her sickness. Pancreatic cancer is a horrible disease. She felt the pain each and every day. She was staying at her sister Antonia's house on Long Island. All her children went there for her and held vigil. When her time came, as much as we all dreaded losing her, we knew her suffering was finally over.

Nobody owed her as much as I did, but it was never about money. The Guiliani family, all of us, had never concerned ourselves with money. It was easy enough to make, one way or another, whenever we needed it. What I owed my mother was peace of mind, something I couldn't deliver before she passed. One might think her getting sick would spark me into sobriety, if for no other reason than as a last act of contrition, but it didn't. If anything, my mom's death had the opposite effect. It hit me like a hammer.

Mom was buried on her sixty-eighth birthday.

That night, after the family had gathered for dinner, I did what I always did when I was down on myself. I wound up bar hopping on Jamaica Avenue, except this time when my binge was over, Lena was ready to dump me for good. She'd been great throughout my mother's sickness, but once I disappeared after that family dinner, she'd had enough. She gave me an ultimatum once my head was clear again.

"Either you grow up and get serious about your life or we're done," she said. "I love you, James, but I can't go through this every other month."

"So, I finally chased you," I said. "I guess it was a matter of time."

"And maybe you're deliberately chasing me," she said. "Maybe you can't handle love. Maybe you're too comfortable screwing up. Be a man, James. If you want to leave, then go, but if you want to stay, then tell me and this time make damn sure you intend to follow through."

"Of course I want to stay," I told her. "And I'm sorry for fucking up again. What else can I say?"

"You can stop apologizing and start taking responsibility. Do something that will keep you out of those fucking bars."

"More responsibility like what?"

"Like a business. Something to keep you occupied during the day so you don't wind up in a fucking bar instead. Since you're out of work with your back, you have too much time to fuck up."

"What, animal rescue?" I said. "Is that what this is about?"

"I'd love that, James, don't get me wrong, but animal rescue isn't a business. You don't do that for profit. I'm talking about a business. I have the boutique, but you can do dog grooming. The store next door is empty now. We can rent it. It would be something you can do to earn money without having to do whatever it is you're doing behind my back."

I wasn't about to start lying about dealing steroids and cocaine, so I kept my mouth shut and did what the lady wanted. She was my last chance. Lena had endured a lot living with me, and I still owed her. If it was a dog-grooming business that would keep her in my life, so be it. I'd still piss and moan about it, because I was still a street guy and I knew bars a lot better than dog grooming, but when push came to shove, I went where Lena pointed.

I opened our second store, the one for grooming, at the address next door to Lena's pet boutique on the corner of Seventy-sixth Street and Thirteenth Avenue. We merged the two stores into one and named our business The Diamond Collar. Three years later, we'd move one more time, to the corner of Seventy-first and Thirteenth Avenue, where The Diamond Collar has been ever since.

Chapter 6

Same Old, Same Old

My last few months in prison were good ones. I'd been a model inmate. I played cards every night and engaged in the bullshit sessions with other inmates that kept us busy enough to ignore our confinement and the shitty living conditions. Prison blows, don't get me wrong, but for a whacked-out junkie, it can serve as both a rehab and a refuge. Looking back at my time in Riverhead, it was definitely better than where I was headed on the street.

Most jail releases occurred between Monday and Thursday. When inmates were being released, they were brought to the facility at Yaphank. When my time was up, the warden processed me out on a Friday morning. I think he had a special place in his heart for me, especially since my 9.2 dive off the loading dock into a laundry boat. Until my Friday-night Halloween release in 1995, weekend releases were unheard of at Yaphank.

Some guys want to take everything they've accumulated while inside prison with them when they leave, but I gave away all my stuff to friends I'd made inside. My CDs, Walkman, cigarettes, and so on, all of it went to the guys I was closest with, the guys who'd had my back.

I was still worried about what might happen once I was out. Although some time had passed, I had violated one of the unwritten laws among mobsters by keeping the hijacking to myself. The guys from Our Friends Social Club might still be holding a grudge. Angelo Sforza had caught a beating from the Our Friends crew and suffered a broken jaw when he was bailed out two years earlier. I could only hope enough time had passed for the rest of the crew to give me a pass.

On the morning of my release, an announcement was made over the facility loudspeaker: "Guiliani, roll up." It was prison-speak for a release.

I was brought to the Sally Port, where my paperwork was being handled by the guard inside the bubble office. While I was there, I received the traditional good-bye cleansing from some inmates as they dowsed me with water from cups, buckets, cans, and anything else they could store water in.

A CO walked me to the front gate and gave the traditional parting message, "Don't look back."

I remembered the superstition about looking back—if you did so, you'd return to prison. I didn't look back, but neither was I looking forward.

I'd told everybody inside about my upcoming trip to Atlantic City and how my friends would be waiting for me with a limousine, but once I was outside the prison gates, I had to wait almost an hour before they showed up. In the meantime, while I stood there like a fool, the guys inside were giving me shit by shouting out the window.

"Hey, James, still waiting for that bus?"

"James, stick your thumb out and catch a ride."

"That's some nice limo, James. Can it fly, too?"

Eventually, when my friends did arrive, it was in the biggest, longest stretch limousine I'd ever seen—a white Continental, one of the newer models. I walked over to it like I owned it, stripping my clothes off as I did so. A brand new Michael Jordan tracksuit was tossed out the rear window of the limo to me. I put it on and did a runway modeling routine for everybody looking down from their windows.

When I finally stepped inside the limo, Ralph Salzano and Fat George were smiling ear to ear. I wasn't even sitting yet when Fat George handed me an eight ball of cocaine, a mirror, and a rolled-up $20 bill. Ralph had already poured me a highball glass filled with vodka and ice. An ice-cold Heineken was also waiting for me in a cup holder.

The driver rolled up the tinted partition glass so he couldn't be blamed for anything if we were stopped for whatever reason. The next thing I knew, my head was buzzing from the snort I took. Then the car was moving and prison was behind me. We were on our way to Atlantic City.

I alternated between snorting cocaine and downing vodka. Fat George and Ralph wanted to hear prison stories. I wanted to be filled in on the neighborhood and what was going on at Our Friends Social Club. Fat George told me about the latest mob busts, which wiseguy had become the latest snitch, which ones had gone away, and which ones were going away. Ralph told me about his latest failed attempt to quit drinking.

"So you're getting me drunk," I said.

"Misery loves company," he said.

"I'll drink to that!" I said.

I told them about the kid whose face was cut because he'd disrespected a Latin King. I told them about the COs, the lousy food, the different sections of the dorms we'd named, and how there just wasn't all the rape and other bullshit they heard about.

Then the ball breaking started. Fat George wanted to know how many times I'd been caught giving head. Ralph wanted to know how good the prison homemade wine tasted.

"Fuck the two a'you," I said. "Gimme another line."

"Wait," Fat George said, "you didn't give one blow job while you were in there?"

"Nah, they brought your mothers in on weekends for that stuff," I said.

"It sounded like there was crying coming from the prison when you left," Ralph said. "You gonna be missed, Head?"

"Nah, I told them about you two. They were pro'bly crying because they wouldn't get their turns."

It's what we did whenever we were getting wasted. Ball breaking was common and expected. When I was younger, we used to call it "ranking out" one another. When I hit the streets as an adult it was called "breaking balls" or "ball breaking," and nobody ever did it better than street guys.

I was back in the saddle snorting cocaine and drinking vodka. Ralph and Fat George were happy I was back out again. It was party time.

The ball breaking continued long after I was too fucked up to speak. God knows what I sounded like getting trashed so quickly after being straight for two years.

"Oooh, oooh, seh, fra, it," I'd say, and Ralph and Fat George would laugh hysterically.

I was completely trashed before we made it to the city limits in Queens, about sixty miles from prison. It only got worse as we headed further south to Atlantic City. Somewhere along the Garden State Parkway, Fat George and Ralph told the driver to stop at a rest area so they could take a piss, but there was no way I could make it inside to a bathroom. I pulled myself out of my pants and pissed between parked cars instead. Ralph and Fat George thought it was the funniest thing in the world. They were laughing so hard, they couldn't stand up. Fat George fell forward onto his knees, and Ralph fell back against one of the parked cars, then slid down to the asphalt. In the end, the driver had to help all three of us get back inside the limo.

I had to feel for the poor bastard. All he wanted was an easy payday, and he was stuck with three stoned assholes he probably wished he'd never met.

The trip resumed and whatever Ralph and Fat George talked about was lost on me. I doubt they understood each other. All I know is one minute I was pissing between cars and the next minute we were pulling up to the Tropicana Casino and Resort. A few days later Ralph told me that I was so stoned, it took them half an hour to get me out of the limousine.

Somehow they brought me upstairs to the suite they'd booked. I must've staggered inside because Fat George and Ralph had to help me into the bedroom, where two drop-dead gorgeous women were sitting on the bed wearing nothing more than G-strings and smiles.

I was lucky I could see, never mind fuck. I'll never be able to remember their names, but I can still see them. One was a natural blonde with a huge chest, and the other was a short, dark-haired Hispanic with tiny tits. They were Atlantic City escorts Fat George had hired through one of the Gotti crew back in New York. They'd checked into the suite earlier the same day and made themselves comfortable. There were two open bottles of champagne, a giant plate of nuts and fruits, and two room-service tables loaded with sandwiches, fries, and salad.

To be fair, the women did their best to wake me from my drug- and alcohol-induced impotence, but I was way too far gone. There was nothing they or anybody else could've done to give me an erection. What we did was sit on the bed and play cards instead. Ralph and Fat George spent most of the night losing their money in the casino.

When it was time for the girls to leave, I let them split the $500 Ralph and Fat George had left me. One of the hookers wrote her name and phone number on the bathroom mirror. I never made it downstairs to the casino and wound up spending the rest of my homecoming celebration staring out the window and missing my bunk back at Riverhead.

Ralph and Fat George came up to get me for the dinner reservations they'd made at some swank steak joint inside the casino, but I'd been flying on cocaine for more than eight hours already. I couldn't have eaten with a gun to my head.

When we returned to Queens, I had a big headache waiting for me, but it wasn't from the Gotti crew. My mother couldn't have been more pissed off at me if I'd robbed our church. She couldn't believe I'd gone to Atlantic City first thing out of the joint.

"How could you not come here first?" she wanted to know.

"I'm sorry, Ma, I wasn't thinking."

"Yeah, no shit, James. If you could think, you wouldn't have gone to prison in the first place. I guess nothing has changed. Two years in prison and you're right back to the same shit."

She was right. I owed her a lot more than a stopover to say hello. I owed her my ass, but once I had a few lines and a few drinks in me, I was James the junkie-alcoholic. I continued trying to apologize, but Mom wasn't hearing it. She didn't talk to me for two weeks.

I finally got her to listen to my bullshit about trying to straighten out, but I'm pretty sure she knew that I was saying things I knew she wanted to hear and maybe even trying to convince myself that I was being serious.

I returned to work the following week, more than fortunate to still have that option in my life. The union had saved my ass more than a few times. Mostly it was because of the influence wiseguys still maintained in construction unions, but I was more than grateful for the chance to earn some clean money. At least for eight hours a day I would be doing something constructive. I owed my mother a ton of money for what she'd done, and there was no other way for me to repay her than to work my legit job during the day and hustle at night.

I had to assume that my indiscretion with the attempted hijacking was given a pass at Our Friends Social Club because I didn't catch a beating, but it was obvious that I was being treated like an outcast. Guys would nod or say hello and very little else. Then I made the ultimate mistake of repeating my first big offense in not showing up to a wiseguy's social affair. This time it was a christening, but instead of showing up stoned, the way I had at a Gotti wedding, I didn't show at all.

It was something you just didn't do, ignore a wiseguy christening. I became persona non grata the very next day.

It was almost 1996 and my Gotti days were behind me. John Gotti Sr. was sentenced to life in prison and his son was about to go away for seventy-seven months. Our Friends Social Club was closed down. I was finished with a mob life, but not finished being a thug. I was still a junkie and an alcoholic. I still needed cash. I was still working as a union laborer, but I spent my paychecks faster than I earned them.

My specialty was robbing shit. Houses and drug dealers were my main targets, but I always had the same goal in mind when ripping something or somebody off: cash, or something I could turn into cash, so I could buy drugs.

I wasn't some animal that did push-in jobs. They were too dangerous. Unpredictable shit happened when you threatened a family. Way too much could go wrong, like someone getting injured or killed, even if by accident.

I only hit houses where nobody was home, and I'd only take what I could sell for instant cash. Once inside a house, I made mandatory stops in the bathroom to check for drugs in the medicine cabinet, and then the bedrooms to check for any other prescription drugs. I'd rifle through drawers for cash, but it was rare to find more than a few bucks. Cash and jewelry were what I wanted most, but sometimes I'd grab a stereo or radio, or anything that at least looked like it was valuable.

Usually I worked with a partner, but sometimes I'd go solo and really screw up. One time I took a bunch of statues I thought were from that fancy Spanish company, Lladró. I'd already gone through most of the house and had come up empty, except for some Percocet I found in the medicine cabinet. Then I spotted six statues in the dining room and I hustled out of the house holding them against my chest like they were precious. I must've looked like a fool doing so, but I looked even worse when they turned out to be *fugazi* knockoffs. The guy at the pawn shop just laughed when I set them on his counter.

"What's funny?" I said.

"This shit," he said. "What am I supposed to do with it?"

"It's that Spanish stuff. It's worth a lot of money."

He picked up one of the statues and turned it upside down. "It's Taiwan stuff. It's worth spit. Nice try."

Another time I decided to hit the house of a former two-date girlfriend. We didn't get along the two times we went out, but she'd made the mistake of mentioning that her mother had a taste for gold jewelry after I complimented her on the chain she was wearing.

"Oh, it's my mom's," she'd said. "She has a ton of this stuff. I borrow from her all the time."

Bells had gone off in my junkie head. SCORE, was all I could think. We broke up after our second date and I waited a full two weeks before making my move. I went back with Fat George to rob her mother's gold, but I'd just made my pass in the upstairs bathroom medicine cabinet when Fat George heard the front door open. The both of us went out a second-story window, but I nearly broke my ankle when I landed on a toy fire truck in the yard.

I wound up getting nothing that night, not even an aspirin.

The most desperate break-in I ever did was with Mike Murphy the day we decided to hit a friend's house while he and his roommate were away on vacation. As horrible as that sounds, it's the way junkies get when they're desperate. Nobody is safe.

Originally, we broke in because we needed a place to hang out after making a score off a drug dealer that I robbed on Atlantic Avenue. It was a Housebreaking 101 rule violation: never break into a house without a purpose. We had drugs and cash, but it was pouring outside and we knew our friend, Gerard Kennedy, was on vacation. We also knew his house wasn't wired with alarms, and that his basement windows provided easy access. Mike went in through one of the basement windows and then let me in through the back door.

At first all we did was hang out doing the cocaine I'd scored and drinking Gerard's liquor. We put on the stereo and listened to music and watched a little television. By the second day, we'd run out of drugs and we were desperate all over again. Neither of us wanted to leave the comfort of Gerard's house, but we both needed to get high. We'd searched the medicine cabinets and Gerard's bedroom but hadn't found anything. I decided to perform another search. Thinking like the junkie I was, I went to the refrigerator and opened the freezer. I rummaged through, moving frozen vegetables and ice trays around until I hit the mother lode.

Bada-boom, bada-bing, I thought. *SCORE!* Two balls of tinfoil were in the back of the freezer. I grabbed one and immediately opened it. The mother lode indeed. I rolled a $20 bill, jammed the open end in the powder and snorted hard and fast. I was expecting a huge hit, but what I got was nothing. I took another hit and nothing again.

"What the fuck?" I said.

Into the kitchen comes Mike Murphy. "Wow, nice find, James," he said.

"Yeah, but nothing's happening," I said.

"Huh?"

I pushed some of the powder around with the $20 bill and dropped the thing on the floor as soon as I saw it—a dead lizard. Gerard had put his stupid dead lizard in the freezer with the powder as a preservative.

I freaked out. I started screaming like a little girl. I ran to the sink and tried to push water up my nose while Mike laughed hysterically. I was never so fucking scared in my life. I thought I had killed myself. I didn't know what would happen, except Mike was busting his gut laughing to the point of tearing up.

"Fuckin' asshole!" I yelled at him. "I could die over here."

"You're killing me right now," he said.

I was pissed off when we finally left the house later the same day. I left his dead fucking lizard on the floor where I'd dropped it.

Drug dealers who worked the streets didn't carry their stash of drugs on their person. Most kept their drugs in a safe place they never disclosed, not even to friends. It was usually a nearby stash they could get to quickly to make a transaction. It was all about a potential arrest; dealers never wanted to get caught holding their stash if or when the police grabbed them. The differences between possession of drugs, and possession of drugs with intent to sell, were major. Undercover narcotics cops did their best to find dealer stashes; it was simply a bigger bust.

Maybe I should've been a narcotics cop because finding drug stashes was my specialty. I'd invest enough time watching a street dealer operate to figure out where his stash was and then hit it as soon as I had the chance. I'd blend into the street scenery long enough for the dealer to relax. Once he ignored me, I'd follow and eventually find his stash. Sometimes it was out on the street and sometimes it was inside a building. Most times, however, I was able to rip off drug dealers in bars because that's where most of the buys went down, usually in the men's room. I'd crouch while standing on a toilet seat and wait to see which ceiling tiles were moved so the dealer could get at his stash. As soon as he stepped outside the bathroom to make his deal, I'd do some quick maneuvering and grab whatever I could reach.

If I was caught by some accident—and it happened a few times—I'd make believe I was looking to deal myself and was looking for a place to stash. I'd either bullshit my way out of it or wind up in a fight, but fights came with the territory.

Sneak thieving didn't always work, but nailing a stash was usually good for a few days. I would take what I thought was good and sell what I thought I could step on and dilute to sell to suckers. When times were desperate and I was anxious to get my hands on cocaine for myself, I'd take a trusty Raven .25 with me to rob a dealer straight up.

"Give me what you're holding," I'd say, while showing him the gun. "Drugs and cash, right now."

Most dealers didn't argue at the sight of a gun, but some did go into a form of drama that could attract attention. Some would raise their hands while backing up, saying, "I don't want no trouble, man."

Maybe they thought they were in the Wild Wild West.

"Put your fuckin' hands down, asshole!" I'd say. "Just give me what you're carrying and shut the fuck up."

Robbing dealers at gunpoint wasn't something I did with any regularity. It was dumb shit that was too unpredictable to trust. First off, if you weren't watching the street long enough, you might not notice when a dealer had backup, and maybe they were carrying a gun. Second, if the cops were watching from somewhere you couldn't spot and you were caught ripping off a dealer with a gun, it was back to prison for armed robbery. It wouldn't matter that it's a dealer you're robbing, armed robbery is what it is. I already had a prison record. Armed robbery would mean an extended stay in prison the next time.

There was one dealer on Jamaica Avenue I really hated, a guy named Big Mike. He was a cocky SOB who liked to talk shit and was a cheap bastard. I knew he sometimes stashed his product behind the juke box or the Joker Poker machine at Doyle's, but I never had the chance to sneak-thief it.

Around 1997, the cocaine gods smiled down on me in the form of two tough guys from the neighborhood, Freddy Stalls and Big Jimmy Sheehan. They were local muscle, known to put serious beat-downs on anyone who crossed them. They had their own drug trade and were looking to expand, so when they wanted to add Doyle's to their route, they took down the guy I hated and unknowingly gifted me my biggest drug score ever.

It happened one week after my kneecap was broken in a bar fight at the Wee Pub on Atlantic Avenue and Lefferts Boulevard. That night I got into it with some drunk at the bar over a bullshit fight he was having with his girlfriend. He called her a nasty name and I was feeling my oats from the cocaine I'd already snorted. He took a swing and I took one back. We wrestled for a few seconds and then I had him pinned on the floor and was taking potshots at his face when his girlfriend stepped into a dozen or so kicks that nailed me in the right kneecap. I guess she wasn't as angry at her boyfriend as I'd thought. The tip of her pointy cowgirl boots had cut my knee to ribbons. Although I was able to get home on a slight limp that night, the next morning I couldn't stand on the same leg. Anthony took me to the Jamaica Hospital emergency room where I was X-rayed and learned I had eight holes in my kneecap.

So when I limped into Doyle's with my cane and sat at the hook of the bar, I wasn't even thinking about pulling a sneak-thief move on Big Mike, not in my condition. I was thinking I'd get drunk and maybe bum some blow off whoever was carrying. Then in walked Freddy and Big Jimmy. They said hello and warned me to keep an eye on the people at the bar while they talked to Big Mike. The translation was obvious: Big Mike was about to catch a beating.

All I could think of was his stash. I'd already seen him duck down to tie his shoes near the Joker Poker machine that night. I knew he had put at least some of his stash there.

Freddy and Big Jimmy took Big Mike into the bathroom and a few seconds later all you could hear were screams. A few of the women in the bar seemed upset but were quickly reassured by the bartender. I didn't have to do a thing except keep my eye on the Joker Poker machine to make sure nobody hit Big Mike's stash before I got to it.

When the beating was over, Freddy and Big Jimmy came out of the bathroom wiping blood off their hands with paper towels. They proceeded to the bar and spoke with the bartender, but I saw him shake his head. Freddy and Big Jimmy frowned and started for the door. Freddy winked at me as they passed, and I hopped off the bar stool to head to the bathroom. When I opened the door, Big Mike was laid out in a puddle of his own blood. His face was a bloody mess and his nose was flat. I let the door close and told the bartender to call for an ambulance. I waited near the Joker Poker machine until the ambulance arrived and Big Mike was hauled off, still unconscious. Once he was out the door, I pushed the Joker Poker machine a few inches away from the wall and discovered the Promised Land. Big Mike must've just picked up from his supplier and stashed his product that same night. All I know is I walked out of there with more than $5K worth of street-value drugs, everything from Percocet to cocaine.

I sold what I didn't use, mostly the Percocet and some of the cocaine I stepped on for resale. The rest went up my nose, as Vinnie Barbarino used to say, "with a rubber hose," except I used a rolled-up $20 bill or whatever cash was handy.

John Fairbanks was a huge, tough dude I knew from the neighborhood. At six foot six and 250 pounds, he was intimidating to look at, never mind fight. I'd seen him destroy guys his own size and two and three guys almost his size at the same time. One day we were hanging out in a Forest Hills bar looking to score some cocaine. Once I spotted a dealer in the bar, I approached him to buy a couple of bags. He was young, maybe twenty-five or so, and he had a crowd of even younger kids hanging around him. He directed me to the men's room, where he proceeded to pull out a bag of cocaine from a baggie inside the front of his pants.

I'd been snorting and dealing the same drug way too long to ignore that move. Most dealers kept two separate stashes for sale; one for users who knew better and the other for suckers. He didn't know me from Adam, so he took his shot.

"Now show me the good stuff," I said.

"What do you mean?"

"Don't be a jerkoff. Show me."

He gave me his best frown, then pulled the baggie holding all his stash out from his pants. I grabbed it and told him, "Thanks."

"What the fuck?" he said as he followed me out of the bathroom. "Hey, what the fuck, man?"

I winked at John and motioned toward the door. John blocked the path behind me as I walked out of the bar. John followed me outside, and then the dealer came out the door yelling. We started to run. I went about twenty feet before glancing over my shoulder to see what was going on. I saw that the guys that had been hanging around the dealer inside the bar had come outside. John and I ran as fast as we could on Austin Street, heading toward Continental Avenue, where I'd parked my car, but the younger crowd was already in pursuit and catching up fast. When they were maybe ten yards from us, John said, "Head, get to The Jug. I'll meet you there later."

I kept running but wasn't comfortable leaving John behind. I'd taken about three steps when I heard a loud thump. I slowed down and looked over my shoulder and there was John standing his ground, one of the chasers flat on his back.

"John!" I yelled.

"Go!" he yelled back, then floored another guy.

I took off again. By the time I was in the car and had it turned around, John was walking backward with just two or three guys following him. The rest were either on the ground or staggering against cars. I beeped the horn, but John waved me off. I couldn't leave him, so I double-parked and stood at the car, the bag of drugs I'd taken under the front passenger seat. Then I heard a siren, and I knew I had to get out of there. I was the one carrying the drugs.

Maybe an hour later, John walked into The Little Brown Jug with a big smile on his face. "Buy me a drink?" he said.

On an icy-cold Friday night in February 1999, I was getting wasted with Jimmy Murphy, Mike Murphy's older brother, at one of our local watering holes on Jamaica Avenue. We'd both come straight from work and were still wearing our Carhartt construction jumpers. It was bitter cold out, the temperature below zero. A Canadian cold front had slammed into the Northeast earlier in the week and it wasn't going anywhere.

The bar was getting ready to close, but neither of us was ready to go home. We decided to hit an after-hours joint nearby, Carmine's on Jamaica

Avenue and Lefferts Boulevard. It was owned by a local tough guy who enjoyed taking center stage with a microphone. He was doing karaoke before it became famous. The tough guy liked to sing, but he also liked to break balls and issue challenges.

That night all everyone was talking about was how cold it was and how much they all wanted to be on a tropical beach somewhere. Jimmy heard one too many people say they wished they were on a beach and said, "So, go already! Stop fucking talking about it and go!"

"Go where?" I said.

"To a beach," Jimmy said.

"What beach?"

"I don't know, a tropical one."

"Where?"

"The fuck is wrong with you?"

I laughed. I was looking to break his balls and he fell for it.

"Nothing, but why don't we go?"

"Where?" Jimmy said. He was looking at me like I had six heads.

"To Puerto Rico," I said. "They got some nice beaches there, bro."

"Yeah," the crowd behind us started in. "Why don't you two go?"

Jimmy wheeled on them and said, "What, you think we won't?"

At that point, the tough guy grabbed the microphone and asked for everyone's attention. He must've heard the yelling going on back and forth, because he decided to issue a challenge.

"Okay, everybody, Head and Jimmy Murphy say they're going to Puerto Rico. I say they don't go anywhere. I say it's worth a thousand bucks if they do go."

Jimmy looked at me and said, "Fuck this, we're going."

I yelled up at the tough guy, "You're on, asshole. One G soon as we get back. Don't forget."

The tough guy waved me off. "Yeah, yeah, go home and sleep it off, Head. Puerto Rico is a fantasy. You'll be right back here tomorrow night."

Jimmy was already paying our bill while the crowd egged us on.

"Don't worry," the tough guy said into the microphone. "My money is safe."

Jimmy said to me, "Let's take a ride to JFK and book us out of here. This asshole is paying for it."

"Sounds good to me," I said.

What happened next had to be told to us by everyone we interacted with during what amounted to our three-day blackout. All I could remember was standing on line at JFK and then waking up in a bed at the El San Juan Resort and Casino.

Fortunately, Jimmy had credit-card receipts that told some of the story, and then there were the people we dealt with who told us the rest. A $600 bill attached to Jimmy's credit card for phone calls made from our first-class seats during our flight helped decipher the start of our trip. My boss at work told me I called to tell him I was flying over the worksite now but that I would try to make it back for work Monday. Jimmy's mother told him that he claimed he'd met a priest on the flight to Puerto Rico and that he said he was going to change his ways and become a man of the cloth. My mother said she hung up on me several times because she knew I was drunk. Jimmy's younger brother told us he couldn't stop laughing once he realized we were really going to Puerto Rico.

There was also a car-rental credit-card charge from the airport in Puerto Rico, which explains why the hotel concierge at the El San Juan had tried so hard to explain why we had to move our car from their front lawn before it was towed. I remember the guy pleading with me and Jimmy. We looked at him as if he was crazy.

"What car?" we said.

There were also charges at the hotel stores for clothes and incidentals. There were cash advances and restaurant charges and in the end, three days later when we tried to book a return flight, Jimmy's credit card was rejected for more than several thousand dollars in charges.

"What the fuck we do now?" he said to me.

"I don't know," I said. "I can't call my mother again. She keeps hanging up on me."

"Fuck, my mother's pissed off, too."

"Shit."

"How much money you have left?"

We had less than $6 between us when Jimmy was forced to call his mother again. She was merciful and wired us the money for return-flight tickets, but when we returned to Carmine's to collect our $1,000, the tough guy said he was just joking and never paid us a dime.

The next year was another wash-and-rinse cycle for me and my demons. I was living with my brother Anthony back in Richmond Hill. He did his best to get me into a gym to train and stay straight, but I wasn't ready to grow up yet. I was still a big kid living an irresponsible life that consisted of working when I had to work, and getting high or drunk afterward. Laborers were paid on Fridays and I was usually broke before Sunday.

Even when Anthony convinced me to work out with him at the gym, I'd show up racing on cocaine. Seeing how buff my brother was, I wanted to get there as fast as possible. I cheated for the sake of results. I was using steroids to build bulk and define my muscles, another expense I couldn't afford without dealing on the side or robbing someone. Anthony was a pure lifter and disciplinarian. He'd been a marine and he didn't cheat or miss out on his workouts. He was also street smart enough to know that I would have to reach bottom before I was ready to heal myself.

It would take another few years for that to happen. In the meantime, I'd go weeks at a time without missing workouts, pumped up on anabolic steroids and often flying on cocaine. I was looking good, getting buff, catching looks from the ladies, and kidding myself no end, because eventually I'd stop at one of our local drinking holes and launch myself on a two-, three-, or four-day bender. Sometimes I'd miss work as well as workouts.

I'd straighten out again after a few days and return to the gym for another short cycle of pumping weights and doing the right thing (if you didn't count the steroids and cocaine), and then I'd stop at a bar after work in the city, or one of the local joints in Richmond Hill, and I was back to bingeing.

I was looking good on the outside while tearing my body to pieces on the inside. Lifting on steroids can be dangerous, but adding cocaine to the mix can make you think you're a lot stronger than you are. Pulled muscles were an eventual guarantee, and once I had an excuse not to hit the gym, I had an excuse to sit in a bar.

Wash, rinse, spin . . . over and over again.

Anthony carried me financially when I was out of work, but I couldn't go to him for money to get high. I went where I knew I could score, back on the streets. Sometimes I'd find a drug dealer working a corner and sneak-thief him. Sometimes, when I was feeling desperate, I pulled a gun. Other times I'd hang out in bars and follow some poor bastard I saw flashing his cash. I usually used a gun with an empty clip for the sake of safety and criminal charges, but it was still a dumb-ass move to make.

Then again, I was James being James.

The entire world was shocked by what happened on September 11, 2001, and I was no exception. I was working my construction job as a laborer at a Prada store job site a little over a mile away on the corner of Prince and Mercer Streets. I was pushing a cart of debris into the street when I heard the sound of a low-flying airliner. I looked up and said, "Holy shit!" A few seconds later, at 8:46 a.m., American Airlines Flight 11, traveling from Boston to Los Angeles, struck the North Tower of the World Trade Center.

My first instinct was to run toward the crash site, but my supervisor, Miguel, grabbed onto me and said, "Hold up, James. We don't know what happened yet."

The screams followed. All around people had come out into the street and were trying to get a view of the tower. Sirens filled the air as the fire department and police began to respond. It seemed like only seconds later, but at 9:03 a.m., United Airlines Flight 175, traveling from Boston to Los Angeles, struck the South Tower.

Miguel and I were in the street outside the Prada store trying to learn what we could from passersby, when we saw huge crowds rushing our way. It was complete chaos less than an hour later when the North Tower collapsed. The dust and debris from the falling tower went through the streets like a dust storm. People were covered in dust, gasping for breath and crying hysterically. All the sheetrock that had been used in the collapsed building had been pulverized into dust that was sweeping through the streets of downtown Manhattan.

Word spread fast that the two jets had been hijacked. Once it was obvious it had been a terrorist attack, the panic level escalated.

"There are bombs planted all over the city!" one guy yelled, and that started another wave of craziness like I'd never seen before.

Miguel shut down the job and asked me to help him secure the equipment. We worked fast, but once we were finished, there was no way to get home. Traffic in and out of downtown was halted. The subways south of Canal Street had been shut down. People were walking over to the

Brooklyn Bridge and crossing it to get home or just out of Manhattan as quickly as possible.

I'd driven a friend, Rocco Buzzi, into work, but my car was in a restricted area and couldn't be moved. Businesses were shutting down all over, but we managed to find a bar open near Canal Street. Buzzi and I went in, sat down, and started pounding drinks as if we hadn't had any for a month. It was probably one of the only bars around that remained open, but it was so packed with people, they literally ran out of booze before sundown.

At that point, people filed out of the place like lemmings, one after another, until all that was left was me and Buzzi and the guy who owned the joint.

We thanked him for the last drink on the house, left him a fat tip, and then started our walk toward the Brooklyn Bridge. There were still hundreds of people making the same trek east, flooding along West Broadway and Broadway, moving across Chambers Street toward the bridge. Everyone was eventually funneled into the walkway, and somehow Buzzi and I were separated. I tried calling his name a few times as I crossed with the flow of pedestrians, but it was no use. There were simply too many people moving in the same direction to find any one person.

On the Brooklyn side of the bridge, one block past Tillary Street, I spotted a bus flying on Johnson Street. I flagged him down and the driver miraculously stopped.

"You were downtown, my man?" he asked me.

"Right near there, yeah," I said. "It was some crazy shit."

"You need a ride?"

"If you don't mind, sure. I just walked across the bridge."

"Where you headed?"

"Queens. Richmond Hill."

He waved me on. "Get on," he said. "I'm headed back to the depot in Jamaica."

I couldn't have been happier unless I found a bag of cocaine on my seat. I didn't, but the ride back to Queens was more than appreciated. The driver was a black dude, maybe ten years older than me. He said he'd heard things from riders, but he never had a chance to see anything until he saw all the smoke downtown from the Promenade in Brooklyn when he took his lunch break.

"What was it like?" he asked.

He was a cool dude, more interested in what I'd seen than getting the bus back to Queens. We wound up shooting the shit for the next two hours as he maneuvered in and out of traffic. He finally dropped me off on Woodhaven Boulevard alongside St. John's Cemetery. I couldn't thank the guy enough.

I still had a good walk to Jamaica Avenue and my feet, even though rested from the bus ride, were in pain when I stood on the sidewalk again. I saw a crowd of men hanging out near Frank's frankfurter van on Woodhaven Boulevard and I asked a guy who'd just pulled up if he was going near Jamaica Avenue. He was chewing on a frankfurter and held up a hand for me to wait. I watched him swallow what he'd chewed off and smiled.

"These are fuckin' good, man," he said. "I come here every day."

"You and a thousand other people," I said.

Then he nodded. "Yeah, I can drop you on Jamaica. I'm heading home, Howard Beach."

How lucky was that? If I'd been a betting man back then, and I still thank God I wasn't or I probably would've had another addiction to overcome, I would've gone to a track and bet long shots all night.

The guy had an exterminator van. I sat up front with him as he drove. I could still smell the frankfurters and onions on his breath. Like the bus driver, he asked me about the towers collapsing and I gave him a brief rundown.

"That's some fucked-up shit," he said.

It wasn't something you'd read in the papers the next day, but he'd said exactly what everyone was thinking.

He was a nice guy and he went one better than Jamaica Avenue and Woodhaven. He dropped me off in front of Doyle's. I offered to buy him a drink, but he was anxious to get the van back to the depot and himself home. In fact, there was nobody in the bar. Everyone had gone home to watch the television coverage of the attacks and the buildings collapsing. I was still drunk and in desperate need of some cocaine to even myself out, but there was none to be found anywhere in Richmond Hill.

Half an hour later, I was resting my feet on a pillow on the couch and watching the endless video reruns of the two planes slamming into the Twin Towers. It was even more horrific to watch on television than it had been to hear that first explosion. All that jet fuel blowing through the buildings and the people who had jumped to avoid burning to death. It was truly horrible.

I tried to call Miguel to see if we were working the next day, but the phones were out. I decided to take a nap and try again when I woke up. The walk across that bridge must've knocked me for a bigger loop than I figured, because when I woke up, it was five o'clock in the morning. I took a quick shower while the espresso pot did its thing in the kitchen. I downed a few cups and then headed downstairs to catch the train into the city. I had to switch trains twice before I was back in Manhattan, and then I had another long walk to the job site. When I got there, Miguel was outside securing the plywood. I helped him finish that, but the job was still shut down.

Most of the downtown area was cordoned off by the police, so it wasn't easy to get around. Everything south of Fourteenth Street was off limits, except for rescue and recovery workers. When I saw a flatbed truck heading south on West Street with a bunch of ironworkers on it, I flagged them down and asked them if they needed any help. It wasn't a heroic act. There were a lot of people looking to help. I was simply wearing the right clothes and standing in the right place at the right time.

"Hop on, buddy," one of the ironworkers said, then helped to pull me up on the truck.

The truck left us as close to the site as the police and fire department were allowing. From there we walked to the outskirts of the rubble, where a fire chief assigned people different jobs. I was with a group of guys searching for bodies. We were told to be extra careful where we stepped and to run for our asses as soon as we heard a shrill whistle that was serving as a warning in case another nearby building was about to collapse.

There were also a few hundred working dogs, the largest deployment of dogs in the nation's history, at the recovery site. I spent the next eighteen hours in what I can only imagine hell must look and smell like. It was truly horrendous, especially when we came across a body, or in most cases, a body part.

There was a river of water surrounding the rubble we were searching through, so when the warning whistle blew, it was difficult to navigate our way out of the mess. At one point after fifteen hours or so, I fell in the water while retreating from the rubble after the warning whistle sounded, and I swore I could taste blood on my lips. I knew then that I was getting close to meltdown. Sometimes the things we'd seen at the site were so horrific it was difficult to imagine seeing anything worse, and then we'd see just that, something worse—a body that had been torn in half, just the torso to head lying face down.

At one point I found a purse with a tiny bottle of Chanel No. 5 perfume inside. Without realizing it, I was saying a Hail Mary. I had an image of the woman who owned the perfume dabbing some on before leaving for work that day. I imagined her anxiousness getting to work. Maybe she was running late. Maybe she was going on an interview.

The enormity of the disaster hit me in the gut. The perfume's owner was likely dead somewhere in the rubble. I stood looking around myself for a long while, wondering where she might've died. I decided to keep the perfume bottle as a remembrance of what I'd witnessed that day.

There were other horrific sights I witnessed, but watching the firemen and policemen line up and salute their fallen brothers was particularly sobering. I'd always accepted that the police were doing their job during my stint as a criminal. Living outside the law didn't mean I was blind or unfeeling. Seeing firsthand what had happened to so many first responders was shocking; seeing their brothers' and sisters' response was overwhelming. Just recalling what I'd seen still brings tears to my eyes.

It took me a few days to get over my experience there, and at no point after that first night did I want to get high or drunk. The two hijacked planes had struck the Twin Towers on a Tuesday morning. I'd spent most of Wednesday, September 12, and some of Thursday, September 13, at Ground Zero, helping to locate and remove bodies. After that, I didn't step outside my apartment until Sunday.

I was glad I put in the time I did helping search for bodies, but by September 14, I was grateful I didn't have to return. I'd gone in with the ironworkers and come out alone. Most of those guys remained behind, catching naps when they could, then going back into the mess of twisted steel to work their magic. God bless them.

Six days after the attacks on the World Trade Center, the job at Prada was back in operation, except now we were under big-time pressure to complete the work on time. It had to do with Miuccia Prada and her promise to open the new store on her husband's timetable. A spare-no-expense edict was ordered and the construction, set back six days because of the 9/11 attacks, went ahead full throttle. I put in fourteen- to seventeen-hour days, seven days a week. The beauty of all the work, aside from the paychecks that were accumulating without any time to blow them on cocaine and booze, was the fact that it kept me sober. The job took a few months, during which I didn't miss a single day. It was nonstop work, with many of us sleeping on inflatable mattresses on the job site rather than making the commute to and from our homes.

There is always some good that comes from bad, and 9/11 was no different. I saw people helping each other everywhere. The atmosphere in general was solemn, but people went out of their way to aid and assist one another. There was also a new measure of respect for the first responders that was great to see. Knowing how many firemen and police had been killed at the World Trade Center afforded both departments a renewed appreciation.

Toward the end of the job, when things lightened up a bit and we were removing the last of the construction debris, I spent a few nights in a couple of the city's dive bars, Hogs and Heifers and Red Rock. They were places to get myself up to speed so I could blow all the money I'd just saved working so hard for so long. As it turned out, I met a woman I'd date for another couple of months at Hogs and Heifers. She turned out to be a little crazy, maybe even crazier than I was.

One of the bartenders at Hogs and Heifers, Mike, told me that the gorgeous woman at the end of the bar wanted to know my name. He said her name was Susan. Of course I introduced myself about thirty seconds later. We spent the night together in her uptown apartment, which had to be worth a couple hundred grand. Susan was not only beautiful, she was rich as well. We began dating on a regular basis, meaning I was sleeping at her place a few nights a week and going to work in the mornings, which turned out to be a very short commute.

One day when I asked her how the hell she made all her money, she slapped herself on the ass with both hands.

"With this, honey," she said.

Susan was a top-shelf call girl. The nights I didn't spend with her, she was working investment bankers from Wall Street and big-shot lawyers, and whoever else could afford her. She was worth a couple grand a night, but she was also lonely. Susan wanted a boyfriend and she'd picked me. The problem was, Susan didn't use drugs. In fact, she hated drugs and she hated the fact that I did drugs. After a few weeks of back-and-forth beefing over my use of drugs, I couldn't take it anymore. I started ducking her calls and going home instead of to her apartment on nights when she wasn't working.

One day when I got home from the Prada site, my brother Anthony asked me, "Who the hell is this broad keeps calling?"

"Ignore her," I said. "Just tell her I'm not home."

"Yeah, fine, but she showed up here last night before you got home. What's up? She stalking you? You rob her or something?"

I had to laugh. "No, I didn't rob her."

"Then call her up and break it off or I'll have the number changed. She rings all fucking night."

I decided to meet her and try to break it off, but Susan gave me a surprise I'd never expected. I never kidded myself about why I was going out with a call girl. It had everything to do with my low self-esteem. I didn't have a girlfriend. Most women might talk to me and share a laugh, but who the hell would be interested in me beyond a few laughs? For at least a few weeks, Susan had been somebody I could talk to and hang out with. She'd been a comfort to me when all I had were my addictions. The sex wasn't bad either, but that was almost secondary to what I really wanted in my life.

When I sat down with Susan to break it off, before I could get a word out, she told me she'd fallen in love with me and that she wanted to have my baby.

What the fuck? I thought. *This broad is crazier than me.*

"What?" I said.

"I'm in love with you, and I want a baby before it's too late for me," Susan said.

I must've stuttered for five minutes before I could finally explain to her that I was still a junkie and an alcoholic, and that I couldn't be trusted to be a parent at that stage of my life. I had no intentions of giving up my addictions, and parenthood was not an enticement.

"But if we have a baby, you'll have to give them up, James," she said. "You'll be a parent."

"No," I said. "I don't want to have a baby, Susan. I'm not responsible and I won't be just because you get pregnant. Chances are I'll wind up back in the joint someday, or maybe dead from an overdose. No, we can't have a baby. And you shouldn't love me. I'm the last person you should fall in love with."

We broke up that day, but Susan continued calling and showing up at the apartment until I dodged her enough times for her to finally give up. Thus ended my 9/11 love affair with a high-end hooker and any chance I'd ever be father to somebody's child.

As things returned to what could be considered normal, and the downtown area slowly opened up again, I caught the attention of a reporter from *USA Today*. Olivia Barker was writing an article, "Ground Zero's Manly Men Are Turning Heads," and she featured me in it.

She wrote:

> Women used to cross the street to avoid James Guiliani. Now they're crossing the street to ogle him.
>
> "You get it a lot now," says Guiliani, 34, the head foreman on a construction site in swanky SoHo, a couple of miles north of the World Trade Center site. There, the Queens resident dug and hauled debris during a 19-hour shift two days after the terrorist attacks. "You see them eyeball you, you eye them back. You get a few 'How are you doing today's?'"

I remained on the job and relatively sober. The Prada store was completed on time. Because it was such a high-end store, I met a few celebrities, including George Hamilton, Rod Stewart, George Clooney, and my favorite, Julia Roberts. I even helped console Britney Spears the morning I found her sitting in a limousine crying her eyes out. I think it had something to do with Justin Timberlake, but all I know is some big bodyguard approached me when he saw I was talking to Ms. Spears to tell me, "Back away from the car, sir."

This guy was as big as Melvin back in Riverhead. "Sure," I said. "No problem."

I doubt 9/11 will ever be forgotten, but over time, as the city struggled to recover, things ultimately returned to what they'd been before the attacks.

Unfortunately, that included my behavior. I had accumulated more than twelve grand in saved paychecks during the work frenzy to finish the Prada project. Twelve grand was pure dynamite for a junkie-alcoholic. I set off the dynamite during a monthlong break from work, hitting every local watering hole on Jamaica Avenue, as well as the after-hour joints like Carmine's.

At the start of 2002, I was back to being James the junkie-alcoholic, and it didn't appear as though anything would change anytime soon. I was in a prison of my own making, and it appeared as though I'd be serving a life sentence.

Chapter 7

Rescues and Heartbreak

I wish I could say that my love for animals was something I recognized and acted on throughout my life, but you already know that's not what happened. Maybe it was my addictions, or maybe it was ignorance, but I would be dishonest if I didn't admit being late to the game. One of the worst things about addiction, and there are many, is that it makes the user selfish. It is always about the next score or drink; everybody and everything outside of that goal is nonexistent. My addictions led me to make the wrong choices over and over again.

I've already mentioned the true catalysts for my transformation from junkie to animal advocate—Lena and Bruno. Whatever good was hiding inside of my selfish nature, they brought it out. Lena's fierce determination to protect and nurture animals was something she was born with. For me, it took intervention and self-discovery.

One day while we were having one of our coffee chats on Thirteenth Avenue, I asked Dr. Pernice how and when he recognized his love of animals.

"I was ten or eleven," he told me. "Our family had a summerhouse in Shirley, Long Island. A small place, bungalowlike, but it was surrounded by thick woods where I used to take hikes. Sometimes I'd catch salamanders under the scattered deadwood in the woods. Sometimes I'd bring the salamanders I'd caught home and put them in a tank. I'd do my best to mimic their environment, to try and recreate their habitat for them. I'd go back into the woods and find dead wood, cut it up and bring it back. My constructions weren't always very good, but I wanted them to feel at home. I guess I learned at a young age that animals of all kinds had a special place in my heart."

Sal also told me how much he loved dogs and cats, but that his family couldn't have one where he lived. He said he did the next best thing and offered to help out with one of his neighbors who had a dog. He'd take it for walks, play with it, and give the dog the extra attention it craved. Sal knew early on that he wanted to be a veterinarian. He said he went through most of his school years wanting to care for animals and that he couldn't wait to apply to a veterinarian school. When he finally had the chance, he applied to a school in Milan, Italy, the Università degli Studi di Milano. Sal left New York in August 1983.

He had some Italian-language background, but nothing near what he'd need to keep up with the speed of native Italians. He'd taken high school and college Italian courses, and when a neighbor of his grandparents who ran a business on Thirteenth Avenue in Brooklyn offered to help him out, he took private lessons from her a few times a week. She was a seamstress and knew the language well, but practicing a language was one thing, speaking it at two hundred miles an hour was another ball game altogether.

When he got to Italy, Sal lived with a relative for five months just outside of Milan. He said it took him that long before he was comfortable enough to move out on his own. He did so when he met another American studying at the same university. They took an apartment in Milan together and both learned the language by speaking it with relatives and friends, and to each other.

Once he earned his degree, some ten years later, Dr. Salvatore Pernice returned to New York in November 1993.

When I asked him about some of the worst things he'd ever witnessed, Sal told me that when he was a young teenager and his family was celebrating the Fourth of July in their summer home on Long Island, he saw a cat crying and staggering through a beach parking lot. When it was close enough, he could see that some piece of human garbage had jammed a firecracker in the cat's rectum. The cat was bleeding from a gaping hole where its rectum had been. Sal says the image of that poor cat continues to haunt him to this day.

He didn't say so, but I have to figure it was another reason he'd become a veterinarian, so he could save animals that had been treated so cruelly.

"There's a different type of abuse, and sometimes it's one of the most difficult things to call," he said. "I'm not really sure it can be considered animal cruelty, but sometimes veterinarians are confronted with the love some people have for their pets, a love that exceeds the most humane way to treat a dying animal. But who am I to tell them what to do?"

He said sometimes people cling too long to a pet who is ready to die and the pets wind up suffering unnecessarily.

"But how do you tell someone who loves their pet they should probably let their cat or dog, or whatever kind of pet they have, go? We can only hope they ask our professional opinion."

He and his colleagues at the BVG, most of them also graduates from the university in Milan, offer internship programs to students around the world. Several from his former school often come to New York to learn what they can in the environment here in Brooklyn. He's the first to say, "Not that we're experts, but it's always good to see different methods of treatment."

All I know is that I thank God for Dr. Salvatore Pernice every single day. He's the most humble man I think I know. He never brags, never gets overanimated, and never tries to bully his clients into doing something for his own profit. He's a true hero and animal advocate, and I don't know how I could've done my rescues without his skill, compassion, professionalism, and support.

The Diamond Collar was showing profit by 2007. We had anywhere from two to four groomers working weekends, depending on reservations made earlier in the week. We were moving the healthier brands of dog and cat food, and selling enough animal outfits to keep our heads above water. Lena was taking care of the books for our business and house, and I was falling harder and harder for her dream of one day owning and operating an animal sanctuary. It was a noble dream, but the money involved in undertaking something as big as a sanctuary just wasn't in our reach yet. We'd have to start small and operate an animal shelter, but even the cost of a small shelter was prohibitive at the time.

For a guy who never thought twice about animals in his more reckless days, I'd become someone determined to rescue and save as many as I possibly could. I was also learning more and more about people and animals with each new rescue. For the time being, I was taking the dogs and cats I rescued to one of two places; the BVG or the basement of our store. One of the more unpleasant things I noticed was the difference in how the public reacted to dogs versus cats. Puppies and kittens are cute to pretty much everyone, but puppies get more attention from adopters. When it comes to full-grown dogs and cats, there's no comparison. Dogs are always first to be saved. Cats lag way behind.

I was rescuing animals at a rate of one a week or so by 2007. As my reputation grew, so did the number of calls I'd receive asking for help. Like I said, if Dr. Pernice had the space at the BVG, he'd provide them with a temporary haven. Some of the more dramatic rescues I was involved with during that time had to do with pit bulls, the dogs most often feared by the general public for all the wrong reasons. Another dog I rescued was a beautiful black-lab mix named Star.

In the summer of 2007, a massive heat wave lasting from late June into the first weeks of August struck North America. Heat strokes resulted in more than fifty deaths. Temperatures sat at, above, or just below 90° for more than six weeks. Those without air-conditioning, especially the elderly, suffered the most. The streets of New York were literally steaming as the asphalt cooked under nonstop sunlight.

On the streets of Brooklyn, it sometimes looked as though the road ahead was moving. I later learned that what I was seeing were waves of heat rising from the asphalt. The few times it rained, you could see steam rising off the roads. Buy a bottle of soda and the plastic bottles would literally sweat with condensation. Touch the road with a bare hand and you'd burn yourself. Imagine how homeless animals fared roaming asphalt streets during the heat of the day?

This was at a time when I began rescuing animals I couldn't always keep or adopt out. Seeing dogs and cats in the street during the heat wave was tough. Stray animals have to search for shade and water, which makes them extra vulnerable to danger. Cats seeking shade under cars were in an obvious danger. Thirsty animals drinking polluted water were also in a potentially deadly situation.

On one of the hottest days in early August, a man named Willie Garrison made a frantic call to The Diamond Collar. He said that a dog had been hit by a car and was dying in the middle of Sixty-sixth Street off Twelfth Avenue in Brooklyn.

Willie's daughter used to bring her dogs to us for grooming and told her father about us. Willie also knew that I rescued animals, and he had often offered his help if I needed him.

I immediately grabbed my truck keys from behind the counter and headed out. I raced to the scene as fast as I could, running yellow and red lights, until I pulled up to within a dozen yards from where the dog was lying in the street. Even with the air conditioner blowing inside my truck, I was sweating profusely when I stepped outside.

There was a crowd of people standing along both sides of the street watching, but nobody was going near the dog. Willie told me that he'd put a bowl of water near the dog, but the dog must've been frightened because he was hurt and had moved away from the water. When Willie tried to push it closer to the dog again, the dog started to growl and Willie stayed back.

The rest of the people standing around watching were probably afraid the dog might lurch out and bite if they got too close. I could see the dog was a black-lab mix and that he was lying in a pool of his own blood. A dog with a black coat lying on black asphalt on one of the hottest days of the year was a deadly combination. The closer I got to the dog, the more I could see steam rising from the dog's blood.

I could tell he was in terrible pain as he suddenly tried to crawl toward the bowl of water Willie had set on the road, but the bowl remained out of the dog's reach. Seeing the dog in that kind of pain, and knowing that every minute that passed lessened the likelihood of his survival, I went into rescue mode. I wasn't concerned with getting bitten or anything else. Getting the dog to the BVG was what had to be done. I went straight to the water and pushed the bowl in front of the dog's mouth. As he lapped up the water, I put myself into position to pick him up. It was then I could see how much of his legs had been torn up. There was no hair or skin, just bone and blood. The dog had been dragged by a car or thrown from the window, and whoever had done it hadn't bothered to stop.

I picked the dog up and carried him to my truck as he continued to cry in pain. Willie came along for the ride and stayed in the back with the dog to keep him calm and hold the bowl of water for him to drink from. I called the BVG on the drive there. I could still hear the dog whimpering from his pain. There's no sadder sound.

When we got there, it was like a scene from a television ER. Technicians were waiting in the street to take the dog. Dr. Pernice already had a room prepared for the dog's arrival. They treated him for his severe injuries while Willie and I waited nervously outside. An hour or so later, we were told the dog was doing fine. I looked at Willie and the relief was all over his face. He looked like an expectant father who had just learned his kid was born healthy.

In fact, he was so happy to hear that the dog's healing process had begun, Willie offered to pay for the operation out of pocket, but the BVG refused payment. Willie couldn't stop thanking Dr. Pernice and his team. On the way back to the store, he asked me what he could do for the good people at the BVG for all the kindness and professionalism they'd shown the dog.

"I don't know, Willie," I said, "buy them lunch or something." It was more an offhand comment than something he should take seriously, but the next day that beautiful man, Willie Garrison, sent over a catered lunch for everyone at the BVG.

It would take three months of constant treatment, during which the dog's wounds had to be re-dressed every day to prevent infection, before the wounds were fully healed. Not long afterward, the dog was adopted by a beautiful family who named him Star. They continue to provide each other with love and companionship to the present day.

And guess who has become a lifetime friend of mine? Willie Garrison continues to bring his dogs to our store for grooming and general good conversation and companionship. The world will always be better because of people like Willie Garrison.

In early 2008, I was heading for the Belt Parkway to meet up with some old friends of mine in Richmond Hill. I was driving on Eighty-sixth Street and Fourteenth Avenue when I noticed a truck directly ahead of me swerving all over the road. I assumed it was some drunk and kept my distance. The last thing I needed was to have an accident, especially with Princess riding up front with me.

I remember thinking this guy had to be the luckiest SOB in the world the way he was driving without getting stopped. As we approached Dyker Beach Park, I saw something small flying out of the driver's side window. There was a loud bang before I saw a can of some kind that had bounced off a parked car. It rolled out into the middle of Eighty-sixth Street.

"Fuckin' nut," I said.

Then I saw the truck slow up ahead, and the next thing to fly out the window was a dog. I could feel my eyes open wide as the dog hit the ground and the truck took off. Half of me wanted to chase the prick down and beat the shit out of him, but the dog looked stunned in the middle of the street. I slowed up so as not to scare it, but then it took off like a shot and chased the truck that was speeding away. I couldn't believe what I was seeing. What kind of piece of garbage does that to an animal?

I was livid as I tried to head off the dog. I had to drive into an oncoming traffic lane to get ahead of the dog. I did so at about sixty miles per hour until I was far enough ahead to pull back into the right lane, stop the car and get out. Once again, I was in rescue mode and not thinking at all. The dog was a seventy-pound red-nosed pit bull, a thick, fierce-looking bundle of pure muscle, and he was charging straight at me. I didn't know if he was going to attack or race by me, but I stepped in front of him and managed to grab him in a headlock. I went down to one knee from the force of the dog's power. I held him tight against my body, his mouth inches from my face. He seemed to calm down in my grip, but there was no way I could let him go.

My other problem was what to do next. With Princess in my truck, I couldn't bring the pit bull in there, because I didn't know if he would attack her or not. If he did, Princess would be dead before I could do anything about it. I was in my own state of panic as I looked around me and started to yell for help.

Fortunately for me and the pit bull, some guy was having a smoke on his stoop because his wife wouldn't let him smoke in the house. He was an absolute gentleman, and he came to our rescue as soon as he heard me.

"What's going on?" he said before he saw me holding the dog in a headlock. "Oh, shit," he said next.

"Yeah, bro, some piece of shit threw him out of a truck window. I was driving behind the guy, but I can't put him in my truck because I have a small dog in there."

"No problem," the guy said. "Let me get a rope and my car keys and I'll take him. Where we going?"

"Just follow me, brother," I said. "And thank you for this."

Twenty minutes later we put him in my store, and the next morning I brought him to the BVG. Dr. Pernice kept him there to make sure he was healthy and a good adoptee candidate. Two weeks later, the mechanic who does my oil changes took the dog and named him Hershey. They remain pals to this day.

In the summer of 2009, I was following shelter posts on the Internet when I noticed a beautiful pit bull was about to be put down. According to the post, the dog was doomed if it wasn't adopted by the end of the day. I drove to a Brooklyn animal-care center with plans of rescuing the dog before it was euthanized. The first mistake I made when I stepped inside the shelter was to tell the woman working the front desk that I was there to rescue the pit bull.

"What do you mean 'rescue'?"

"Keep it from being killed," I said.

"We're an adoption agency, sir," she said. "We don't let people rescue dogs here. We don't do false adoptions."

I was frustrated, but wasn't about to give up. There was no way I was walking out of there without that dog.

"Look, all I want to do is save the poor thing. I'll keep him with me."

The woman shook her head. "Sorry, it doesn't work like that."

It was then I noticed the sign alongside her immediate area and the plastic five-gallon jug beneath it.

CONTRIBUTIONS

Bada-boom, bada-bing, I thought. My street instincts kicked in and I moved over to the plastic jug they used for donations. There was maybe fifty bucks in there, counting the change; not even two inches of cash.

"Can I at least make a donation to the shelter in the dog's name?" I said.

"Of course," she said, this time giving me a huge smile.

"Thank you," I said.

I made sure the woman was watching me as I opened my wallet and very slowly, very deliberately, removed three $100 bills and pushed them into the plastic jug. Fifteen minutes later, I was carrying the pit bull outside to my truck.

I took the dog to the BVG for a checkup. He was treated for severe kennel cough and some minor skin issues. There was nothing serious to worry about, except I didn't really have space at home for him. Dr. Pernice came through once again and housed the pit bull at the BVG.

By this time, Sal had already taken in several of my rescues and I felt I owed him at least some relief whenever I had the chance. I saw that the pit bull was genuinely a gentle animal and the perfect companion to accompany me and Princess on our daily runs. This way the BVG had at least one empty cage during the day and the pit bull had some human contact. It turned out to be a great idea, except I was quickly getting attached to the dog.

When I told Lena about the pit bull, she felt terrible, but she said we just didn't have enough room at the house. She was right, of course, so I continued to take the dog with me during the day and then brought him back to the BVG nights before they closed.

Fortunately, one of the interns at the BVG, a student from the same Milan veterinarian school that Sal had graduated from some twenty-plus years earlier, fell in love with the pit bull. Aksell Ottanta was the name of the intern. He'd taken an apartment near the veterinary office when he first moved to New York. Because he was so fond of this pit bull, he started taking the dog home with him nights. He'd return the dog in the morning and I would pick him up and take him out for the day. Because the dog was living in Brooklyn full time, I named him Brooklyn.

Between Aksell and me, Brooklyn had human contact and company, not to mention genuine love and affection just about the entire day. The new routine was great, but I knew that sooner or later, we'd have to find a permanent home for him. I tried word-of-mouth and online networking, but I was striking out. Most times when it comes to rescued pit bulls, people have the wrong impression. Most assume pit bulls are always rescued from dogfighting rings. Although it is sometimes true, not every pit bull has been trained to be vicious. In fact, no dog is born that way. Much like humans, dogs are products of their environments. You abuse a dog long enough, it will turn on you. You move a dog from one environment/ owner to another, over and over, the dog will be confused and unsure what to expect.

I'm sure that this is the problem many shelters have in finding homes for rescued pit bulls, and it was no different for Brooklyn until a friend of mine called me one day with a lead. Kim said she knew of a young family on Long Island who were interested in adopting a pit bull.

"Kim, you're a savior," I told her. "The guy who was taking him home nights, one of the interns at the BVG, just returned to Italy. The dog has been caged again nights. What do you know about this family?"

Kim told me that they were a youngish couple with one kid, a young son about ten years old, and that they owned a beautiful home with a white picket fence. I was visualizing the perfect American family, minus the dog. They sounded like the perfect fit for Brooklyn. I told Kim to have them get in touch with me and that I'd gladly adopt Brooklyn out if they checked out okay.

Kim showed the couple pictures of Brooklyn and then called back to say they loved him and couldn't wait to pick him up.

"Great," I said. "Bring them to Cafe Amici in Queens."

"Why there?" she asked.

"Because he comes everywhere with me," I said. "I go there a few times a week and he's always with me. This way they don't have to come all the way to Dyker Heights, *capisce* (understand)?"

"Great," Kim said. "What day?"

"I know Sal is gonna want to have the dog neutered, so why don't we make it for next week, after his stitches heal?"

"Oh, no, James, they want the dog right away," Kim said. "This week if possible."

"Shit, okay. Let me talk to Sal. Maybe we can turn him over with instructions to let the stitches heal before they get too rough with him."

"That would be great, James. I'll call them now."

"*Aspettare*, wait a little," I told her in Italian. "Hold on until I talk to Dr. P. I'll ring him now and call you right back."

It was all working out, and the young happy couple from Long Island met me at Cafe Amici in Queens a few days later. Dr. Pernice had neutered Brooklyn, but he'd also removed a wart from one of his paws. There were stitches in both areas, the dog's groin and one of his paws. I had Brooklyn sitting on the floor alongside me, his stitches still clearly visible. The couple showed up on time, a good sign.

I could sense they were a little nervous, but I figured it was because of where they were meeting with me, in an Italian cafe filled with guys who at least looked like they were connected. Let's face it, some of them looked like the tough guys they were. It also could've been my look or my voice, which is gruff. Whatever it was, I had the sense the entire time I was speaking to them that they weren't really paying attention. They both looked as though they wanted to run out of there as fast as possible.

In the meantime, I was trying to get across how important it was for this nice young couple to treat Brooklyn gently until his stitches healed. Not only for the dog's sake, but for their sake as well. It wasn't like Brooklyn was some ten-pound shih tzu.

"Please, whatever you do," I told them, "make sure there's no rough-housing with the dog until the stitches are healed. You know, keep the dog off limits for certain kinds of playing. Most people don't understand how pets aren't toys. They think they can play with them a little rough sometimes, and sometimes the animals get pissed off."

"Also, make sure the dog isn't put into an uncomfortable position for him. Let him get used to you and your family first. Don't bring him around too many people, or let too many people visit him right away. Brooklyn has been bounced around a lot. He's been staying with me days, somebody else nights, and then caged nights. Give him some time to get used to you guys. And remember, he just had surgery in two places. He's gonna be tender in those areas at least until the stitches heal. You definitely want to avoid his getting an infection or pulling the stitches out. And you don't want anyone going near those stitches while they're still healing. He might snap at someone and you definitely don't want that to happen."

"No problem," the husband said. "We'll take good care of the dog, trust me. You have my word on that."

"The only other thing, and this is very important to me, so please pay attention. Should this arrangement not work out for some reason, whatever the reason, please, I beg you, please bring the dog back to me. Don't give it away to a friend, or bring it to another shelter. Just give me a call and I'll come pick him up, any time, day or night."

"No problem," the husband said. "I'm sure everything will work out great, but if it doesn't, we'll call you."

"Okay," I said. "Fair enough."

I stood up and handed over Brooklyn by his leash. I can't tell you how much it hurt to do it. I was all tears as the couple walked him back to their car. Brooklyn was a special dog. I'd enjoyed our time together, every day for almost a month. I knew that the dog was already missing Aksell, especially during the night when I'm sure the intern and Brooklyn shared their best times together.

I went home that day a little upset over losing Brooklyn, but glad that he appeared to be going to a young couple who at least seemed to want him. The next day while taking a look at Facebook, I saw a picture of Brooklyn on a beach.

"What the fuck?" I said aloud.

"What, James?" Lena said.

"Look at this."

I showed her the picture of Brooklyn on the beach. He appeared exhausted, his tongue hanging all the way out of his mouth. The caption above the picture read: "Jogging with my new dog, Brooklyn. Two miles? A piece of cake."

"Piece of shit," I said. "Never mind cake."

I couldn't believe it. The woman had taken Brooklyn to the beach in his condition, and then ran him for two miles?

Not wanting to be overbearing, I called Kim instead of the family and asked her to give them a call. "Please, Kim, tell them to go easy with Brooklyn. He shouldn't be out on a beach in this heat, never mind jogging. He still has stitches that need to heal."

Kim was surprised at how the woman had treated Brooklyn and said she'd call right away. I spent the rest of the day into the night worried that something bad might happen. My gut instincts told me something was wrong. The next morning when I looked on the woman's Facebook page I was relieved to see nothing bad going on. I felt somewhat relieved. Maybe she'd gotten the message and would do the right thing going forward.

If only my hopes could've turned to reality.

At one point later the same night, I decided to check the woman's Facebook page again before going to bed. I cursed loud enough for Lena to hear me from where she was in our bedroom upstairs.

"What the fuck is wrong with these people!" I yelled.

There was Brooklyn surrounded by a dozen or so people in a yard filled with maybe two dozen more people. They were having some kind of barbecue while showing off their new dog, but the dog was clearly not happy, not even in the picture. His tail was between his legs and he seemed to be cowering away from two people who were reaching out to him when the picture was taken.

"You believe this nut job?" I said to myself.

This time I wrote on her Facebook page to remind her of Brooklyn's surgeries and stitches. The next morning when I checked to see if she responded, I saw that she hadn't. Maybe she hadn't read it yet, or maybe she was ignoring me. Either way, Brooklyn had been put in danger, not only for him, but for all the people at the party. I waited a few hours and called Kim again. This time I told her to let them know that I'd seen the Facebook picture and I was very worried that the dog was getting way too much of the wrong kind of attention.

"Remind her that Brooklyn's been abandoned a few times," I told Kim. "The dog doesn't understand going from one set of owners to another. I had him during the day and I'm gone. Aksell had him during the night and he's gone. The BVG had him in between and they're gone. The dog isn't used to his new family yet. All those people will just confuse him more."

"Okay, James, I'll tell her. And I'm sorry they're being like this. I wish I knew better."

"Alright, look, maybe it'll work out. Maybe I'm overconcerned for nothing. Brooklyn is a tough dog. Maybe he's handling it."

Two days later I saw a picture on the woman's Facebook page of her son lying on top of Brooklyn, his face right alongside the dog's face, his feet touching the stitches around the dog's groin. Needless to say, I flipped out. I didn't want to bother Kim again, but there was no way I could let this go on. I wrote on the woman's Facebook page again, this time saying (in all caps): "THAT ISN'T A GOOD IDEA. THE DOG STILL HAS STITCHES. YOU NEED TO BE MORE CAREFUL, PLEASE!"

Once again the woman never responded, but the next day the post was gone. Later that same night I received a frantic call from Kim.

"James, the woman just called. They're trapped in their bedroom. Brooklyn went crazy. They called the police and they're on their way to shoot the dog."

"Shoot the dog?" I said. "They should shoot the people. Where do I go? I'm on my way."

"No, James, they're afraid of you," Kim said. "They think you're still a gangster because of where you met them. The father said he doesn't want you at his house."

"Fuck him," I said. "I want my dog back. You call him back and tell him to give me my dog back or there will be trouble. That piece of shit. What the hell happened?"

"The mother claims she was running the vacuum cleaner near the dog and Brooklyn went berserk. He started chewing on the vacuum bag and growling and she got scared and grabbed her son, and they locked themselves in a bedroom. Then she called her husband and the idiot came home and slapped the dog. Brooklyn attacked him."

"Good, I hope he took a chunk of his fucking leg off, the moron."

"No, James, it's serious. He called the police."

"You call him back and tell him to back those cops off. I'll come out there and meet you someplace. Can you get the dog out of the house?"

"They managed to coax him into their yard. I'll have to get him from there."

"Okay, just be careful. Then we'll meet up. Long Island, right?"

"We can meet off the exit on the Long Island Expressway, yeah. Exit 60."

"Alright, I'm on my way. Just make sure that asshole doesn't let those cops take my dog."

"I'll try. Okay, see you later. Call me when you're near the exit."

Over the next hour or so I was in a complete panic. What if the police got there first and Brooklyn growled at them? What if they killed that poor dog? The assholes who'd adopted him had done everything they weren't supposed to do and the dog was probably fed up. I blamed myself for giving him up, but if something happened to that dog, I was going to do something about it.

I was pulling up to Exit 60 on the expressway when I spotted Kim's SUV. I pulled off to the side and was looking for the dog, but I didn't see him. I was so friggin' nervous, I yelled out my window: "Kim, where's my dog?"

It was like a miracle, Kim later told me. She had Brooklyn in the back of her SUV, but he was lying down and not moving, as if he were in shock of some kind. She said the dog left the yard with her through the gate, because he refused to go back inside the house. I don't know what that ass-hole guy did to make the dog attack him, but he was lucky Brooklyn didn't rip his throat out.

He was lucky I didn't rip his throat out.

Kim said as soon as Brooklyn heard my voice, his head popped up and his tail started to wag. He jumped up into the front seat and out the pas-senger window. I was a nervous wreck because if he ran onto the express-way he'd get run over for sure. I opened my passenger door and Brooklyn jumped inside my truck. He kissed me half a dozen times and then jumped into the back. Two minutes later, he was out like a light. Brooklyn was feeling a sense of security he hadn't felt since I turned him over to those morons at Cafe Amici less than a week earlier.

I had tears streaming down my face. I couldn't believe how he'd reacted. This wasn't a vicious pit bull. Brooklyn was a loving dog looking for genuine affection. The assholes who'd adopted him had never listened to a word I told them about Brooklyn's surgeries or his stitches. They were obviously the wrong choice for pet adoption. I learned a few valuable lessons that day, but the first was, Don't judge a book by its cover. They could shove their white picket fence up their collective asses. This nice young couple with their nice new home—they were idiots when it came to caring for an animal.

Of course I wanted to keep him. Who wouldn't after that experience? The problem was, there still wasn't enough room at my house for Brook-lyn, and Aksell, who had loved and cared for Brooklyn, had already finished his internship at the BVG and was back in Milan, Italy. I couldn't bear the thought of Brooklyn in a cage all night again. As happy as I was to have him back, I was equally upset at the thought he no longer had a permanent home.

Over the next few days, the crazy family who had adopted Brooklyn trashed me and the dog on their Facebook page: "James Guiliani gave us a vicious Pit Bull to bring home. The dog attacked my family. Don't adopt from him. He's a gangster."

It was bullshit, bullshit, and more bullshit. I responded with a post of my own, explaining *exactly* what had happened after they took a dog with stitches from two surgeries and basically tortured him for six days. A day later I received a post from a neighbor of the whack-job family on Long Island. The neighbor said the same family had already given up a purebred bulldog after just two weeks because they claimed they couldn't let it pee on their living-room rug. They never even bothered to try and train the poor thing. They just gave up and gave the dog away.

Another lesson learned. I swore that from that point on, I'd do a little more investigating into families about to adopt an animal I rescued. Just like the movie *Blue Velvet*, what goes on behind closed doors and/or white picket fences isn't always as bright as the facade.

While I continued to worry about what would happen to Brooklyn next, Aksell, from his home in Milan, had also read the posts about Brooklyn.

The next day at the store, with Brooklyn and Princess on the floor behind the counter with me, who walks into the Diamond Collar yapping one hundred miles a minute in his native Italian? I didn't understand a word Aksell was saying until I heard him say *Brook-a-lyn*. The dog also understood his own name, even in broken English, because as soon as Brooklyn heard Aksell's voice, up he jumped. Their reunion was incredible. The dog was happy—crying as he licked Aksell's mug all over. Aksell continued speaking Italian that I didn't understand, so I called Lena and had her translate.

"What's going on?" I asked her.

"It's great, James," Lena said. "Aksell wants to take Brooklyn back to Italy with him,"

"Serious?" I said.

"Yes, it's why he came back. He wants to take him home tomorrow."

"Holy shit, Lena. I'll have to contact Sal. He's gonna have to get the dog certified for a trip like that, I think."

"I'm so happy for Brooklyn, James," Lena said. "At least now you can rest assured he'll be taken care of. He'll be loved."

It was true, make no mistake, but a little of my heart was broken because it meant I'd have to say good-bye to Brooklyn one more time.

Today, Aksell and Brooklyn remain family in Milan, Italy, and I can never express how much it means to me to know that Brooklyn is loved by someone who would travel across an ocean to bring him home. *Viva Italia! Viva Aksell! Viva Brook-a-lyn!*

In 2010, one day while I was hanging out with Dr. Pernice at the BVG office, I received a phone call from one of my older gangster friends on Eighteenth Avenue. A bunch of the guys were at the cafe there when they heard screeching tires followed by the screams of a wounded cat. Someone who had witnessed the accident said they saw the cat get hit in the left lane before it was knocked into the right lane, where a second car ran it over. My friend told me there was a big crowd standing around the cat trying to keep it from moving, because it was on someone's front lawn. It was trying to crawl away and one of its legs appeared to be mangled.

I raced to the scene on Eighteenth Avenue and Seventy-fifth Street, double-parked my truck, and tried to clear a path to the cat. It was the first time I heard my name being whispered by some of the onlookers.

"Hey, that's that guy," I heard someone say.

"Guiliani, right?" someone else said, "that gangster guy saves animals."

I guess some word of mouth was spreading around Brooklyn, but I was more concerned with the cat than my image. I asked one of my friends if the cat belonged to anyone.

"Nobody spoke up yet, James," my friend said.

"Alright, fuck it," I said. "I have to get him to Pernice."

I knew to be careful, because the cat was probably feral, and a wounded animal is usually a dangerous animal. The cat was a beautiful black-and-white with a tuxedo coat, and a tiny black mustache that reminded me of Charlie Chaplin. As I drew closer, I could see his leg was indeed mangled. I reached out a hand and he hissed loud and long.

Shit, I thought. *This is gonna hurt.*

And it sure did. As soon as I was close enough to scruff the cat up into my arms, I did so and pinned him against my chest. Of course he bit the first thing he could, which was one of my nipples, and brother, did it hurt. He clamped his teeth down and wasn't letting go. In the meantime, the three paws he could still use were embedded in my skin as he pulled for all he was worth. Genius that I am, I didn't think to put on a sweatshirt or something with long sleeves. Not me. I was wearing my trademark wife-beater T-shirt, except it was being torn to pieces along with my skin.

My friend yelled at me to be careful, but it was way too late for that. Blood was gushing from where the cat had gripped me with his claws.

I yelled for someone to get my carrying case from the truck. Another mistake I'd made was not taking it with me when I first got out of the truck. When the case was down on the ground alongside me, I had to drop to my knees to position myself and the cat in such a way as to make the cage his only escape route. That quickly turned into a wrestling match that had to look comical—a 240-pound man and a six-pound cat.

Fortunately, after a few more lacerations, the cat was safe inside the cage. He was still hissing and in obvious pain, but at least I could bring him to the BVG. When I got there, the technicians at the office were as concerned about the blood still seeping from my wounds as they were about the cat. Dr. Pernice stitched both of us up, but the cat's right front leg had been shattered and would remain deformed for the rest of his life.

The cat was indeed feral, and Sal had to treat him for worms, parasites, fleas—you name it—but in the end, he was healthy and probably healed faster than the scars he left all over my chest, arms, shoulders, and neck. Because of his tiny black mustache and where I'd rescued him on Eighteenth Avenue, I named him Chaplin 18, and he's still with me—a happy, healthy cat with one deformed leg.

My mornings almost always start with a stop at Cafe Isabella a few blocks from our store. If I'm not running late, I have my espressos right there. Otherwise I grab them to go, and then down them in my truck. One morning while I had a few minutes, I was talking to Philomena, the girl who works the counter at the cafe, basically shooting the shit, when she suddenly remembered something she had to tell me.

"James, I've been meaning to tell you about a cat that I find out here in the mornings. I'm not big on cats or anything, but this one really breaks my heart. I always find it crying outside the store in the mornings, just sitting out there looking at the front door next door, the one to the apartments upstairs. I'm afraid it's gonna wind up dead one day."

"Talk to me," I said. "What's going on?"

"It's the guy upstairs, his cat," Philomena said.

"And it's outside in the mornings?"

"He throws it out every night."

"What?"

Philomena shrugged. "I think he lets the cat inside when he goes to work, to let his kids play with it upstairs. They must feed it and everything, play with it, I guess, but then when he gets home, he throws it out. I asked him once and he said he doesn't let cats stay in his house during the night."

"You're kidding," I said. I couldn't believe it.

"No, I think he's a real prick, the guy. He throws it out and sometimes when I'm here closing, I can hear it crying. He just leaves it out there to cry all night long."

"Who is this moron?" I said.

"He lives upstairs. Maybe you could talk to him and see what's up."

"Talk to him? I'll take his cat with me is what I'll do."

I left the cafe to open the store, but after closing that night, I headed back to the building where the cafe is located and waited until I could get upstairs to talk to the moron who was throwing his cat out every night. How he considered it his cat was already too much to comprehend.

I found a few kids in the hallway playing with the cat, but it was close to seven o'clock and I wasn't sure if their father was home yet or not. When I asked one of the kids, he went inside the apartment and brought back his father.

"Yeah, what is it?" he said, with an attitude that deserved a smack.

I started off polite, thinking maybe the guy was just a stupid son of a bitch and didn't know any better. He was a foreigner, and sometimes people in different cultures don't treat their animals the same as we do.

"I'm wondering about the cat," I said. "Do you really throw it out every night?"

"Of course," he said. "I don't let animals sleep in the same house as my family."

"Are you aware that the poor thing is out there crying all night?"

"It's a fucking cat," the guy said. "Who cares if it cries?"

"I care," I said. "I'm taking her with me."

"You can't take her with you, she's my cat."

"Not if you kick her out on the street every night, she's not."

"Who the fuck are you to tell me that?" he said.

At that point I had to smile. "Excuse me," I said to the kids playing with the cat, then picked her up and started down the stairs.

"Hey!" the guy yelled.

I turned, smiled, told him to go fuck himself, and brought the cat out to my truck.

The next day I brought her to the BVG and left her there to be examined while I returned to the store. It was a Saturday afternoon, just about closing time, when Philomena gave me a call. She said the guy had gone to his landlord and told him about my stealing his cat. The joke was on him, because the owner of the building was the same guy who owned the cafe. The moron was told there was a no pet clause in his lease anyway, so the cat couldn't be returned.

The next day, a Sunday, he was waiting for me when I opened the store. I ignored him, but he followed me inside.

"I want my fucking cat back!" he demanded.

"Go fuck yourself," I said. "And get out of my store."

"Fuck you!" he yelled. "You stole my cat. I'm gonna call the cops."

"Go 'head, you moron, you can't even have a cat in that building."

"You're a thief."

"And you're a dick, but I'm not wasting any more time on you. Get out."

"No. I want my cat!"

"Listen to me, bro. You didn't want the fucking cat. You threw her out every night. What the fuck do you want her for? To abuse? To hear her cry outside all night? She could get killed out there on the street. She could get run over by a car, or attacked by a dog. What the fuck is wrong with your brain?"

"You're a fucking thief!" he yelled. "Thief, thief, thief!"

It was all I could take. I stepped around the counter and he backed up.

"What?" he said. "I'll call the cops."

I shook my head. I was dealing with a complete lunatic. I told him if I had to throw him out of the store, I'd kick his ass back to where he lived three blocks away.

"Is that what you want?" I said. "Just so you can have me arrested? For a cat you didn't want anyway? You want to wind up a cripple? It's fine with me, if that's what you want."

I don't know how or why, but it worked. He took a few steps back, gave me the finger, and walked out.

I named the cat Princess and she still lives in my store.

Unfortunately, not every rescue story has a happy ending. I can think of none sadder than the day a litter of kittens would break my heart. It was probably the closest I've come to wanting to get wasted in the four years I'd been sober.

It was the winter of 2011 and I was walking with a friend, Jennifer, on Seventy-fifth Street, when we heard what seemed like baby screams. It was difficult to hear clearly because it had started to rain.

Jennifer said, "Stop, James. Listen to that. It's a baby screaming."

I stopped and turned toward the noise, but it wasn't a baby. The screams were jumbled, one on top of another.

"Sounds like cats to me," I said.

"No way."

"Yeah, I think so. Let's go see."

We jogged down a driveway toward the noise. When we reached the end, we saw a deck behind a house. The cries were coming from under there. A litter of jet-black kittens, maybe a week or two old, was lying in about an inch of ice-cold rainwater that had seeped through the deck. They were surrounded with white rice, soy beans, vegetables, and noodles.

"What the fuck?" I said.

"What?" Jennifer said.

"Look at this shit. Somebody is feeding them Chinese food."

I went to take them out of the water when an Asian woman stepped out onto the deck.

"What you doing?" she said with a heavy accent.

"There's a litter of cats under here," I said. "I'm going to try and save them."

"No touch cats," she said. "They okay. I feed them."

"They can't eat this stuff," I said. "Where's the mother?"

"Mother come back," she said.

"Where is she?"

"Mother come back."

I turned to Jennifer and said, "Fuck this. I'm taking them."

The woman went crazy and started throwing towels at me, but I handed off three kittens to Jennifer and grabbed the other three, and we bolted from the yard back out to the street. We brought them to the BVG, but Dr. Pernice had already left for the day. One of the vet technicians, Melissa, was just about to close. Once she saw the kittens and the condition they were in, she helped me try to save them.

Their body temperatures were very low and they were starving. They were also covered with fleas. We cleaned them off and then used blow-dryers to try and get their temperatures back up to normal. Then we individually bottle-fed them with warm milk. We used hot-water bottles, warm blankets, and a heat lamp to keep them as warm as possible afterward.

Before we left, they were huddled together. They were the cutest thing I'd ever seen, and I left the BVG office feeling very good about myself. To my mind, I'd just saved six beautiful, innocent kittens from a horrible cold death.

On the way home, I doubled back to the address where we'd found the kittens on Seventy-fifth Street. I decided to ask the neighbors about the cats. I wanted to find the mother as quickly as possible, but what I found out was that the mother had been run over in the driveway a few days earlier. That meant the kittens had been on their own, out in the cold without the food and the warmth they needed, for at least a few days. The Chinese food wasn't doing them any good whatsoever.

I was upset, but I still felt good about what we'd done earlier in the day. Saving those kittens meant a lot to me. I told Lena about them and she was heartbroken.

"I just hope they survive, James," she said. "Sometimes there's nothing you can do for them. If the mother's been dead for a few days and they were out in the cold, they might not survive."

I tried to blow off what she'd said, but it bothered me all night. The next day I stopped at the BVG to see how they were doing and was devastated when I learned that one of the kittens had indeed died.

"Fuck!" I said. "I thought we saved them. All of them."

Sal tried to explain the same thing to me that Lena had said. He also told me that kittens are born with very weak immune systems and that once removed from their mother's care and milk, the immune systems are basically nonexistent.

"Well, at least these five are making it," I said, being my usual stubborn self.

Sal didn't say anything, but I could tell he didn't want to upset me. I guess it has to do with how sometimes too much love can make an animal suffer more than it was meant to suffer.

The next day, another of the kittens died. They were getting lots of care and attention at the BVG, but Sal had been right about their immune systems. On the third day, the third kitten died. Another died on the fourth day, leaving just two of the kittens still surviving. By the fourth death, I was a complete mental case. It was killing me to go home every night not knowing if another kitten would be dead when I went to check on them the following day.

I was back to praying on the fifth morning. I prayed all the way to the BVG office, but one of the two remaining kittens had died during the night.

"Tell me this one won't die!" I said to Dr. Pernice. "Please tell me that."

Sal just shrugged. "I wish I could, James, but I can't. It's out of our hands now."

That night I went from angry at God to praying to him, back and forth. Lena tried to console me, but I felt as if I was going through another Bruno multiplied by five. I couldn't face the sixth kitten dying.

In the morning I went to the early mass at St. Ephrem's Church on Seventy-fifth Street. I prayed on my knees, put a $100 bill in the poor box, and begged God to spare the last kitten's life. When it was time to stop at the BVG, I could barely make myself walk inside. Melissa had just opened up. I could tell what had happened from the look on her face.

Neither of us could speak until she finally managed to say, "I'm so sorry, James."

Each of my rescues, whether successful or bittersweet, eventually galvanized my resolve to save and care for animals. I'll never understand how some people can treat animals with such ferocious cruelty. We've all seen television commercials by the American Society for the Prevention of Cruelty to Animals (ASPCA) showcasing dogs and cats that have been treated horribly. We've all heard and read about horrendous dogfighting rings like the one Michael Vick was once involved with. If nothing else, Vick's crimes helped to expose the savagery of dogfighting. Today the general public is much more aware of those kinds of horrors.

It wasn't long ago that I saw a story on social media about a kitten that had been dropped into a pipe and had cement poured in behind it so that only its head and the top of a paw were exposed. Thankfully, one of the construction workers heard the kitten's cries and dislodged the pipe from the ground to free it.

We're left wondering what would possibly make someone do something so cruel to something so helpless. I often wonder what in the world is wrong with us. I don't know the answer, except that the abuse I too often hear about and sometimes witness always infuriates me. I like to think that I've become a better man because I can now recycle that fury and use it to fuel my commitment to care for abused and abandoned animals.

Chapter 8

Natural Disasters and Dogfighting

On October 29, 2012, Superstorm Sandy crossed the eastern coastline near Brigantine, New Jersey, slightly northeast of Atlantic City. At the time it was considered a post-tropical cyclone with hurricane-force winds. Sounds bad, but it was a lot worse. The storm struck during high tide. A full moon supercharged the storm surge and brought a world of hurt on everyone and everything in its path. Thousands of animals were not spared.

It was estimated that some 15 million dogs and 14 million cats were in Hurricane Sandy's path. Aside from pets that found themselves home-less from the storm, there were thousands more animals whose fate was unaccountable, feral cats and stray dogs especially, animals that were either displaced or killed from the massive flooding. No one really knows just how many animals were permanently lost because of Hurricane Sandy.

The hurricane caused damage in twenty-four states in total. New Jersey and New York received the most severe damage. When the surge hit New York on October 29, streets, tunnels, and subways were flooded. Power was cut off throughout the metropolitan area. The only animals to benefit from the massive flooding were rats, and with most feral-cat colonies uprooted, the rat population only thrived.

A year later, the number of Sandy pets that remained in need was stag-gering. Some animal owners made the mistake of leaving their pets to fend for themselves, while others who lost their homes made sure their animals ended up in shelters.

A few days after the storm, I received a phone call at the store from one of the rescue groups on Long Island. I was told they needed assistance at Midland Beach on Staten Island, where the storm seemed to have done the most damage. I was also told that there were animals all over the place, but not enough people to help round them up. I later witnessed for myself how most people were rescuing dogs, while ignoring cats, all too often a common occurrence when it comes to rescues.

The most upsetting situation that was brought to my attention concerned a house in Midland Beach where an estimated fifty cats were trapped. The caller said, "The people there are saying that the woman who owns the house is a known hoarder. She has a ton of cats, they're saying upwards of fifty, but people were afraid to go inside to check on them. The house has been severely damaged and is flooded."

"Of course I'll help," I told the caller. "I'll get there soon as I can with supplies and I'll try to round a few volunteers up."

I immediately put out word on Facebook and made calls asking for donations. My people really came through. They brought all kinds of supplies to the store: food, cages, blankets, treats, everything you can imagine displaced animals might need. I removed most of the food from my shelves and started loading my truck. Once I had everything packed and had arranged for people to cover for me at the store, I was on my way to Staten Island. I drove about two blocks before I remembered that I needed gas. My fuel gauge was sitting on a quarter tank. I was going to get gas the day before but had decided to head straight home instead. I figured I'd get it in the morning, never expecting to have a problem. Big mistake.

I headed for the gas station I usually used but quickly learned that getting gas wasn't going to be so easy. The gas station was closed. So was the next one I drove to, and the one I tried after that. Getting gas was my first of many problems that day. All the gas stations were either sold out or without electricity to run their pumps. Gas had become a high priority throughout the city, but it never dawned on me until I had to make the trip to Staten Island.

The next thing I did was call up everybody I knew who might have a lead on where to get some gas. I called friends, family, and gangsters to see if they had access to a gas station someplace nearby. It must've taken me fifty calls before a former gangster friend called me back with a lead.

"James, there's a guy who'll sell but it isn't gonna be cheap," he said.

"How much?"

"He's asking ten bucks a gallon."

"You're kidding me? And he's a friend of yours?"

"James, you know how these guys work. This is business to them. You want the gas, you're gonna have to pay his price."

"Alright, fine. I'll pay it. Tell me where to go and I'll be there soon as I get the cash."

I headed back to the house, grabbed a handful of cash and headed out to the station. And $300 later, I had a full tank again. Rescues on Staten Island after the storm would eventually cost me more than $900 in gas.

Getting gas was one expensive nightmare, but getting through Staten Island was another kind of nightmare. I called Dr. Pernice, who lives on Staten Island, as I crossed the Verrazano Bridge. I told him what was going on in Midland Beach, and he said to pick him up on my way.

Getting to his side of Staten Island was almost impossible, but once I'd picked him up, getting through Midland Beach was like driving through a war zone. Aside from police roadblocks all over the place, there was so much debris in the streets, it was nearly impossible to make a pass. Furniture, clothes, boats, cars, porches that had become separated from their houses, everything you can imagine was blocking our way, including downed power lines. It was an obstacle course. I couldn't drive any faster than five miles per hour. The storm surge had destroyed so many homes, people had to pull whatever they could salvage out into the streets. It was horrible to witness so many people trying to pick through and save what they could from their shattered lives.

It was surreal, but one of the other things I noticed going on all over the place was barbecues, but not the celebratory kind. People had to eat but couldn't use their homes. There were still live fires raging from gas lines that had ignited where houses used to stand. People had moved their barbecues out to safer areas to cook whatever food they had left.

Driving along one street, on the left was total devastation, and on the right were Red Cross tents serving as temporary shelters. It was like being in a bombed-out city. There was so much going on, it was nearly impossible to make any headway. At one point, it took me three hours to drive three-quarters of a mile to get to the site where I was to meet up with a rescue group.

When I got to the house where the cats had been hoarded, there was an amazing guy named Vinnie Olito. Vinnie is a CPDT-KA, a certified professional dog trainer. He had three girl volunteers who'd been slugging it out with the toxic-swamp-like conditions. The entire area surrounding the house was a mess. Vinnie and his volunteers had been rescuing animals since the storm first hit, and there they were trying to access the house where the cats were rumored to have been hoarded. As it turned out, it wasn't just a rumor.

Vinnie and I, Dr. Pernice and his son, and the three girls all made our way into the house, which was a bigger disaster area than what we'd dealt with outside. The stench alone was overwhelming. God only knows what kinds of diseases were at work inside those walls. Mold had already started to climb up the walls above the waterline, and the water was still deep, in some places up to our knees. I immediately felt overwhelmed. I'd already seen how most people were searching for dogs and ignoring cats, but here I was confronted with a horror house filled with cats, dead and alive.

Supposedly, the house was owned by an elderly woman who'd once been a seamstress for Broadway theaters. She'd become a hoarder over time, and the people in the neighborhood claimed she had more cats than could be counted.

They weren't kidding.

All of us assumed that most of the cats were already dead. At first look, it appeared to be a floating graveyard. Cats had been drowned, and we could see some of them were still in the water. Some I could feel under my feet; those that had died and sunk to the floor. Many of the drowned cats had been caught in the yarn the former seamstress must have kept in her living room; they had become entangled and couldn't free themselves. Many had drowned that way, their legs outstretched and enmeshed in the material.

Still, we could clearly hear that there were live cats as well, but none of them were easy to reach. The kids did a fantastic job of cornering most of the cats so we could scruff them and bring them out of the house. Time was of the essence, so we worked as quickly as possible to extract the cats that were still alive.

Most of the cats were in very bad shape. They were covered in feces, mud, and whatever else was floating in the water inside the house. They were also completely infested with fleas, every single one of them. Dr. Pernice explained that we had to get them back for treatment as fast as possible. They were probably sick from whatever they'd ingested over the last three days. The living conditions before the storm must have been horrible, along with the terrible flea problem, because the cats we were rescuing were all undernourished and dehydrated. Some were missing eyes.

The last cat rescued from the house was the most difficult to catch. Vinnie took on the monumental task and somehow managed to catch him. All of us cheered Vinnie's efforts. At the end of the day, seventeen cats were rescued from the house, why I came to call them the Staten Island 17.

We all knew before we brought the cats for treatment that there would be very few, if any, takers as far as adoption went for these cats. The translation being: I'd have to provide for however many managed to survive.

Fine, that's what I was there for, but it still bothered me that it took volunteers to provide the extra-special efforts required to rescue the cats. Why weren't other rescue groups involved? Vinnie Olito had called a number of them. As rewarding as rescuing animals can be, it can also at times be very frustrating. The case of the Staten Island 17, at least for me, is a constant source of frustration whenever I think about it.

The next stage of our cat rescue was nearly impossible. We had gathered the cats in three massive cages that wouldn't fit inside my truck. We tried six ways to Sunday to figure something out. In the end, for the sake of expediency, I tied the cages to the roof of my truck in order to get the cats to a veterinarian as quick as possible. The trip back to Brooklyn was too dangerous, especially having to go over the Verrazano Narrows Bridge. The strong winds passing through the bridge might further harm the cats, not to mention the time it might take to get off Staten Island. I doubted the cats could afford the three-hour drive it might take to get back to the highways, some of which were still being monitored and road-blocked by the police.

Like usual, it was Sal Pernice to the rescue. He called a veterinarian friend, Dr. Michael Alpino, at the Boulevard Veterinary Group, just a few blocks away from Midland Beach on Staten Island. Dr. Alpino was another hero who went out of his way to help treat and house the animals affected by Hurricane Sandy. He told us to bring the cats to his office as soon as we could. Two minutes later, we were on our way.

It had to be quite a sight, all of us unloading the three giant cages of cats from the roof of my truck. We had to form a chain of people to offload them, like a production line. Once we had the cats inside the Boulevard Veterinary Group office, the first order of business was to kill the fleas each cat was completely infested with. Getting the cats to swallow a Capstar pill wasn't an easy task. They'd already been through severe trauma from the storm. Most of them weren't very willing to let us stick a pill into their mouths. Needless to say, we each received a lot of scratches and bites trying to kill fleas.

Once the pills were administered, we still couldn't feed them, because of how overstressed they'd become. We didn't know how long their stomachs had been empty, and we had to take precautions. Feeding a sick cat might make matters worse. Until they were fully examined and tested, we had no idea what kinds of illnesses they were carrying. Drs. Pernice and Alpino did what they could, putting some on IVs with antibiotics, but it would remain touch and go for another few days.

It was midnight before we all called it a night. I returned to Brooklyn knowing that we'd saved seventeen cats so far. As exhausted as I was, I returned home feeling good about our combined efforts.

I told Lena about the day, and how hard it had been from start to finish. Then I told her about the cost of the gas and apologized for taking so much cash.

"Are you kidding me, James?" she said. "Take whatever you need, whatever we have."

It took me about two seconds to fall asleep that night. Between trying to find gas, fighting the storm-made roadblocks, the conditions we'd worked in, the struggle to get the cats out of the house, getting them to Dr. Alpino's place, and then the struggle to get the cats to swallow the Capstar flea pills, I was totally spent. My gigantic head hit the pillow, my eyes closed, and the next thing I knew, the alarm was ringing.

"Good morning," Lena said.

I probably cursed.

An hour or so later, I returned to the Boulevard Veterinary Office to check on the cats. Luckily, all seventeen were still alive, but the next stage of rescue would require we clean all the gunk, feces, and dead fleas off each cat. It required us to dip each cat in a bucket of warm-water solution before hosing it off. Each cat deposited so much blood from the dead fleas and ticks, the water turned red. It was truly disgusting to see how infested each cat had been.

We used blow-dryers to dry them, then Drs. Pernice and Alpino gave the cats more antibiotics.

We prepared food for each cat and although they were hungry, some of the cats still wouldn't eat. Those we assumed were still too sick to even try. Once the antibiotics kicked in after a few days, we were able to nourish most of them. We almost lost one that wouldn't eat, but she pulled through after a few more days. Her name is Mama.

Ultimately, the cats would require a full week of treatment before they could be released. There was no way we could adopt them out before a week passed, because the old lady was still their rightful owner. Chances were nobody would take them anyway, especially after they learned what the cats had been through.

The only thing going for us to eventually adopt them out was the fact that the woman's house where they were rescued was still flooded a full week later. We still had to have some kind of clearance from her, or she had to ignore them long enough for us to consider them abandoned.

So while the cats recovered at Boulevard Veterinary Group, I continued heading back to Staten Island doing rescues, by then paying $30 a gallon for the gas to get me back and forth, and losing a lot of sleep. Dr. Pernice was also doing more than his fair share, and all of it voluntary work. One day, on our way to try and save a pig we heard was stuck in that toxic mud, we spotted a giant sea turtle off to the side of the road. Its shell had been cracked and we could smell gasoline in the midst of the mud. There was also the runoff from the flooded sewers of Midland Beach. Someone said the turtle had been hit by a truck. It was pathetic to see something so helpless slowly dying. Sal and I managed to get the turtle into my truck, and we immediately drove it back to Brooklyn to try and save it. Sal did what he could, including mending the giant shell, but a few days later, the turtle died.

It was one of so many heartbreaking Hurricane Sandy stories, but it did not deter us from moving forward.

On day three of my rescues, I received a call from someone in Brighton Beach in Brooklyn. Coney Island and Brighton Beach had also been devastated by Hurricane Sandy. This rescue involved another hoarder, except she had left the cats in a cage in her house when she evacuated. When I found them, the mother and three kittens were still alive. Three other kittens had drowned. I was furious. How could anyone leave their pets behind? How could they not think about animals they'd been keeping? The truth of the matter was that way too many people did exactly that when the storm surge flooded their homes.

One afternoon, while I was about to leave Doctor Alpino's office at Boulevard Veterinary Group, a woman approached the front door pulling a dachshund by its leash. The dog was clearly up in age, and I noticed right away that his teeth were all black. I asked her what was wrong and she said she was bringing him in to be put down.

"Why?" I asked. "He still looks healthy enough."

"No, you don't understand," she said. "Louie always stayed in the basement. He never came upstairs, but our basement is flooded and we can't leave him there anymore. He's old now anyway."

I couldn't believe what this whacko was saying, but I knew better than to get into an argument with her. I tried diplomacy instead.

"What if I take him? I live in Dyker Heights in Brooklyn and we weren't affected by the flood."

"No, I wouldn't want Louie to be a bother to someone else," she said. "He's old now. He's been with us for thirteen years. He's had a good life."

I wanted to explode, but I knew I had to haggle with her a little more. I promised I'd make a donation in Louie's name if she let me take him.

"I don't mind," I told her. "Even if he only has a few weeks or months or a year left. Let me take him and I promise I'll take good care of him."

She finally agreed and I immediately brought him back into the office for Dr. Alpino to examine. He managed to clean the dog's teeth and get him healthy again. Two days later, I adopted him out to a wonderful family that took great care of him. It was a great feeling, because I knew this family would do the right thing. The family, including their two kids, fell in love with the dachshund, but unfortunately, Louie died just three months later. Because of the way he was treated by his new owners, we called him King Louie, because his last three months weren't spend in some basement. He was truly treated like a king.

I'll never forget when I got the call from the family that had adopted him. I felt so bad for King Louie and for them. Their kids were especially upset. They truly loved that dog, so I did what I do best—found another pet for them. When I brought them their new family member, another rescue dog, I told the kids that King Louie was in heaven and that he would watch down on them and their new friend.

One of my last calls from Staten Island came from Vinnie Olito again. A somewhat confused pit bull was running wild in the streets when the police shot him with a sedative dart. The problem was that the dart was lodged in the pit bull's throat and Vinnie feared he might choke to death. Dr. Alpino was overwhelmed with other rescues at the time and no other vets were willing to treat the dog, so Vinnie called me and I called—who else?—Sal Pernice. We took the pit bull to Brooklyn where Sal performed surgery and removed the dart from the pit bull's throat. A good friend, Christine Scarolla, fostered the dog until it was adopted out six months later. It was a happy ending amid so many horror stories about pets that had died during and after the hurricane, and so many more that went unaccounted for.

On the eighth day after we rescued the Staten Island 17 from the hoarder's house in Midland Beach, the owner hadn't reclaimed them. I took fifteen of the cats with me back to Brooklyn. Two had to stay behind because they were still too sick to leave the veterinarian's care. One of them, a tortoise-colored cat, Dr. Alpino kept as the office house cat. He remains there to this day. I picked the other one up as soon as Dr. Alpino gave it a clean bill of health.

Once I was in possession of sixteen rescued cats, I had nowhere to bring them except our home. Lena's adult son had been living in our basement, but once she knew the cats had no place to go, she asked her son if he wouldn't mind moving in with Lena's mother, his grandmother. He appreciated what we were trying to do and the cats took over our basement.

We did manage to adopt one cat out, one we'd named Edward, but that wasn't for another few months.

Things went okay for a short while, but then the cats developed a mysterious illness that was affecting their eyes. They often bled from their eyes and nose. Maybe it was from the environment they'd had to survive, the years of neglect, or what they'd been exposed to after the storm, but we never figured it out. Dr. Pernice examined the cats several times but there was no way to diagnose what it was that was making the cats sick. We even brought them to the Veterinary Emergency and Referral Group in Cobble Hill, Brooklyn, which is open 24/7 and offers specialist care. Even the medical director at VERG, Dr. Brett Levitzke, was unable to discern what was ailing the cats, and he's one of the best veterinarians in the world.

Lena wound up spending six to seven hours a day nursing the cats, because many were blind and required special care. They'd become her new kids, and she wasn't about to give up on them. She even went so far as to consult holistic vets and ordered holistic medicine. It soon became a monstrous undertaking, but that was Lena's specialty, caring for the hopeless. I'm probably the best example of that.

As Lena became a woman possessed with making the cats healthy again, the frustration of their illness was taking its toll. She was worrying so much she wasn't sleeping much. Every morning, first thing, she was down in the basement feeding and nursing the cats. When they started doing worse, Lena become depressed. I had sick cats and a depressed Lena on my hands. I told Sal what I was facing and like always, he came through, except there wasn't much to be done.

One of the problems facing private rescues is the lack of donation funds and supplies. Because I wasn't a registered rescue agency, the cost and time and effort involved with caring for these rescues would have to be mine and Lena's alone. As I said, Dr. Pernice did what he could, but nobody else seemed to care much.

Finally, we caught a break and the holistic medicine seemed to be working. After a week of continued improvement, we let them upstairs to mingle with our other rescues, their new brothers and sisters. When all was said and done, fourteen of the cats survived. Two died on us, and the one we adopted out also died, but the remaining Staten Island cats, fourteen of the original seventeen, still live with us today.

One of the nicer things that we experienced from all our work with the rescues from Hurricane Sandy was the response from an Ohio-based pet supply store, Monstrous Havahart. They donated twenty brand-new cat traps for our continued work after the storm.

This world can use more charity like that provided by Monstrous Havahart.

If Hurricane Sandy didn't cause enough problems for feral and other animals displaced by the storm, Mother Nature slammed us with a couple more backhanded storms, the first just two weeks later. Winter storm Athena, a nor'easter packing near-hurricane-force winds and freezing rain, also dumped almost five inches of snow on Central Park in New York City. The surrounding metropolitan areas, the same areas ravaged by Sandy, were also affected. Power lines collapsed faster than Con Ed could repair them. On Long Island alone, 184,000 customers were without electricity. The Long Island Power Authority upped the number of those without power to 199,000 by the end of the day.

Then, just three months later, on February 8, 2013, yet another nor'easter struck—this one named Nemo.

The storm affected more than 25 million people and God only knows how many animals. Once again, power outages were widespread and extremely difficult to repair. Central Park snow accumulation totaled 11.4 inches. At LaGuardia Airport in Queens, it was 12.1 inches. Because of the high winds throughout the blizzard, snow drifts were as high as seven feet in some areas.

One of the hardest-hit roadways was the Long Island Expressway. Many people found themselves stuck in snowdrifts that left them with no other choice than to abandon their cars. The roads had become impassable, and the LIE was officially shut down to all but emergency vehicles. The snow cleanup and towing of abandoned vehicles went on for two days. Parts of the expressway, between Exits 57 and 73, were closed for nearly three days.

After the storm dropped the first six inches on the New York area, I received a call from a cat lover I'd come to nickname Catwoman out at her cat sanctuary on Long Island. She was frantic about the weather forecast. Her sanctuary featured a large, fenced-in backyard with landscaping that included a tree house, benches, scratching posts, plants, grass pots, and mesh netting that extended out from the tops of the fencing so the cats wouldn't wonder outside of the enclosure. The flooring was concrete and plywood, graded downward so water from rainfall drained out of the enclosure into storm drains. There were also cubbyholes for feral cats that prefer hiding spaces, and a large doghouse serving as a feline shelter. Although there were indoor areas for the cats, most of the sanctuary was subject to exposure. Catwoman was afraid some of the cats would be trapped in some of the tiny shelters inside the sanctuary. The cubbyholes and the doghouse were particular areas of concern. She asked if I could come out to the sanctuary to help make sure none of the cats were trapped by the accumulating snow.

"Of course," I said. "Let me see if I can find some volunteers to help out and I'll get there soon as they reopen the roads."

"Reopen them? I was hoping you could come out tonight."

"Honey, I'd need a fuckin' helicopter to get out there tonight. The roads are all closed. Trust me, as soon as I can get there, I'll be there. In the meantime I'll try and round up some people to help. Soon as they open the LIE again, I'm there."

"Okay, keep me informed," she said. "I'm really panicked about this. The snow is piling up in the corners now. Snowdrifts. The entire sanctuary is covered. I'm afraid I won't be able to save them otherwise. The shelters will be buried in another few inches."

I assured her I'd get there as soon as possible. I made a few calls to find out if there was an alternate route to Long Island, but it was a no-go. Sunrise Highway, the Meadowbrook Parkway, the Grand Central, the Southern State, they were all one big mess from accidents and cars that had already been abandoned. The LIE had been closed between exits I had to traverse to get to the sanctuary. There was nothing to do but gather some troops and stay ready for when we could make the trip.

I made calls to several animal-rescue agencies and put out word through Facebook about Catwoman's sanctuary. I needed volunteers and supplies. Catwoman had about three hundred cats at her facility. Close to one hundred at a time remained outdoors. If the snow kept falling and the wind kept howling, many of them might die. We'd need food and cat sweaters and towels to dry them off and keep them dry. We'd also need shovels. I wasn't sure if Catwoman had enough shovels to go around, so I played it safe and headed to Home Depot, where I bought six shovels and a few ice picks.

The next morning, the weather had worsened. The snow accumulations were close to a foot, with huge seven-foot snowdrifts. At one point the rain had turned to freezing rain, which meant some of the early snowfall would turn to ice. I checked Facebook for messages and not a single rescue group had responded to my post. Nor did anyone else offer to volunteer. I checked the news and was frustrated by the official highway closings. There was no way to get to Catwoman and her cats for at least another twenty-four hours.

I knew I had to stay prepared for a green light to hit the highway, so I packed my truck with supplies and headed to Petco to pick up cat blankets. It was another expensive day, but I knew the cats at the sanctuary would be cold and wet and in need of something that would keep them dry and warm. Four hundred dollars later, I was packing the blankets in the back of the truck.

When I returned home, there were a few Facebook messages, but only two from people willing to volunteer. Two of them said they'd meet me out at the sanctuary and to let them know when I'd get there. Vinnie Olito, one of the heroes from Hurricane Sandy, called and said he'd come with me out to Long Island whenever I was ready.

I thanked Vinnie again and again, then told him that come the morning I was leaving, no matter what.

"Sounds good to me," Vinnie said.

The next morning Vinnie met me bright and early and we were on our way. It was a seventy-one-mile trip, door to door, but it wasn't going to be a routine drive out to Long Island. The roads in Brooklyn were already destroyed with potholes you could lose a tire in, but once we made it to the Long Island Expressway we were confronted with a giant mess. Sections of the expressway had yet to be cleared. Thank God for some of the residents of the local townships on the island, is all I can say. Those that had snowplows on their SUVs and pickup trucks were out hustling to earn a few extra bucks, which Suffolk County was more than willing to pay to get the roads cleared again. In the meantime, I had to plead with municipal officials who were directing traffic off the closed sections of the LIE. Once I told them I was on a mercy mission to save cats buried at a sanctuary, they let me pass, but the next three hours in my truck became a series of getting stuck, getting pushed out, getting stuck again, and getting towed or pushed out, over and over. By the time we made it to our exit, it had been six full hours since we left Brooklyn. The last stretch of road near the sanctuary was iced over and as treacherous as any road I'd ever driven. My truck was hydroplaning ten yards at a clip. It became impossible to steer and eventually I had to grease a guy with a plow on his pickup truck fifty bucks to push me out of a ten-foot snowbank I'd skidded into.

When we finally reached the sanctuary, the outdoor area was barely visible. Catwoman was standing out in the street waiting for us. She had tears in her eyes. Behind her was nothing but snow. All the netting inside the sanctuary was down. The stockade fences were visible only where snowdrifts hadn't covered them. She told me she couldn't account for all the cats; some of them had to be outside, trapped beneath the snow. I remember thinking if those cats were still alive, it would be a fuckin' miracle.

Fortunately, two minutes after we arrived, three of the people I'd contacted through Facebook showed up: Susan Brown, Cecilia McFadden's son Billy, and his friend Loren Rodriquez, and later two local volunteer firemen. Vinnie Olito and Catwoman and I struggled to get inside the sanctuary. The snow went from knee-deep to shoulder-deep where the drifts climbed up the fences. We could see track marks where at least a few of the cats had escaped the sanctuary, but everything except the tree house was buried under the snow.

I decided the only way we could get the snow out of the sanctuary was to take down some of the fence. Otherwise, all we'd be doing was shoveling snow on top of snow. We had to use a neighbor's yard, and to get there we had to go through a bamboo field with six-foot snowdrifts. When we finally made it to the stockade fence, we yanked down a small section. Once we had the fence down, we at least had someplace to shovel the snow—someplace to dump the snow from inside the sanctuary back outside.

We started at point A with a game plan to shovel to point B. Vinnie went ahead of us and used a long stick to try and pierce the snow for signs and sounds of the cats. He struggled through waist-high snow, tripping on some of the cubbyholes, potted plants, and other items on the floor of the sanctuary. The various small shelters Catwoman had built for the cats' cover from rainfall had become obstacles we all tripped on from time to time. Vinnie continued poking the snow, fighting through some drifts that were up to his shoulders. He poked and prodded until we heard something, and then we all worked as fast as possible until a group of cats were freed from the blanket of snow covering their tiny shelters.

We were nervous as we continued to shovel for all we were worth, all six of us, but after an hour we'd cleared maybe six feet of snow and freed a dozen or so cats. I decided it was fruitless to try and shovel the snow without a more specific game plan.

I asked Catwoman where the biggest shelters were located. Where were the cats most likely to congregate?

"There are cubbyholes along the fences," she said, "but there's also a few in the middle of the sanctuary. The doghouse is in the middle. I was more worried about cats that might've strayed outside the shelters."

"Yo, honey, we can't be worrying about one or two cats," I said. "We're on a clock here. We have to get to as many as possible as fast as possible."

Catwoman pointed out where the shelters were inside the sanctuary and we started digging again, this time with a more specific plan. The closer we made it to each shelter, the more cats we rescued. We hit air pockets around the enclosures and found up to fifteen cats at a time. Most of the cats had at least tried to get to the tiny shelters. Still, it was going too slow.

I asked Catwoman for the number of someone with a backhoe. A farmer friend of hers who dug out pools during the summer lived nearby. He wanted $500. I tried to negotiate him down, pleading with him for the sake of the cats, but the guy said it was business and I had to give in. I knew Catwoman was broke, so I forked out the cash.

The farmer moved more snow from outside the stockade fence, so we had a bigger space to dump the snow from inside the sanctuary. It was a long, tiring process, more than fourteen hours, but when all was said and done, there were only a few missing cats, and five that had died. The ones that had passed had been crushed by snow and ice. The freezing rain Mother Nature had dropped overnight had made the conditions inside the sanctuary much worse.

I wasn't happy with how many had died, but the truth of the matter was, if we hadn't made it to the sanctuary when we had, and if not for our volunteers and Vinnie Olito, Catwoman's sanctuary would've become a cat graveyard for as many as one hundred cats.

Needless to say, once we finished, everyone was soaked and cold, and in dire need of warmth again. By the time I made it home, after dropping Vinnie off, I was exhausted. Lena had a bed and blankets ready for me. I know I told her we were victorious and I remembered her smiling. I'm pretty sure she was talking to me when my eyes closed and I fell asleep.

Ten hours later, when I finally woke up again, Lena was sitting right beside me with a fresh pot of espresso.

She said, "So how was it?"

I shook my head. "Fuhgeddaboudit," I said.

"Forget about it good or bad?"

"Tough. Hard. Exhausting. But we saved most of the cats."

"Cats?" she said. "I thought you went to see that movie."

I felt my eyebrows draw together. "What movie?" I said. "The hell are you talking about?"

"*Victorious*," she said. "That's what you told me when you came home last night."

She tried to keep a straight face but couldn't. Once she started to smile, I couldn't help but laugh. We laughed hysterically until we were both crying, but they were happy tears. We really had been victorious. Most of the cats had been saved.

The situation out on Long Island had me discussing something with Lena she'd always wanted, an animal sanctuary of our own. We didn't have near enough money to think that big yet, but maybe we could start smaller and open an animal-rescue shelter. We've always been concerned about how animals are treated in most shelter environments. Neither of us were fans of cages, the red tape too many shelters require of potential adopters, and the time limits some shelters have before an animal is euthanized.

Lena and I knew that our way of running a shelter might be considered radical as compared to some shelters, but we were more than comfortable knowing that however many animals we would rescue, none of them would ever live in a cage. Nor would there be red tape for people looking to adopt. And there's no way in hell we'd set time limits for our animals. If they weren't adopted, they'd live their lives out with us.

With that game plan in mind, expediency became the priority for me. Lena was all for it, as long as we could afford it, but I became obsessed with the idea. I'd been warned more than once, and by more than one person, that former addicts often replace one addiction with another. Well, if my new addiction was saving animals and opening a rescue shelter, so be it. At least it would be doing something constructive.

Less than a month after the snowstorm, I began my search for a space I could use for an animal shelter. I was looking in the Red Hook section of Brooklyn when I ran into a friend from back in the day, Matty Lynch. We exchanged hugs and spent a few minutes talking about the old days. Matty had heard of my rescues through some mutual friends, and he said everyone was happy for me. He offered to buy me a drink, but I told him I'd gone sober since 2006.

"I heard about that, too," Matty said, "but tell you the truth, I didn't believe it."

I shrugged. "It's true," I said. "No need for that shit anymore."

He slapped me on the shoulder. "Good for you, Head," he said. "I mean that."

Matty saw I had Princess and a recently rescued pit bull in my truck. He pointed to the pit bull and said, "Where'd you get that one from?"

"Abandoned," I said. "People get divorced and sometimes neither side wants the responsibility. You interested in adopting?"

"No, but he reminds me of what's going on in the old neighborhood," Matty said. "On Jamaica Avenue. A dogfighting ring."

I knew the neighborhood had changed a lot over the years, but I was still surprised to hear something like that. "You serious?"

"It's what's I heard," he said.

In the summer of 2012, some guy in the Bronx had been caught with more than forty pit bulls he'd been training and using in dogfights in his basement, but the truth of the matter is dogfighting rings aren't as prevalent in New York City as they are in more remote areas, especially down south.

I asked Matty if he knew for certain there was a dogfighting ring or if it was just a rumor.

"Head, it's what I heard, but I've heard it from a few people now. It's fucked up, but the neighborhood isn't the same. Word is it's a Spanish gang running the thing, but that could be one of those cultural things. Some people grow up with that shit, don't think there's anything wrong. It's like a form of gambling to them. You know, like cockfighting or whatever."

"That's another sick fucking thing, cockfighting," I said. "They attach razors to the roosters when they do that sick shit."

"That is sick," Marty said.

I asked him if he knew the address where the dog fights were going on and he said he'd ask around some more and get back to me. Two days later, I assumed it was another rumor spurred on by some movie about a dogfighting ring, or maybe I'd missed something about dogfighting on the national news. For all I knew, it had to do with the publicity Michael Vick brought to the world when he was convicted for his involvement with dogfighting.

After a week, I didn't give the dogfighting story another thought. It was eight or nine days after I saw Matty that my cell phone rang and I recognized his number.

Matty had an approximate location on the border of Woodhaven Boulevard and Richmond Hill, at Seventy-seventh Street and Jamaica Avenue. I asked him if he knew anything more, but all he'd heard was another confirmation that it had to do with some Spanish gang. I thanked him and said I'd check into it and let him know what I found.

I spent the next few days parked half a block from Seventy-seventh Street and Jamaica Avenue looking for pit bulls being walked in the area, but there were none. I knew I couldn't ask anyone because anyone running a dogfighting ring, or anything else illegal, would have their own set of informants. If there was dogfighting going on in the area and word got out that someone was asking about it, the ring would pack up and move elsewhere. I wasn't a gangster anymore, but I could be mistaken for an undercover cop if someone was paranoid enough.

By the third day, I was getting fed up sitting in my truck like a moron. I'd move it around a little, parking on Seventy-seventh Street one day, on Jamaica Avenue another day, but if there were dogfights going on, they were well hidden. After two hours of sitting and watching, I decided to take a walk up to Forest Park to see if I could find something out a few blocks away. Maybe somebody had heard something and they might be able to confirm one way or the other if there was a dogfighting ring in the neighborhood.

Forest Park is where I used to deal drugs and hang out with my old 112 street gang, but I doubted anyone would recognize me so many years down the road. There was a group of kids playing two-hand touch football that I approached with my pit bull. They liked the dog but were clearly nervous.

"He a fighter?" one of them asked.

I chuckled. "What makes you ask that?" I said.

"He's diesel, man," he said. "He looks fierce."

"He could be fierce, but this one isn't," I said. "They only get like that when you train them to be fierce. Go ahead and pet him. He won't bite. He's a good dog."

First one kid petted the dog, then a few of the others. I got a kick out of how fast they got over their fears of a pit bull. The dog's tail was wagging like crazy and he licked every face that got close enough to his tongue.

After a few minutes, I felt comfortable enough with these kids to ask them if they heard about a dogfighting ring anywhere in the neighborhood.

"You're not gonna put this guy in the ring, I hope?" one kid asked.

"No way," I said. "I'm just curious. That's not my thing, but I have a friend who fights dogs. He's looking for a place."

They did a lot of looking at one another before one of them said, "Yeah, but they aren't from here. Some gang from East New York fights dogs in a building on Seventy-seventh and Jamaica. They bring the dogs there to fight."

"No shit?" I said. "Then he's in luck, my friend. Can you show me which building?"

"We'll point it out to you, yeah, but we're not going inside."

"No problem," I said. "I appreciate it."

Once I knew the exact building, I drove home and came up with a game plan that didn't involve the police or Lena or anyone other than my brother Anthony. First of all, the police might bust the place and wind up destroying any dogs they found. Going to Lena would mean a long discussion and lecture, and her trying to talk me out of doing anything.

I called Anthony and asked him to take a ride with me the next day. When I picked him up, he'd just come from the gym. His arms and chest were all pumped up. He looked like he'd just stepped off a bodybuilding contest stage.

"You're looking good," I said.

Anthony winked at me. "I knew you'd come around some day," he said. "I was always better lookin' than you. It's about time you admitted it."

He asked me where Princess was, and I told him I couldn't take her where we were heading.

"Uh-oh," Anthony said. "James has his thinking cap on again."

I had to laugh. My brother knew me inside and out. I told him what was going on as I drove back to Woodhaven. When I was done filling him in, Anthony looked at me and said, "You got a clear fuckin' head, James."

I had to smile. It was Anthony shooting straight again.

"You realize the psychos that do this shit, fight dogs, they're all strapped up, right?"

He meant they'd have weapons.

"Yeah, I know, but we're just gonna go inside and see for ourselves. I'm not looking to barge in while they're fighting. I just want to confirm this isn't some bullshit rumor. The kids pointed me here, but for all I know, they're just going off rumors."

"Fine," Anthony said. "Let's go and get this over with."

Twenty minutes later, we were down in the basement laundry room of the apartment building. There were four washers and four dryers, one with a handwritten sign that read: Out of Order. The sign looked like it'd been there for years.

There was a long hallway off to the right that led toward the rear of the building. At the end of the hallway was a door that led to another room maybe six times the size of the laundry room. As soon as we were inside, we knew we'd discovered something. The smell made both of us gag. I turned on a light and saw several thick coiled springs hanging from the ceiling on one side of the basement. There were also wood cages, pet carriers, small treadmills used for dogs, harnesses and muzzles, and a case filled with what looked like raw meat, but no dogs.

It looked more like the type of place where dogs were trained to fight than where the fighting actually took place. Then again, it was a big enough space to convert in a short amount of time, especially if the fencing they used for a ring was portable.

"Now what?" Anthony said.

"I don't know, bro. I guess I have to report it now."

No sooner did I speak than a tall Hispanic kid in his early twenties was standing in the doorway with a lead pipe in one hand, a cell phone and leash in the other hand. On the end of the leash was a red-nosed pit bull and it was growling.

"The fuck are you doing in here?" the kid said.

I have to admit I was surprised and a little nervous. Either we'd tripped some kind of makeshift alarm when we opened the door or the light, or we were in the wrong place at the exact wrong time. I wasn't worried about this one dude with his lead pipe, but usually where there's one gang member, there's another dozen somewhere close. The other thing I was worried about was the pit bull. If it was trained to attack, Anthony and I were fucked.

"I said what the fuck you two doing in here?" the kid repeated.

"Easy does it, brother," I said. "We're just looking."

The dog continued growling and the kid wasn't stopping him.

"Looking for what?" he said.

"I heard there were fights here, that's all. Dogfights. We're not looking for trouble."

"You break into this room and you're not looking for trouble?" he said. "You cops?"

"Come on, bro," I said. "I look like a fuckin' cop?"

There was some activity back down the hallway, either someone in the laundry room or more of his gang coming to the basement as reinforcements. Anthony looked at me as if to say, "Now you did it, James."

"Look," I said to the kid. "I'm an animal rescuer, okay? I can't allow dogfighting, especially in this neighborhood. I used to live nearby. It's wrong, brother."

"Who the fuck are you to tell me what I can and can't do?" he said. He'd puffed his chest out, but there was something missing in his body language. Call it a street instinct I have, but I knew there wasn't much determination behind this kid's words. Either that or I was reading him ass backwards.

"I call my boys and you're both dead," he said.

It was then I noticed he had a name tattooed on his neck: Jesus.

"Your name Jesus?" I said.

He pronounced it *Hey-Zoos*.

It was time to step up and take a chance. I said, "Well, Hey-Zoos, let me tell you something. You call your boys and you'll win, no doubt about it. They'll come down here, we'll have at it, you and your boys against me and my brother, your dog there rips one of us up, and you'll win in the end, but you and somebody else will be missing your eyes when all is said and done. I'm no slouch, my friend, and look at my brother. He's no joke, either. He's not going down easy. We're not looking for trouble, but we're no punks. I want to be reasonable with you. There's no need to have a brawl over this, but what you're doing down here is fucking wrong, man. Dogs shouldn't be treated like this. No animal should be treated like this."

"And I know you don't want to kill me and my brother over this bull-shit. You got the name 'Jesus' tattooed on your neck, no matter how you pronounce it, and you're fighting dogs? That's just crazy, bro."

Jesus was still trying to look tougher than he was, but he still had that cell phone, the lead pipe, and his growling pit bull.

I said, "Look, bro, all I'm saying is this bullshit you're doing is so fuckin' wrong. How can you pet a dog one day and send it out to get mauled the same night? How can you train dogs to maul each other? That's sick, bro. It's fuckin' wrong. You tell these guys from East New York it's over at this building. No more."

As soon as I mentioned East New York, I knew I'd made a mistake. So did Anthony, because I could see him close his eyes and mouth the words "Fuck me."

"The fuck you say about East New York, motherfucker?" Jesus said. "I'll cap both your asses." The louder the volume of his voice, the louder the pit bull growled. "You both best get the fuck out of here right now and never come back."

I swore I'd talked him down, but now he was pumped up again. He stepped up to me, within a couple of feet, but he'd tightened and shortened his grip on the dog. I knew to be prepared for that pipe, but if the dog went for me, there'd be nothing I could do. If he swung the pipe, I was going for an inside-out move with my left arm, so he'd at least miss my head.

The shouting must've drawn the attention of two women who were in the laundry room. At least it wasn't someone else from his gang. One woman was older than the other, maybe in her midforties. The younger one could've been her daughter, maybe in her late teens.

"What's going on in here?" the older woman said.

"Jesus?" the younger one said.

Both women held their noses from the stench.

Jesus went silent. He moved to the other side of the basement and put the dog in one of the cages. The dog barked a few times before Jesus gave it a command and it stopped and lay down. The younger woman was shaking her head at what she was seeing in the basement.

The older woman looked at all of us, one at a time, then directed her next question at me. "This about the dogfighting?" she said.

"Yes, ma'am," I said. "We're trying to talk him out of doing it."

"*Dios mio*," she said. "Thank God. I know this boy all his life. He's a good boy until he start with those men with the dogs. They pay him for this bullshit."

I could see that Jesus was uncomfortable catching shit from the woman, and I was sure that I could pull his punk card again as soon as she finished.

"Why you do this, Jesus?" she said to him. "Why? These poor animals. For money? What, you gonna be rich from this shit? You gonna buy a BMW someday? You still living with your parents. You're not paying rent. What the hell you doing this shit for?"

She was doing better than I had, but I also knew it was time to add something extra. The trick was not to sound threatening and talk to him like a man.

"Look, bro," I said, "we're not going anywhere until you promise to stop this shit, okay? My brother and me, we're not letting you fight dogs here anymore. You kill us, the cops come and you go to jail for two hundred years. So let's not talk that shit, you're not gonna shoot us. And if you did shoot us, the guys paying you to use this place, they'll pay somebody else and you'll be jerking off in jail upstate someplace. Attica or Fishkill, or Sing-Sing. You really want that?"

He huffed, partly from frustration and partly because he knew we were right. We had to let him save some face, especially in front of the women, so I decided to back down a little.

"Look, we're gonna go, okay?" I said. "We'll leave now, but we know what's going on here and we'll be back. Maybe with the cops and maybe with some friends of ours. Either way, the dogfighting is gonna stop. One way or the other, you gotta do the right thing here. Tell the guys paying you the site is compromised. Somebody ratted them out. Whatever. They won't take the chance of coming back to fight if they think they might get pinched."

Jesus wasn't speaking, but the two women were. They kept at him; the older one crying as she did so.

"You're a good boy," she said. "I know you are. You can't do this shit anymore. It's not right. Please, Jesus. Don't let them use this place anymore. Throw this shit out and make them find someplace else."

It went on a little while longer. Jesus seemed to be folding where he stood, his body shrinking as he lost his confidence. When I saw he was beat, I pulled out my wallet and offered him $200 for his dog.

"Take it," I said. "I'll buy that dog off you right now. I'll take him with me and find him a new home. I'll adopt him out so he's never involved in this shit again."

"I don't fight him," Jesus said. "Not yet. I'm training him."

"Then let me untrain him," I said. "No dog should be trained to kill. Let me take him and you can have $200. Here, take it."

When I saw him hesitate, I thought it was because maybe he actually liked the dog, but then when I offered him $250, he nodded.

The dog came home with us that day. I named him Jamaica 77 because of where we'd bought him on the avenue. I returned to the building and sat on it a few days a week to see if there was any suspicious activity. Then I saw the younger woman I'd met in the basement. I asked her if the dogfighting had stopped and she said it had. I asked her if Jesus was okay and she assured me he was.

"He told them what you said to tell them and they get scared," she said. "He told them somebody went to the police. They don't come back again."

I thanked her and left her my card from the store. I told her if there was ever any more trouble with dogfighting to please give me a call. When she asked about the dog, I could tell she expected me to say it had been put down. I made her smile instead. I told her how I was trying to reacquaint the dog with a more normal environment. I told her I'd find a good home for it soon, and that it was being well cared for in the meantime.

"Oh, I'm so happy," she said. "Thank you for doing that."

"Wanna know his name?" I said.

Her smile was as bright as they come. "What? Jesus (pronounced *Hey-Zoos*)?"

"Jamaica seventy-seven," I said. "Because of your building, the corner it's on."

The young woman was still smiling as she nodded over and over. "I like that, too," she said. "I like that name."

The lessons both storms taught me were invaluable as I continued my search for a property I could use as our first rescue shelter. Likewise, the situation with the dogfighting ring in Queens reminded me about the dignity every animal deserves. Seeing those coiled wires hanging from the ceiling that were used to strengthen a pit bull's jaws and neck, seeing the raw meat the dogs were fed, and the cages the dogs were housed in—it all reminded me of how dependent on us animals really are.

As I searched for a space for my rescue shelter, I kept the following in mind: it would have to be a structure that was safe from Mother Nature; it would have to be conveniently located in order for it to be practical; it would stress a quality-of-life atmosphere for my rescues rather than quantity, which meant letting my rescues roam freely in a cageless environment. I'd been caged myself in prison and I had no intention of doing the same thing to my rescues.

Chapter 9

Building a Shelter While Rescuing Animals

I didn't realize how much my reputation as an animal rescuer had grown since we moved the store to Seventy-first Street. I was aware of people in the neighborhood using my name, either from grooming customers at the store or from word of mouth on the street, but I had no idea that my personal story had reached across the ocean. I'd received a few calls from Hollywood production companies about filming a documentary over the years, but I never took any of them seriously. I knew people from my old life as a gangster who were constantly being hounded for stories about John Gotti and the Gambino family. The Hollywood companies seemed to be opportunists looking for a high-profile story to sell. Like most of my old friends, I wasn't interested.

In late 2012, I received an overseas call from a guy named John Farrar. He said he was with NERD TV, a London-based production outfit looking to film a documentary in the United States.

"How'd you hear about me in England?" I said.

"From a few different sources," John said. "News articles from the states. Now that we have a New York office as well, we learned from word of mouth on your side of the pond. People come to us with ideas all the time. They know we're looking for new projects. Your situation there in Brooklyn interested us soon as we heard about it. Then we did some research of our own. You were a former gangster, correct?"

"Yeah," I said. "I was with two gangs, actually."

"And you've done prison time."

"Two years."

"And now you're an animal rescuer."

"Yeah, that's me. I'm going to open an animal-rescue shelter soon as I find the right space."

"Seriously?"

"I don't joke about rescuing animals."

"That's great, James. If we go through with this project, we'll need to set up cameras inside the shelter while it's under construction and so on."

"Well, if you're really interested, you'd better move fast because I'll be looking for a shelter soon. Don't take it the wrong way, but I'm not waiting for cameras."

"No, no, I'll get back to you soon as I can."

"Fair enough," I said. "In the meantime, I'm checking real-estate ads and putting out the word. I don't know when I'll find something, but I can tell you this much, brother. It's no cheap trick, opening an animal rescue. It's gonna cost."

Of course I was hoping he'd offer to pony up some cash, but that isn't how those things work. There'd be no money from NERD TV. If they filmed the documentary, it wouldn't mean a dime for us unless it was sold.

The telephone line went blank for a few seconds. I didn't know if we'd been disconnected.

"Hello?" I said.

"Sorry, James, I was just thinking," John said. "From Goodfella to Dogfella. That's a great story, James. A great human-interest story."

"Yeah, but it's about the animals, John. I don't do this to pat myself on the back."

"No, no, of course not. I'm talking about how it'll sell. If it sells. Goodfella to Dogfella, I mean."

I had to laugh. Goodfella to Dogfella. I hadn't thought of my life in that way. First off, I wasn't a made guy, so technically I wasn't a Goodfella, but I had been a gangster, and my life had changed from one of crime and addiction to rescuing animals. I guess "animal fella" wasn't as catchy.

John and I talked for another half hour or so. Since he wasn't promising the world, like the reps at some of the other production companies that had called, I liked what he had to say. He was a straight shooter. When he called again a few days later, we talked about my past, my family, friends, and so on, and how I'd come to be an advocate for animals. John said he was interested in my past but more interested in what my life was like today. "The day-to-day machinations of life as a Dogfella," was how I think he put it.

I told him about the store and some of the aggravations of being a small-business owner. Hiring staff, training them, dealing with the public, and the rest of it. I told him it can get pretty comical at times, but mostly it was just another job.

John said that he'd like for NERD TV to film me while I performed rescues, worked at the store, and my home and after-hours life.

"After hours?" I said.

"I read somewhere you play cards. You still hang out at social clubs and so on. Still have friends from your gangster days."

I was surprised at how much John knew about my life, but I wasn't so sure I wanted people filming me at the house.

"I read where you have fifteen cats and a few dogs at your house. Is that right?"

"More like thirty cats and five dogs," I told him.

"Then we'll want to watch how you operate around all those animals. Your daily routine, what you do."

I shrugged on my end of the line. "Sure," I said. "Okay. Why not? How you gonna do all this filming?"

"We'll use portable and stationary cameras," John said. "In a few days you'll forget they're even there."

"Stationary cameras at the store?" I said. "How? Where do you put them? I still have to run a business."

"It should help business, I'd think," he said. "People see the cameras they'll want to be on television."

"Yeah, and maybe clog up the store. We'll have to see how that works out."

"We'll also use portables, handheld cameras, but the stationary one will be out of your way. We'll mount them on the walls and over the doors, in your car, and wherever else. The mounted ones will be out of your way."

"What happens with the thing once you're done?"

"Filming? We'll try to sell it, but there are no guarantees. Maybe nothing. We'll see, but it's your story that's interesting to us. How you went from gangster to animal rescuer, how you run the store, how you live."

"Okay, but I'd want the focus to be on the animals. Rescues. Not for my reputation. To save animals. I want people to see and understand how dependent animals are on us, all of us. They're no different than kids. You don't beat a child if it pees its pants, if it dirties itself. You don't beat a child and you shouldn't beat a dog, either. You don't put a kid outside and let it freeze when it does something wrong. Most of the time the kid doesn't know it's done something wrong. Same with a dog or cat. That's the message I want people to get from what I do. To treat animals with the same respect they give one another. Dogs and cats give us the unconditional love we all crave. We need to do the same for them."

John got the message, but filming wouldn't start for another seven to eight months. In the meantime, I had animals to rescue. The problem was I was running out of space to house them. I had already overwhelmed Dr. Pernice at the BVG and there wasn't room for another animal in our house. It was time to get serious and find a space so we could open our animal-rescue shelter.

I'd started searching for a space for an animal shelter the week I first learned about the dogfighting ring in Woodhaven, Queens. Immediately after that issue was resolved, I was back at it, calling real-estate agents and searching the real-estate ads in all the local newspapers and weekly bulletins. Months and months passed as I became frustrated by high rents and impossible locations.

There were several reasons for my wanting to open a shelter so soon, including what I'd witnessed at the cat sanctuary on Long Island, and what we'd seen in Midland Beach after Hurricane Sandy, but there was no greater reason to open a shelter than to give Dr. Pernice some relief. Sal Pernice was and remains a saint when it comes to animal care, but I'd been overburdening him with rescues at the BVG for far too long. I knew both the office and Sal Pernice needed a break.

There was no way I would soil my relationship with Sal, and I told him so the day I realized just how much of a pain in the ass I had become.

I'd just brought him another cat I'd rescued when he put his hands up and waved me off.

"I'm sorry, James, but I can't do it this time," he said. "We don't have any empty cages. We're filled to capacity right now."

I understood and nodded. "I understand," I said. "I do, so don't apologize, please."

"I am sorry, but you know how this place is," he said. "If I had the space, of course I'd take the cat, but I don't this time. You have to start thinking about finding another place for the rescues. I know how overcrowded you and Lena are at home, but maybe you can find another rescue shelter. Someplace to take the rescues we don't have the room for."

I'm not sure if Sal was playing me then, because he knew how I felt about most rescue operations. I hated the idea of animals being left in cages. I hated the coldness of those operations and some of their policies. I resented the application forms some rescue operations made a potential adoptee fill out, and that they often rejected people for the lamest of reasons.

If you live in an apartment and/or your job requires you work long hours, some rescues may reject your application. I say, "What the fuck?" Cats are fine on their own and so are most dogs, provided you give them some attention once you're home. And what difference does it make if you live in an apartment or not? Unless an apartment building isn't zoned for animals, or if a private rental doesn't allow pets, who cares? So long as you love your pet and do the right thing by it, what difference would living in an apartment make?

Then there's this little rule that makes me crazy: If you have infants, some rescues will reject your application because a dog or cat might respond poorly to roughhousing. Hey, guess what? Dogs and cats don't jump into cradles just because they were roughhousing with a parent. Seriously, what the fuck?

Another dumb-ass rule some rescue shelters use has to do with home owners and the security and height of any fence you might have. Seriously? You can own a home, but if your fence isn't high enough, no animal adoption? Sorry, but unless you're training dogs to be vicious, that's just nuts.

And then there's the length and scope of some applications. How about one that went on for ninety-nine questions? That in itself is enough to turn potential adopters off. Or how about applications that require you to provide your annual income, employer information, and/or your Social Security number?

Listen to me, that's all bullshit. Of course you want to know as much as possible about potential adopters, but if you look at just that, what about me? If someone looked at my past alone, they'd turn me down. I was a junkie-alcoholic and a convicted felon. According to those types of regulations, I couldn't adopt a pet. How fair would that be to an animal living in a cage?

I learned it myself the hard way that appearances aren't always what they seem. The morons who nearly had the pit bull named Brooklyn destroyed because they couldn't follow simple common-sense advice had a beautiful house with a white picket fence. They turned out to be a horrible choice for pet adoption.

Unfortunately, just like nobody knows how good or bad a parent they'll be until they're actually parents, the same goes for those who adopt animals.

My operation was going to have a different set of rules, ones I could only beg potential adopters to abide by, the most important of which had to do with bringing an animal back to me personally rather than taking it somewhere else if things didn't work out. I am more than willing to take an animal back rather than not know what happens to it once it's out of my care.

I think Sal knew this when he suggested I "maybe" take them to another shelter if he didn't have room for any new rescues. What he was really telling me was that I should think about opening my own shelter.

He admitted that to me a year or so later when he said, "I had to make sure that you were serious about this, that it wasn't some spur-of-the-moment thing you were going through. A lot of people say they want to rescue animals and they may mean well, but they quickly learn how much effort, time, and money is involved, and they quickly change their minds. I can't tell you how many people I know start off with the best intentions and wind up giving up in frustration. It's like kids who tell their parents they want a puppy or kitten. They see one in a window someplace and they fall in love. It's a new toy. Then once the dog or cat is home and they're tired of playing with it, that's it. The parents don't need the extra cost or the work it takes. I just had to make sure you were doing this from the heart."

Dr. Pernice spoke from experience. I understood what he was talking about because I'd already seen it for myself—dogs and cats who were adopted one week and returned the following week. With that in mind, I started to look for a space to shelter animals in earnest.

The first dozen or so places I went to see were cost prohibitive. I knew I'd have a lot of freight to carry beside the rent on any space, so I had to budget myself, something I'd never done in my life.

Lena was concerned about the cost as soon as I told her the rents I was hearing.

"James, we can't afford two thousand a month rent," she told me. "Don't forget there's the food and supplies that will be monthly expenses, aside from electricity and heat. And don't forget the animals we have at home. More than thirty now. We have to keep the rent down to a thousand at most, which means a small space."

"I don't care about the size," I told her. "I want quality over quantity. I'd rather we house twenty cats and dogs than sixty, if the sixty have to stay in cages and live imprisoned. I'm not doing that."

"I understand, but you need to keep it in mind, the size and cost. Ask about square footage and try to bargain down based on that. And don't forget, you'll probably need to renovate every space you see. You were in construction. You know what that'll cost."

She was right, but I was determined to find someplace where I could house my rescues.

The next few spaces I looked at were too far from our store and our home. One space, in Far Rockaway, would've meant an hourlong trip without traffic. It was also in a zone that had suffered from Hurricane Sandy, and there was no way I was going to put my animals through that kind of disaster again.

A space in Red Hook, Brooklyn, looked appealing, but the real-estate agent couldn't get the owners to include heat or electricity in their $1,500 a month rent. I'd already been warned that between heat during the winter and air-conditioning during the summer, the cost of operating would escalate another $600 to $700 a month. We simply didn't have that kind of money.

I went to see a moderately priced space near my old haunts in Richmond Hill, but the Jamaica Avenue building had a bad history of water damage from busted pipes during the winter. Apparently the owner was a cheap fuck who let his tenants fend for themselves when temperatures dipped below freezing. There was no way I was putting up with that.

In Ozone Park I found a first-floor space that was long and narrow, but once again the landlord wouldn't budge on including gas or electricity in a $1,300 monthly rent.

Six weeks went by and I was getting both anxious and desperate. I'd rescued two more cats I couldn't ask Sal to house at the BVG. I had to add them to our ever-growing household. Lena was the one caring for our animals at home while I ran the store and tried to find a space for a shelter. Our lives were becoming more and more hectic. I came home one day and Lena said we had to talk.

Listen to me, when a woman says, "We have to talk," it's usually something bad. I swallowed hard and said, "Okay, fine." I sat the table and said, "Talk."

"Maybe it's not the right time," she said. "Maybe we have to wait a little longer. Right now I'm overwhelmed with what we have, James. I know you're trying your best, but maybe we have to wait for rents to come down some more. Why don't you give it up for a few weeks at least, and see if somebody calls you with something. You already put the word out. I'm sure there'll be something you can look at within our budget if you give it some time. You had a call I took today from somebody near Dr. Pernice. Maybe he'll find something for you. Something close, so you don't make yourself crazy driving back and forth ten times a day."

I didn't want to give in, but I understood what she was really telling me. Yes, she was looking out for me, but Lena isn't the type to whine about her own troubles. She was overwhelmed, and I should've recognized it sooner.

"Okay," I said. "I'll give it a break. I'll put the word out one more time and this time I won't even go look unless the rent plus gas and electricity is within our budget."

She smiled at me, then kissed my forehead. I could see the relief in her smile and feel it in her kiss.

"Who was it called, anyway?" I said later.

"Somebody near Sal Pernice. An agency near his office."

"He leave a number?"

"No, but I'm sure he'll call back."

"Okay," I said. "The pasta ready?"

I eat pasta for dinner seven days a week, but not because I'm cheap and looking to save money. It's what we were brought up on as kids most nights because we could only afford so much meat to go around. Don't forget there were eight of us, six kids and two parents. When mom cooked pork chops, she'd flatten them out with a mallet to make them look bigger than they actually were. We'd get one each with a side dish of spaghetti. Most nights we'd get the spaghetti or rigatoni or penne, or whatever pasta shape was on sale. I guess old habits die hard, because all I ever want is pasta for dinner.

The next morning, not thinking about the real-estate agent or a rescue space or anything other than opening up the store, my cell phone rang while I was downing my third morning espresso.

"Hello?" I answered.

"James Guiliani?"

"Speaking."

"I'm a real-estate broker in Dyker Heights. I spoke to your wife. You still looking for a space?"

"Yeah, whatta'ya got?"

"A nice spot that I think will work for you. Can you meet me this afternoon?"

"Make it tonight. I have a store to run."

"Okay, what time?"

We set a time after work. I didn't pay attention to the address he gave until I was pulling up in front of the place.

"Holy shit!" I said to myself.

It was directly across the street from the BVG office. Truth be told, I thought it was some kind of joke.

I met the agent, and he walked me inside what used to be an illegal gambling parlor. The front windows were still blacked out and there was a tiny vestibule area I'm sure was used for security. Once inside the front door, you'd have to stand to the side to open the interior door.

I walked all the way inside and immediately saw the work that would have to be done. It would be substantial.

"Before we waste any time, what are they asking?" I said

"Fourteen hundred," the agent said.

"Too high," I said. "It include anything?"

"Electric."

"Still too high."

"I can probably bring him down to thirteen-fifty. That better?"

"Come on, bro, that's still out of my reach. Fifty dollars?"

"What can you afford?"

"How long's it been empty? Looks like a while."

"Almost a year."

"More like two years."

He shrugged. "It's what he told me."

"Tell him eleven hundred," I said. "Electric included."

"He'll never go for that."

"Then it'll stay empty. It's all I can afford."

I was bullshitting, but I knew his thirteen-fifty was bullshit, too. If the store was empty for any length of time, and it sure looked like it had been, he'd come down lower than thirteen-fifty.

Before we left, I said, "And don't forget, it'll cost me a fortune to renovate this shithole. I'm talking big money to renovate it."

"What do you plan to do here?"

"An animal-rescue shelter."

"That can't be too expensive. You have concrete floors already. All you need are the cages, right?"

"If I was just another rescue shelter, maybe," I said, "but I'm not. I'm not keeping my animals on cold concrete floors or in cages. There won't be any cages in my place, and it'll have a floor and rugs and everything else they'll eventually find in a home once they're adopted out. I'm not opening another prison here. Animals don't belong in cages."

I asked about the building, if it had any citations, then took a quick look at the plumbing and circuit breakers. Everything seemed okay, so when we shook hands and parted, I was secretly hoping the landlord would come down in his rental price. I didn't really expect him to hit eleven hundred, but every dollar would count.

The place didn't have a yard the way I'd wanted, nor was it very wide, but it had a roof and more than enough space to house another couple of dozen animals without squeezing them into cages or making them live on top of each other. There was genuine potential in the space and there was no denying its perfect location. Twenty yards from the BVG. How much better could it get?

There was no call the following day, but two days later I received a call from the real-estate agent. He claimed the building's owner was willing to go down to $1,300.

"Too high," I said.

"He came down a hundred, James," the agent said. "And he's throwing in electricity."

"Bro, I already told you. That's still two hundred more than I can afford."

"Isn't there some wiggle room here? You know, he comes down a little, you go up a little?"

"I don't know what to tell you, bro," I said. "I like the space, but there's no yard and I'll have to do a ton of renovation. That's gonna cost me major coin, brother. He has to consider that, too. Right now, it's a shithole of a shell. Once I'm in there, it'll be all spruced up, and on my dime."

"Alright," he said, but he sounded dejected. "Let me see what I can do."

"Make him understand," I said. "The renovations I'll be doing are to his benefit."

Another two days passed without word, but I'd already told Lena that I thought we found the perfect space. She still wasn't crazy about the cost, because she knew I'd take it at a higher price than the $1,100 I'd said I'd pay, but she also knew that the location couldn't be better. The BVG also had an outside dog run for exercise, and walking rescues across the street for treatment would be worth its weight in gold alone. Trucking them an hour or more wasn't an option.

On the third day, just about the time I started looking at the real-estate ads in the *Daily News* for another space, the agent called back to give me a final offer.

"Twelve hundred," he said. "That includes electricity, but no heat."

"Fuck me," I said. "Let me get back to you, but see if he'll go eleven-fifty. I'll take it for eleven-fifty."

At that point, I knew I was taking it, but I wanted to see if maybe they'd drop it another fifty bucks. I had nothing to lose.

The call came by the end of the day. "Twelve hundred," the real estate agent said. "He won't budge from there."

I tried one more time. "I'll call you back in the morning," I said, "but I doubt it."

That night I told Lena the price and she still wasn't thrilled. She laid out all our monthly expenses on the table. The mortgage, utilities, food for us, food for the animals, and incidentals, and that was just our house. The store expenses were being handled by our business, but adding what would amount to another $2,800 a month to our existing expenses might sink us.

"Come on, Lena, you know I'll take care of this," I told her.

"Yeah, but I don't want you winding up in jail to pay the rent, James. You have to do this on the up-and-up."

"I will," I said, but she knew I was full of shit. I'd do whatever I had to do to pay the freight on our animal-rescue shelter. Once I opened, there would be no turning back.

"Okay?" I said.

Lena shrugged. "If it's what you want," she said.

I gave her my best smile. "Haven't I been a good boy?" I said.

"Don't start," she said.

"Come on, I will hug you and squeeze you and tell you I love you . . . "

Lena gave in and I called the real-estate agent back the next morning. I was still hoping he'd have another drop in price from the landlord, but we settled at $1,200 a month in rent for the space. The next stage of the process would require construction and renovation. I had connections in the industry, but nobody worked for free. I wanted good people, and I didn't want to get robbed.

It's a lot easier to want something than it is to get it.

Once I signed the lease, I had a month to prepare the space for my animals. The first thing I did was get estimates on a total renovation. I wanted an apartment-like atmosphere for my animals, but that would require some serious construction. The first few estimates sounded like telephone numbers: $50K, $60K, $75K. One guy offered to do everything in two weeks for $91,420.

"What the fuck is the extra $1,420 for?" I asked him.

"It's how the math works out," he said. "Don't forget an essential part of the cost is our profit."

I told him, "Bro, next time bring a gun when you want to rob somebody."

The construction costs were astronomical, and when I told Lena she gave me that "I told you so" look.

Eventually, I managed to bring down some of the construction estimates by using outfits that could do more than just one aspect of the renovation-construction. The guy who did my ceilings also handled the walls and electric lighting. The guy who did my floors found me painters. Everything seemed to be lined up, but once I explained that time was of the essence, it was like giving my contractors a green light to add zeros to their estimates. In the end, we worked out an agreement where the construction was done on time and at as reasonable a cost as I could find. My main concern was that there be no skimping. I wanted new floors, walls, a dropped ceiling, a massive paint job, LED lighting, and twilights for overnight. The rest, the furniture, lamps, a big-screen television, a microwave, and storage cabinets I'd handle on my own. In the end, my cost was close to $35,000, a big chunk of the money we'd saved for our retirement. When I told Lena what we were facing, she wasn't too happy.

Then I reminded her about John Farrar and NERD TV. "Maybe they'll sell the show and we can put that money toward the shelter."

"I don't think we should count on anything, James. Assume the worst."

"Except the filming alone in the store should help," I said. It might've been wishful thinking, but people were already excited about a potential documentary in their own neighborhood.

"So, what, you'll be a movie star?" she said. "You may wind up a poor one."

"Maybe, but the animals will become stars," I said. "Think of the exposure we'll provide with something like this. Instead of the ASPCA commercials showing all the abused cats and dogs, people will get to see other people doing something about it. Maybe we'll get some help."

"Help from who?"

"Donations, I don't know. Once people see how hard it is to run a rescue, maybe they'll contribute. You know, help out?"

"Please, James, how many people help out now?"

"Just a few, I know."

"Just a few is right. Willie and Vinnie and some others, but that's it. Not even the rescue shelters went up to help out with Catwoman after that blizzard."

"Maybe we reach more this way."

"Maybe."

"It can't hurt."

"I hope not."

I knew Lena was concerned about me biting off more than I could chew, but I did have a good feeling about a potential documentary. Anything to do with animal rescue had to be a good thing, especially for the animals. The exposure alone would be worth the time and inconvenience.

A few days later, John Farrar got back to me and said they definitely wanted to film in the house. I wasn't sure how Lena would take to the idea of having cameras filming our every move, but she was fine with it.

The film crew from NERD TV showed up shortly after construction began at the space I'd rented. They set up cameras at the store and our house, but they couldn't gain access to the rescue shelter until the painting began. I was on a tight schedule to get the shelter completed because I was still doing rescues, and until it was completed there was no place to house more animals. The film crew managed to catch a few of them, including a few dogs, some ducks, and a pig.

Yes, some ducks and a pig.

We had three cameramen from NERD TV waiting for rescue calls the day I received a call from Staten Island. This time it had nothing to do with hurricanes or a snowstorm. This time it was the aftereffects of Easter Sunday, when ducks are a big sale item. So when a few kids on Staten Island fell in love with some ducks and brought them home, I guess they never expected the ducks to flourish and grow. Soon the ducks were too much for the family to keep. As it turned out, one of my cousins was part of the family looking to save the ducks. They were a terrific family and they'd been very good to the ducks, so how could I refuse them?

It was a sad rescue because I could really see how upset everyone was at having to give the ducks up. It was a house filled with tears when I came to take them. My cousin and I embraced like we were leaving the country. I brought the ducks back to Brooklyn and immediately stopped at the BVG. Dr. Pernice looked them over and gave them a clean bill of health. One of his technicians, Steve Dispenzza, took the ducks and set them in a large basin of water. They took to the water, well, like ducks.

A few days later, another Easter Sunday duck needed to be rescued. This one was from just a few blocks away at Cafe Isabella. Someone from there had a duck he'd named Howard that he could no longer keep. I took Howard to be examined at the BVG and he was also given a clean bill of health. The question was, would the Staten Island ducks take to Howard the way they'd taken to the water? Steve did the honors, placing Howard in the basin with the other ducks, and after a few minutes of trouble for Howard, the Staten Island ducks accepted Howard as one of their own, which he was anyway, right?

Once again, Dr. Pernice came up with a solution. A few days later, the ducks were picked up by a sanctuary in New Jersey that rescued all kinds of wildlife, including ducks, swans, deer, and every other kind of animal you could imagine. They even kept a donkey on the premises. At least I knew that the ducks would be cared for the right way.

The day I received a call from a girl about her pig, I was truly surprised. I'd never rescued a pig before. I wasn't even sure how to go about it. The girl had called from her home in Mill Basin. She'd received a pig a year or so earlier that was supposed to be what is called a "Dandie Extreme," a miniature potbellied pig that would weigh no more than fifteen to thirty pounds when mature. What she'd received as a gift instead was a potbellied pig that had already reached one hundred pounds.

Her family had allowed her to keep the pig in their basement, but it could no longer climb the stairs to get outside and it was too heavy to carry. It had simply outgrown its environment. The girl was devastated that her pig, Curtis, had to leave.

She was sobbing when I carried the pig up the basement stairs and then out to my truck. I tried to assure her that everything would be okay and that I'd find the right sanctuary for Curtis, but her heart was clearly breaking. It was a tough rescue, because once again I could see how much this girl loved her pet. There is nothing worse than having to separate a loving owner from his or her pet, and in this instance there was clearly mutual love between the girl and her pet.

Once I drove away, it was up to me to find Curtis the pig a new home. But first I had to bring him to the BVG for an examination, which I did as soon as I left Mill Basin. Then I asked for suggestions, and again Dr.

Pernice knew of a sanctuary, this one in Pennsylvania. The proprietors required a fee for their lifetime service, so I forked over the cash and brought Curtis to his new home. He would live the rest of his days there. When I called his owner, the girl was crying happy tears that Curtis had a new home, and for the rest of his days. She even wrote letters to the sanctuary in Curtis's name.

I learned a long time ago that on a 78° day, the temperature inside a car can reach 120° in five minutes. On a 90° day, it can climb to 160° inside of ten minutes. The day of the annual Bay Ridge Fifth Avenue Feast in 2013, the temperature was close to 90°, and there wasn't a breeze to be found. The streets were supercrowded with people, food, and game tents. There was even a belly dancer, a pizza-eating contest, wine tasting, live music, children's rides and games, and more sausage stands than you could count.

The BVG had another office on Fifth Avenue from which they hoped to adopt out a few animals at the feast. Dr. Pernice was there, along with several technicians. I called two of my friends to help with the adoption process. Frankie Tank Tops and Nicky T showed up, and we canvassed the crowd with flyers from the BVG.

We were walking through the crowd distributing the flyers when some kid ran up to me and said, "Hey, you're the dog guy, right?"

I nodded. "Yeah, what's up?"

"There's a dog trapped in a car a couple blocks from here," the kid said. "It looks like its suffocating."

"Where?"

He pointed behind him. "A couple blocks from here. The windows are up and its tongue is hanging out its mouth," the kid said. "You gotta do something."

I asked if he knew who the owner was.

"No," the kid said.

"Could be anybody," Frankie said.

"Come on, show us," I said.

We all followed the kid as fast as we could run to a car that was parked in direct sunlight. Just like the kid had said, the dog was lying on its side with its tongue hanging out of its mouth.

I saw there was no time to waste ringing doorbells to find the owner. We busted out the passenger window to rescue the dog. I reached in to lift the dog off the hot vinyl upholstery, and completely confused, the dog bit me. I couldn't have cared less. I pulled him out of the car and we immediately gave him water. The poor thing couldn't lap it up fast enough. We took him back to the feast to Dr. Pernice for an examination.

Frankie went back to the car with a note providing my phone number. If the jerkoff who left the dog in the car wanted his dog back, he'd have to come to me first.

The following day I received a call from the owner, but he could give a shit about the dog. He wanted me to pay for his window. Unbelievable.

"Yeah, fine," I said. "I'll pay you for the window, but I keep the dog."

"Fine," he said. "The window costs seventy-five bucks to replace."

"Come and get your fuckin' money," I said.

We adopted the pooch out a few weeks later, but all I could think about for months afterward was how close to death from heat exhaustion that dog had come. If the asshole who'd left him in the car had told me the window cost $200, I would've given it to him. I might've followed him home that night and broken his windshield while he slept, but he would've gotten his $200. I have to try and contain my anger in situations like this one, but sometimes it's just too much to ask. Fortunately for everyone involved, the asshole was more interested in taking care of his broken window and I was able to barter his dog into my care.

One Saturday morning, I received a call at the store about a Siberian husky that was hit by a car just a few blocks away. I called one of the groomers and asked him to watch the store until I got back. Once I was in my truck, it took me no longer than thirty seconds to a minute to arrive at the scene. There was already a police car there. Two policemen had surrounded the dog with cones. There had to be at least sixty people watching from both sides of the street, some had obviously come from a nearby Burger King. Between the police and the cones they'd arranged, it looked as if a person had been hit by a car.

I heard someone say, "Hey, that's the dog guy."

The police asked me if I was there for the dog.

"Yes," I said.

"Okay, once you get him in your truck, follow us."

I proceeded to scoop the dog up off the street and set him down in the back of my truck. He was whimpering and in obvious pain, but he was still breathing. The police provided an escort from the scene to the BVG office. It was the first time I ever chased the police, but I couldn't have been more thankful for what they were doing. Once we were at the office, I brought the dog straight to the examination rooms and Dr. Pernice. I was still catching my breath as I told Sal what I'd learned at the scene.

Sal was doing the examination, but I could tell something was wrong.

"What?" I said.

Sal didn't say anything, but I could tell from his body language that I'd been too late. The dog was dead.

"It's not your fault," he said.

"There were ten or fifteen people standing around watching," I said. "Why didn't one of them take him? They let the dog lay there for who knows how long before somebody called me."

"It's not your fault, James," Sal said. "Sometimes there's nothing you can do."

I was heartbroken. That dog shouldn't have died. It was all I could think about for the next few days, how that poor animal had remained severely wounded in the street while a bunch of people could do nothing but stare. Had somebody called ten or fifteen minutes sooner, maybe the dog would have survived. Maybe Dr. Pernice could've performed his magic. Instead, they stood around and watched while a dog's life ebbed away.

You would think I could adapt to this kind of loss, but the truth is, I can't. I can never get over the loss of an animal, especially when it could have been saved. Needless to say, I wasn't a pleasant person to be around the next few days.

And then some asshole gave me an excuse to vent my frustrations and save another dog.

Less than a week after the husky died, I stopped at a diner to order breakfast to go. I put the order in and then stepped back outside. There was a kid, maybe eight or nine years old, watching me from the bottom step of the stoop he was sitting on. I figured he was fascinated with my tattoos, because I was wearing a wife-beater T-shirt that exposed my ink. Either that or the kid had spotted Princess in the back of my truck and he was more interested in her.

It was a hot, muggy, morning. The smell of spoiled refuse from trash cans was thick in the air. If you walked past the wrong garbage can unprepared for the odor, you just might puke.

I made eye contact with the kid, smiled, and said, "Good morning, little man."

The kid's face lit up, as if he was waiting for an act of kindness. He reminded me of some of the dogs I'd rescued and how fast their tails would wag at the smallest sign of positive attention.

"Hi," the kid said. He stood up and walked over to me.

I held my smile for the kid. I liked his stones. He wasn't afraid. He came over to me and asked if I was a dogcatcher.

"Kind of," I told him, "but the good kind. I rescue them."

His face brightened. "Really?"

I was still smiling. "Yeah," I said. "It's what I do. You like dogs?"

He nodded. He was about to say something else when the screen door at the top of the stoop where he'd been sitting banged opened. A tough-looking guy, or maybe a guy trying to look tough, stepped outside. He had a toothpick dangling from his mouth. There was some tone to his exposed arms, probably why he was wearing a tank top, but then I saw he was wearing shorts and shoes. I almost laughed at the shoes when I noticed the kid had lost his smile.

"Hey," the guy said to the kid. "You better get upstairs and clean that fuckin' mess your dog made before I strangle it."

I'm not sure if it was the guy himself or the anger I was still carrying from the husky that had needlessly died less than a week ago, but my internal switch was thrown. I felt an adrenaline rush fueled by anger sweep through my body as I pushed myself off the truck and started for the guy. I moved too quickly and bumped into the kid by accident. I had to catch him from falling.

"Sorry, little man," I said.

"It's okay," the kid said.

"Jesus Christ, be careful," the guy said to the kid.

Saying Jesus Christ was a no-no growing up in our house as kids. Momma Guiliani didn't allow us to use the Lord's name in vain, but that wasn't the reason I could feel myself about to explode.

"My bad," I said in the guy's direction. I refused to acknowledge him.

I reached into my pocket, pulled a twenty from the roll of cash I was carrying, and handed the bill to the kid.

"Do me a favor, pal," I said. "Go inside the diner there, ask if Jimmy Head's order is ready, and pay for it with this. Leave an extra two dollars as a tip and you keep the rest of the change, okay?"

Some of the kid's spark returned to his face. "Sure," he said. "Thanks."

I patted his head and watched him walk inside the diner. A moment later, I was in the tough guy's face.

"You're gonna strangle a dog?" I said.

"Hey, back off, buddy," he said. "It's none of your business."

I glanced to my right to make sure the kid hadn't stepped back outside, then I reached around the tough guy, opened the door he'd come out from, and pushed him inside the vestibule. I kept my hands at my sides, which wasn't easy, and then stepped up close so my nose was an inch from his. I said, "You touch that fuckin' dog, or that kid, and I'll open your fuckin' head with a baseball bat. Understand?"

The tough guy was no longer tough. He listened, something he definitely wasn't used to doing.

"I mean it," I said. "I come here a lot, bro. I'll ask around. I'll know if you did anything to that dog or the kid. You do and I'll find you. Understand?"

"Hey, go easy, man," the tough guy said. "We're cool. I was talkin' shit is all. Tryin' to get him to clean up. Nothin' more than that. He's not even my kid. He's my girl's kid."

I could tell he was a coward, a typical bully, the kind who'd pick on kids and small animals, but like most bullies, he was the kind who'd shit his pants when he was called out. I told him to remember what I said and left him in the vestibule. He didn't come back outside, at least not while I was there, but I did what I said I'd do and I asked about the kid in the diner after he brought me out my breakfast.

Nobody knew the family, but the cashier said she'd ask around. I thanked her for lookin' out and was on my way.

Ten years ago, I would've gone to work on a piece of shit like that just for looking at me the wrong fuckin' way, never mind hearing him threaten to strangle a dog.

I was still angry at people in general, because nobody had tried to help the husky I'd tried to save, but I realized that there were people like the cashier and the kid who helped restore some of my faith in humanity. There were still good people around. People like Doctor Pernice, Willie Garrison, Vinnie Olito, Aksell Ottanta, and the love of my life, Lena.

It was time to get over the loss of the dog and refocus my energy. There would always be another animal to rescue.

A day or so later I received a call from a senior apartment center called St. Brendan's Houses in Brooklyn. A woman named Teddy had a dog named Buddy that she could no longer keep. She'd developed some kind of respiratory problem the doctor told her was from the dog. She'd had Buddy for several years and loved him like crazy. I could tell by the way she spoke, her voice cracking on the line, that she was very upset at having to give the dog up.

How could I not take the dog? When I went to St. Brendan's, I saw that Buddy was a little fella, maybe a Chihuahua-mini Pinscher or some kind of Chihuahua-terrier mix. He was very friendly and loving. I also saw that his mother's heart was breaking. I asked her if the condition was something confirmed and whether she was sure she had to let Buddy go. She said it was what her doctor had told her. She'd been having issues breathing and she had to give Buddy up.

She was still crying when I left St. Brendan's. Honestly, so was I. There's nothing worse than having to take an animal from an owner who has done the right thing by his or her pets. In this case, Teddy had no choice.

I brought Buddy home that night and Lena immediately fell in love with him. It was hard not to fall in love with this dog. He was so outwardly friendly, it was impossible not to let him have his way with our hearts. There was a little jealousy from Brock, Princess, and another of our rescue dogs with a biting problem we'd named Evil Eva, but by the next morning, at least Princess was getting along with Buddy. I took him to work the next day with me and Princess, and the two got along fine.

A few more days of having Buddy live with us, and the deal was sealed; he would become one more of our permanent family. Lena even told me she hoped I didn't find another home for Buddy because he belonged with us now.

Just when we were completely attached to him, Buddy's mom called the store to give us the good news: her doctor had diagnosed her respiratory condition as something treatable with medicine.

"If it's not too much trouble, James, can I please have Buddy back?"

I could tell Teddy was nervous when she called, probably fearful that I'd already adopted Buddy out.

"Are you sure?" I asked, not because I was afraid of her giving him up again someday, but because I dreaded the idea of giving Buddy up myself.

"Positive," Teddy said. "I'm just hoping you can do this for me. I know it's a lot to ask."

How could I say no? Here was a woman who clearly loved and treasured Buddy, and for all intents and purposes, she was his mother. It was an offer I couldn't refuse.

I told her I'd have him groomed, on me, and that I'd return him to her the following day. Lena was a bit upset at the news of losing Buddy, but she was totally understanding of the love Teddy had for her dog. Lena and I both cried a little our last night with Buddy, but we also knew that he'd be back with his owner, where he truly belonged.

The next day, after grooming Buddy and putting on one of the dog outfits we sold at the store, I brought Buddy back home to Teddy. The reception Buddy received was something I'd never witnessed before or since. Nearly the entire senior population at the apartment complex was waiting for Buddy in a large common room. They even had a "Welcome Home, Buddy" cake waiting for him. It was the most amazing thing to watch how that dog's tail wagged two hundred miles an hour, it seemed, when he heard Teddy's voice again. It was a bittersweet celebration for me, but I was honored to be a part of it, and I knew we'd done the right thing by returning Buddy to his rightful owner.

As I've mentioned before, one of the saddest situations involving rescues occurs when a couple is going through a divorce. When neither side cares to take responsibility for their pet, the animals are either given away or brought to a shelter. When I learned about a 160-pound Cane Corso that was about to fall through the cracks of another divorce, I couldn't take the chance that it might wind up on some rescue shelter's deathwatch timetable.

There are many names the Cane Corso goes by, including Sicilian mastiff, but it is actually an Italian molosser, which is closely related to the

Neapolitan mastiff. The Cane Corso is actually an older breed than its cousin, the Neapolitan mastiff.

When I arrived at the apartment where the woman lived with her two kids, I was confronted with a monster of a dog they'd named Primo. *Madonna mia*, was this dog big. And wild! Although they'd had the dog for several years already, they hadn't trained it at all. Primo was rambunctious and anxious to play as soon as someone new was on the premises. The problem, of course, was how to slow him down. I mean, it's not like he was some ten-pound shih tzu. When Primo thinks it's time to play and he stands on his hind legs and pins his front paws on your shoulders, he can knock you across a room.

I began by asking the woman if there was any way she could keep Primo. I was more concerned with the dog having to change environments than his rambunctious behavior. I knew I could train Primo the same as any dog. It would take patience, but when it comes to training dogs, there's just no other way.

The mother told me she couldn't keep him. We agreed on a date a few days later to meet at the BVG office, because she wanted her kids to have a few more days with Primo.

Dr. Pernice examined Primo and gave him a clean bill of health. There were some issues with his ears, but nothing medicine wouldn't cure. Still, Sal was concerned about the dog's behavior.

"An untrained Cane Corso could become a problem," he said. "And he's a few pounds overweight."

"A few pounds?" I said. "He looks like he can use a few days at the spa."

So now that we had this huge dog that needed housing, Sal came through again. He would keep Primo at the office overnight, but he wanted the dog to be trained before trying to adopt him out. Primo was a massive package of energy. It wouldn't be easy, but my new job was to calm his big ass down.

The only way for me to train Primo was to be with him. So I worked a rotating shift with the BVG. Princess had to make room for our newest partner, all 160 pounds of him, during the day, and I delivered the big boy back to the BVG at night.

One day, while I was supervising some of the construction work at our shelter across the street from the BVG office, Steve Dispenzza took Primo outside to the dog run to poop. When Steve tried to put a leash on Primo, the dog became very aggressive. I heard the barking and rushed across the street. Fortunately, Primo didn't attack, but he had snapped at Steve.

From that point on, Dr. Pernice left strict instructions, including a poster on the wall inside the office that no one was to handle Primo except me. I had established a relationship with Primo. Cane Corsos are known to protect their area, so we could only guess that when Steve tried to put a leash on Primo, the dog felt threatened and lashed out.

It took a lot of patience to get Primo under control, but after a while he became the gentle monster he is today. He learned to wait for my commands before going off on his own. He learned to heel and lie down when told to do so. He learned to give me his paw, kiss, and stand up on his hind legs, which is nothing to sneeze at. We're talking about a small bear when Primo gets up on his hind legs.

Training him was one thing, but adopting him out was another issue altogether. First off, his size intimidated most people. Even after they met Primo and saw that he wasn't aggressive, they were overwhelmed by his massive head and body. If they managed to get beyond his size, the idea of caring for such a big dog also stopped them from adoption. Primo's food and veterinary bills could be costly. Lastly, potential adopters might not have enough room for such a big dog. Although Primo didn't need a full backyard to roam and was just as comfortable lying in the back of my truck as he would've been in a park, most potential adopters assumed they needed a huge yard or a nearby park.

There were a few offers to adopt him, but I was never comfortable with any of them. One guy I knew managed an auto junkyard. He wanted Primo for a guard dog. We'd recently saved a pug from a junkyard after it was tied to a car bumper overnight and left in a dirty, greasy, gasoline-infested environment. A friend had alerted me to the pug's condition and I went there with Frankie Tank Tops to rescue it.

I wasn't about to let Primo be left out in the cold to guard used auto parts and cars. To this day I hate it when I see a dog locked in a junkyard for the sake of scaring off potential burglars. There was no way that was going to happen to Primo, not in this life.

Over time, it was obvious to me that Primo wasn't going to be adopted.

Of course I'd also fallen in love with him, and when I brought him to the store, he was the instant star of The Diamond Collar. I had people coming to the store just to see and pet the big guy. Within just a few weeks, it was obvious that a star had been born, or in Primo's case, reborn.

It's amusing sometimes how people now react when they first see him behind the counter or lying out on the floor of the store.

"He's just a big mush," they'll say.

"What a big baby!"

"Does he ever move?"

And, of course, there's the usual line of questioning that comes shortly afterward.

"What do you feed this thing?"

"How much does he weigh?"

"I hope he has his own bed!"

"How big a shit does he take?"

"Big," I tell them. "Very big."

So, in the end, I made Primo my dog. He's no longer up for adoption. I wouldn't trust anyone else with him.

When Lena was fifteen years old and living in upstate New York, she and her boyfriend heard some yelping and crying coming from a neighbor's front porch. When they investigated the noise, they found a box filled with six puppies. One of the six clearly had a broken leg, the one Lena immediately fell in love with. They assumed the dogs were for adoption and they knocked on the neighbor's front door.

"The dogs out here, are they for adoption?" Lena asked.

"Hell, honey, you can take any one of those except for the one with the broken leg," her neighbor said. "That one is my crazy brother's punching bag and he has to stay behind."

Lena said she couldn't believe what she'd just heard. The guy's brother was purposely using the dog to take out his frustrations.

"Are you sure?" she asked. "Because I'll take him if you don't want him."

"No, I'm sure, kid. You can take any of the others, but not that one. My brother chose that one already."

"Okay," Lena said. "I'll have to ask my mom."

At that the neighbor closed his door and Lena and her boyfriend immediately scooped the one with the broken leg up and ran home with him. Her first-ever rescue was actually a robbery.

I can't tell you how much I love hearing her tell that story, because it confirms everything I know about my woman—she was born to do the right thing.

Lena named that dog Keno, and by the time her family moved to Brooklyn from upstate, the dog was part of their family. Keno lived a happy life with Lena until he reached about nine years old and developed a strange leg problem. Both his back legs became paralyzed and he couldn't walk. This was before MRIs were performed on animals, so when Lena took him to a local veterinarian, Keno's ailment remained a mystery. Determined to learn what the problem was, Lena took him to several more vets over the next few months, but to no avail; Keno's back legs remained paralyzed and nobody could figure out why.

Lena did as much research as she could. Some of the vets she took the dog to had suggested she put him down, but there was no way she'd ever do something like that. Instead, Lena gave him therapy in her basement, using a small child's pool to bathe him and manually move his legs. Still, it was to no avail. Lena tried taking Keno to New Jersey for acupuncture, but the dog's rear legs remained unresponsive.

It wasn't until a year later that Keno became able to move his legs again. It was like a miracle, Lena said, because it was right after Easter and the dog was suddenly walking. She attributed it to the hundreds of silent prayers she offered God to help her dog.

She thought all was fine again until Thanksgiving, when Keno's rear-leg paralysis suddenly returned. It would be nearly another six months before he was once again able to walk—again, right after Easter. It was a pattern that repeated itself yearly for the next nine years and until Keno finally passed. Lena had that dog for eighteen years in total. A dog that some piece of shit had used as his punching bag wound up living a full and love-filled life because my woman, at age fifteen, wasn't about to let it suffer at the hands of a maniac.

Was there really another name to call our first shelter?

Chapter 10

What We're Doing Now

A few days before the ribbon-cutting ceremony, I had the genius idea of spray painting the roll-down gate that covered the big plate-glass front window of Keno's. I was thinking Old World when I did it, so I bought three cans of spray paint: red, white, and green—the Italian flag. Within a single day of the paint job, I had every elderly Italian man who lived on the same block, Seventy-seventh Street off New Utrecht Avenue, asking me if the card games were back on.

"What card games?" I said.

"The ones used to be here," one gentleman smoking a De Nobili cigar told me. "This used to be a social club for us until a few years ago. The feds busted it up."

Holy shit, I thought. *You gotta be kidding me.*

The next day it was the FBI that came knocking on the front door of Keno's. I couldn't believe it. What the hell kind of card game could it have been?

The special agent asked if he could walk through the facility and I let him. There was nothing to hide.

"Why's it look like an apartment in there?" he asked once we were back outside.

I told him about my belief that animals waiting for adoption shouldn't live in cages, and that I wanted them to be familiar with an apartment or home lifestyle before they were adopted.

"Sounds like a good idea," he said. "Good for you."

I was curious as to why they'd come knocking so soon. I'd only been in and out of the shelter to supervise and help with the construction. If they were watching, they had to have noticed the lack of gaming equipment.

I had to ask. "What made you think there was something else going on here?"

"This used to be an after-hours joint," the agent said. "We're making sure it isn't a backup for one already in existence. Usually, one place gets busted, they overnight it someplace else. We wondered if this place was back in business. And frankly, you don't look like a guy rescues animals. We know you have a record, who you were affiliated with, and so on. And you are wearing the uniform."

He meant my Michael Jordan tracksuit. It's what we used to wear back in our wannabe gangster days. It became a stereotype over time, the same way the special agent was wearing a sports jacket and sunglasses.

I smiled and said, "Yeah, but that was a long time ago."

He shrugged.

"Well, you're welcome anytime," I said. "Let me give you my card from our store, The Diamond Collar." I pulled out one of our store business cards. "In case you need to get your dog groomed," I added. "And feel free to make a donation to this place. It's called Keno's."

I don't think he appreciated my last few comments, but at least he was up front with me. Whatever he was doing there, I was grateful when he left.

I guess if the FBI thought Keno's might be a card room, it made perfect sense when two young wannabes took their shot at me. I was bringing a folding table into the place when I was stopped outside the door by two guys wearing the new wannabe uniform: sports jackets, slacks, leather loafers, and sunglasses. One was tall and thin, the other short and fat.

"Hey, man," the short one said. "Got a minute?"

"A minute, yeah," I said. "I'm busy. What's up?"

"This place here," the tall one said, "the card game. You around anybody on it?"

I couldn't believe what I was hearing. Here were two young morons looking to shake down a card game I wasn't running.

"No," I said. "I'm not around anybody and there's no card game."

"We heard there's a game here," the short one said.

"You heard wrong, bro."

"Then what's the Italian flag for?"

"I'm Italian," I said.

The tall one looked at the short one, then they both shrugged.

"Us, too," the tall one said. "Who you with?"

I wanted to kick the both of them in the ass. Who even knew if they were connected? For all I knew, they were a pair of jerkoffs looking for an easy score. If you were connected, the proper protocol was to find out on your own if someone else was connected. You didn't ask unless you were a made guy.

Maybe he didn't understand me the first time. I said it again. "I'm not with anybody, okay? Not with the guys you think."

Then I played it straight and didn't flinch. I waited for them to give themselves away. I saw they were struggling, so I pointed across the street. "I take my rescues there," I said. "To the BVG."

"Huh?" the tall one said.

"Look, I'm busy today. This isn't a card room. There's no action to be found in here. Just dog and cat shit. It's a rescue shelter."

The two morons looked at one another. I saw they were still stumped, but I didn't have any more time to waste on them. I went back to work.

Once the construction was finished at Keno's, I began preparing the space for its residents. This was the fun part. I set up scratching posts for the cats and put up shelves along one wall for the cats to have some private space away from the dogs.

The first rescue cats came from the BVG. Sal housed a wide variety of rescues there. American wirehairs, shorthairs, bobtails, a Persian, and a Siamese. A few days before we officially opened Keno's, I brought them across the street to their new home.

I rescued a few more cats the day before we opened, including one that was blind. I brought them all to the BVG for examinations. I must've been in and out of their office three or four times that same day.

Keno's next cats came from Catwoman's Long Island sanctuary, thirteen kittens. I swear that 2013 must've been the year of the kitten. We were up to twenty cats, including the kittens, some of which also had ailments that required medicines and extra care. Dr. Pernice was working overtime, it seemed. We were a day from the official opening when he said to me,

"You know, James, I thought I'd be rid of you because of Keno's, but you're around more now than ever."

Sal has a very dry sense of humor. He wasn't smiling when he said that, so I was a little nervous until he allowed the corners of his mouth to raise and form a big grin.

He was right, of course. When I wasn't bringing new rescues to him for examination or to check on an animal I knew was sick, I was there to visit him and the staff.

The afternoon before the opening, I brought in our dogs. Rocco was our very first rescue dog at Keno's. I brought him in before the others because he was deaf and blind. He was a Maltese I'd adopted out of our store some seven years earlier. He was also proof that our honor system worked. Rather than put him down, his owner called me to come pick him up when she could no longer care for him. Although Rocco would only survive another few months, that day his tail wagged as if he were a puppy again.

Once Rocco was used to his new environment, I brought in the rest of our dogs. Our two beautiful pit bulls, 66 and Sarge, were next. They settled into the place instantly and neither seemed to notice Rocco or our cats. Spike, a poodle-schnauzer mix, immediately took to one of the scratching posts and seemed to guard it, so I had to move the post up higher. He barked at first but eventually got over it and found something else to obsess over.

The last dog I brought into Keno's later the same night was an easy choice. How could I not take Primo off the BVG's hands? We'd been spending days together for so long, there was no way I could abandon him. I had trained him to be the pussycat he really is, albeit a 160-pound pussycat with a giant head. Primo still spends his entire day with me wherever I go, including when I'm on the road somewhere, but at nights his home is now Keno's instead of the BVG. In fact, Primo is the king of Keno's, where he has his own huge bed, a queen-sized futon, another gift from Dr. Pernice.

Speaking of Primo, his star has shone even brighter since his move into Keno's. He's appeared on a few news shows with me, including *Huffington Post Live*, *Good Day New York*, *Ali Wentworth*, *The Bettor Show*, *CBS on the Couch*, and perhaps his crowning achievement, Primo and former New York governor, Eliot Spitzer, had their side-by-side faces appear on the cover of the *New York Post* on September 7, 2013, with a headline that read: "Which Dog Has Fleas?"

The following day, June 30, 2013, with the sun shining bright, we held the ribbon-cutting ceremony to open Keno's Animal Rescue. Some of our close friends were in attendance—Frankie Paint Tech, Nicky T, Dr. Pernice, and Father Guy. The crew from NERD TV was also there to film the ceremony, so I thought I'd play a gag on Lena. I gave her a pair of gigantic scissors, the kind you need two hands to hold, but they wouldn't cut. She tried to use them once, then again, then one more time before she turned and gave me the look.

We all had a good laugh before I handed her real scissors and she cut through the ribbon.

As soon as she was inside the space, the dam burst and Lena cried. It had always been her dream to have an animal-rescue shelter—and her dream had come true. Watching her, I also cried. Lena was the person who'd made all the difference in my life. Together, we would make a difference for a lot of animals.

Father Guy brought us a statue of Saint Francis, the patron saint of animals. He set the statue down and we all joined hands in prayer, after which he blessed Keno's.

Earlier in the morning, I'd arranged for two trays of delicatessen cold cuts, a *cassata* cake from Cafe Isabella, and champagne bottles that weren't really champagne—they were actually Martinelli's Sparkling Cider in champagne-style bottles—to be delivered after the ribbon-cutting ceremony. There was no way I could leave that much food inside with all the rescue cats and dogs while we had our formal opening outdoors. Primo alone would've finished off everything inside of ten minutes.

At the end of the day, I couldn't have been happier. I was also proud of myself. Not because I was anything special. I know I'm not, but opening Keno's Animal Rescue was something I had accomplished without depending on others. There were several people involved in the process, certainly all those who had steered me in the right direction, but finding the space, arranging for the construction work, and managing the shelter while still performing rescues was something I could feel good about. Opening Keno's not only proved to me that I could change, it proved to me that I had changed. I was no longer a junkie-alcoholic. There would be no more hounding Sal Pernice for space for rescues, no more trying to convince Lena that we had room for just one more rescue in our house. I had finally accomplished something both my parents would have been proud of—their son doing good for others. Keno's was a facility that would house and protect animals until they were adopted, so they could live their lives out with dignity and in comfort.

These days at Keno's, on average I'm housing anywhere from thirty to forty animals at a time. Unfortunately, there aren't as many people adopting as there are animals in need of a shelter. I'm always happy to find a new home for my rescues. Kittens are usually the first to be adopted, but sometimes a cat that's been with me for a while is adopted by someone who prefers adult cats. It's always when the adults are adopted that I feel the emotional tug all parents must feel when their kids leave a nest.

No less of an emotional tug was the day I found Rocco in a coma one morning. It was three months after I'd opened the shelter, and it proved to be my first real emergency at Keno's. I opened the doors and found Rocco on his side with white mucus leaking from his mouth. It turned out that his lungs were filled with fluids. Robert Hale, at the BVG across the street from us, put Rocco to sleep for me. I knew that Rocco was happy with us at Keno's the last few months of his life, and I was grateful I could provide him with some comfort. My greatest consolation about all rescues that pass, especially those that have lived full lives, is the knowledge and belief that they are all puppies and kittens again, and that they are playing with one another in heaven.

The day after our opening, when I was finally alone in the space with my rescues, it hit me. The time for feeling good was over. It was time to work. Thinking about running an animal shelter is one thing, doing it requires a lot more than thought. First off, I had to establish the rules by which the shelter would be run—my rules. Keno's was Lena's dream, but it would be up to me to run things. I made the list of rules for Keno's and hung them on the wall inside the door. Keno's would:

- remain a cageless environment;
- never require excessive or intrusive applications for potential adopters;
- never require a fee for adoptions;

- be run on the honor system, requiring those who adopt to promise to bring their rescue back to Keno's if things didn't work out; and
- we would never set time limits for any of my animals; none would be euthanized to make space.

Running the shelter required a new level of sacrifice. I had anywhere from twenty to forty animals a day to care for, so there was no longer any extra time to enjoy some of my favorite pastimes. Instead of afternoon card games at Cafe Amici in Queens, I was picking up dog shit and emptying litter boxes. Instead of washing my gullet with a glass of ice water, I was washing and bleaching Keno's floors. Instead of hanging out with the guys, I was hanging out with twenty to thirty cats and two to ten dogs. Instead of sucking down espresso and exchanging pleasantries with customers at our Diamond Collar store, I found myself having conversations with Primo, Princess, Rocco, 66, Spike, and whoever else would pay attention.

Another time-consuming and very necessary chore, especially in a cageless environment, are the head counts I perform twice a day. I hated being counted while I was in prison, but they are a necessary evil in the shelter. The first comes in the morning while I feed my rescues. The second comes every evening before I close and lock the doors. I'm not satisfied until I have an accurate count, twice each and every day.

On top of everything else, I quickly developed a "keep it clean" policy. Everything had to be spotless in Keno's or I couldn't rest. One day I saw myself mopping the floor in one of our mirrors and I thought, *Brother, you are one whipped individual.*

Understand that this was something I never did at home unless Lena was sick or out shopping somewhere when one of our house animals had an accident. My rescues managed to do overnight what Lena could never get me to do—they'd domesticated me.

Because of the potential for parasites, fleas, and whatever else could infect my animals, I took to washing the floors three times a day; once after each feeding and once before I left for the night. I also changed the linens inside Keno's every three days, which meant I had to have the dirty ones cleaned. And don't forget the feedings. Opening upwards of thirty cans of cat and dog food a day will leave you with some nasty scars on your fingers. The tips of my fingers look as though they've been put through paper shredders.

The sanitary aspect of running an animal shelter is no joke. It requires direct and constant attention. Because I don't believe in delegating work to someone else, especially work that I deem essential, I was left to handle most of the chores myself. There were several people who volunteered to help at the shelter, but the truth of the matter is that they didn't know what they were in for. I sometimes wonder if they thought that all I needed was for someone to come in and pet the cats and dogs.

One woman who volunteered one morning asked me what I needed done first. I was in the process of collecting and taking out the garbage. I pointed to the kitchen and said, "Start there. They haven't eaten yet."

She started to open cat food cans and was quickly surrounded by twenty-five cats, all of them mewing and looking up at her as if they hadn't eaten in ten years.

I would've stopped her right then and there, but I was on my way out with the garbage, and I figured it was best she learn the hard way. I returned to the shelter as she set the cat food on the floor. I had to chuckle at the look of horror on her face as Primo bulled his way to the cat food and ate every bit of it.

"Oh, no!" she said. "Why's he doing that?"

"Because he doesn't know he's not supposed to," I told her. "And he always eats first."

"Oh, shit," she said.

"It's okay, I should've told you."

"I don't think I can do this," she said.

"Up to you," I said.

"I don't think so."

And that was the end of that volunteer story—less than one hour.

Inevitably, most of the people who volunteered quickly realized how much work was involved. Cleaning cat litter and dog shit isn't exciting work. Nor is feeding or cleaning so many animals, especially at one time. Most of the volunteers who came to Keno's lasted just a day or two. The few who lasted longer I appreciated very much, but eventually the work and long hours proved too daunting for them, too.

The truth is, I don't think I ever would've been comfortable leaving keys with anyone. I accepted early on that my days of vacationing were over. Keno's would require my attention seven days a week, 365 days a year, and I had no choice but to keep the place clean and make sure the animals were fed and healthy.

The flip side to the labor and effort it cost me was the assurance that everything that needed to be done was done right. A clean shelter is a good shelter, and there's no short-cutting the cleaning process. Nobody likes to shovel shit, but let's face it, somebody has to do it.

Another realization about my running Keno's had to do with our home life. Lena had to get used to the change in my schedule. I was tied up most of the day and into the night caring for our rescues. We also had the store to run, and sometimes the timing of specific chores conflicted. We had animals at home that Lena took care of while I headed to Keno's to feed our shelter animals. The shelter still had to be cleaned after meals. I had Primo and a few other dogs to walk before returning to the store to take care of our business there. My breaks from the store involved driving over to Keno's to check on the animals and to clean again. Plus, I was still fielding potential adoption calls while remaining in rescue mode. At the end of our business hours at The Diamond Collar, I returned to Keno's to feed the animals and clean the place one last time before going home for the night. Fourteen- to sixteen-hour workdays became common. The nights Lena and I used to treasure watching movies and eating ice cream were often sacrificed along with my card games.

Once word spread about Keno's, my rescue calls doubled, tripled, and then quadrupled. There were times when I feared answering our phones at The Diamond Collar store, because I couldn't take another animal at Keno's without jeopardizing the health of those we already housed.

Even some of the rescue shelters that had wanted nothing to do with me, James "Head" Guiliani, were calling Keno's and acting like I was some long-lost buddy.

"Hey, James, congratulations on the shelter!" one guy said. This guy, before I opened Keno's, refused to take my calls about rescues I didn't have space for.

"You think you could take a few animals off our hands?" he had the nerve to ask.

Don't get me wrong. It wasn't that I wasn't looking out for the animals he was trying to get rid of, but this was the same guy who wouldn't have pissed on me if he saw me on fire in the curb. Now that I had a shelter, he was looking to pass off some of his animals. I prefer handling my own rescues. Should I have to seek space for a rescue, I go where I know I'm welcome.

"James?" he said.

I was so pissed off, I couldn't even speak.

"You there, buddy?" he said.

Calling me buddy sent me over the edge. "Go fuck yourself," I said, and then hung up on him.

I know it wasn't the professional way to handle it, but that's my personality. I don't believe in playing games.

One of the most upsetting things that happened after we opened Keno's was finding a dog tied to the traffic light in front of our store. The dog wasn't hurt or abused, but it immediately reminded me of Bruno and how someone had left him tied to a parking meter.

I kept an eye on him while I waited to see if anyone would come back to get him, but no such luck. I thought maybe some moron had gone shopping, maybe in the Rite Aid across the street from our store, and maybe they left the dog tied to the traffic light? Yeah, right. The dog had been abandoned, obviously purposely left close to our front door. Of course I had to rescue him. How could I not take him inside our store?

I brought the dog to the BVG for an examination. Fortunately, Dr. Pernice had some space and the dog remained at their office until it was adopted a few weeks later.

Still, the swarm of rescue requests went on. By the end of the first month, I was receiving hundreds of messages on our Keno's and Diamond Collar Facebook pages about animals in need of rescue. Between the phone calls and the messages, I was frequently left feeling guilty for not responding. I only had so much space at Keno's, and the shelter was quickly filled to what I felt was comfortable for the animals. I didn't want to overcrowd Keno's. There's no easier way for diseases to spread than inside an overcrowded shelter.

Even knowing that, however, some of the many rescue requests got to me and I made a few mistakes by allowing my guilt to trump my better judgment.

I learned early on during the rescue process, long before Keno's, that all rescues had to be brought to the BVG for examination, and treatment if needed. It was simply the best and safest policy to follow. Endangering healthy animals in a shelter by bringing in a sick dog or cat, or one infested with fleas, was to be avoided at all costs. Unfortunately, a few times when I was pressed for time, or the rescues occurred after-hours when the BVG was closed, I made the mistake of bypassing that vital first step in securing an animal—the medical examination.

I once brought a cat into the shelter without an examination because I was in a rush to keep an appointment in Queens. The cat had ringworm, and before I knew it, all thirty of the cats in my shelter had it. Fortunately for me, I did bring the new rescue across the street to the BVG the following day and Dr. Pernice immediately diagnosed the problem.

"He was at Keno's last night?" Sal asked.

I nodded.

Sal shrugged. "You know better, James. We have to treat them all now."

Thankfully, none of the cats were severely infected. Shampoos and ointments remedied the problem, but if you think that's a simple task, try doing it to thirty feral cats.

Less than two weeks later, I was leaving a friend's house around midnight, and there was a kitten mewing not two feet from the front tire of my truck. By the time I made it to Keno's, it was after midnight. The BVG was long closed for the night. I could have brought the kitten to one of VERG's two twenty-four-hour emergency veterinary operations run by Dr. Brett Levitzke, but I was tired and anxious to get home for the night. Besides, what were the odds of this happening to me twice in less than one month?

Obviously, picking winners was never one of my strengths. The kitten had a form of conjunctivitis that required immediate treatment, which included giving an eyedrop solution to all thirty cats. How did I learn this? Who else?—Dr. Pernice.

"This is twice now, James," he said with a straight face.

"I know, Sal," I said. "I'm sorry, man."

"It's gonna cost you this time."

"I deserve it."

"It isn't going to be cheap."

"It shouldn't be. I'm a dope for this again."

"Why didn't you take it to VERG?"

I could only shake my head. I'd screwed up a second time and swore there wouldn't be a third screwup, but I'd always been the kind of guy who had to keep burning his hand on the stove before figuring out the stove was hot.

My third and last mistake regarding health issues had to do with yet another cat I'd brought into the shelter without having it examined first. It was another late-night rescue, after which I almost brought the cat home first, which would have resulted in the same problem, but I decided to drop it off at the shelter until morning. It was another feral cat, except this one had fleas. I left him in the bathroom at the shelter, secluded from the other cats, but somehow he managed to get into the main room. When I opened the next day, there he was sitting on the couch. Of course all the cats had to be treated for fleas.

I crossed the street and spoke with Dr. Pernice. He came into Keno's, saw that two cats were infested and said, "You know the routine."

I sure did. The first order of business was getting the cats to swallow a Capstar flea pill, wait twenty-four hours, and then individually apply flea medication called Frontline to each cat to make sure the fleas were dead and gone. Once that was accomplished, I had to bleach the entire space, another few hours of painstaking and tedious work.

In this case, number three was the charm. My health-issue mistakes were behind me. I would never make the mistake of bringing an animal into Keno's without it being examined by a veterinarian again.

A few days later when I saw Dr. Pernice in his office, he finally cracked a smile.

"You think you got it down yet?" he said.

"Oh, yeah," I said. "Never fuckin' again."

I made a different kind of mistake before we ever opened Keno's by choosing a dropped ceiling.

A few months down the road, I brought a new rescue into Keno's named Sonny. He was an orange tabby, maybe two years old. I'd put him through a process of adapting to the shelter after having him examined at the BVG. Because Sonny was a feral cat, his first two days at Keno's were spent in a cage I'd placed in the middle of the floor. I wanted him to feel more comfortable around the dogs and other cats before letting him roam free inside Keno's. It had worked with other feral cats, making them not quite as skittish once they were free, rather than just dropping them into such a new world.

The morning of the problem, I did my head count while the animals ate, but I came up short one cat. I counted again and was still short one cat.

"What the fuck?" I said.

I then proceeded to turn the place upside down looking for Sonny. I moved all of the furniture out to the center of the room, emptied each and every kitchen cabinet, emptied the bathroom, and put my ear to every foot of wall space to see if maybe Sonny had found his way inside our walls somehow.

At one point I panicked and ran out to the street to check the garbage bags I'd put out. Maybe Sonny had crawled inside one of the bags and I hadn't noticed.

No dice. Sonny was missing and I didn't know what the hell had happened.

"Sonny, where the fuck are you?" I yelled.

Sonny didn't respond.

By closing time I was exhausted and completely defeated. The only possible answer was Sonny had somehow found his way outside the inner door into the vestibule and then out onto the streets when the front door was opened. I had to stop at The Diamond Collar and close the store, so I was extra-exhausted and feeling like shit when I finally made it home. It was close to eleven o'clock and Lena was waiting for me.

"James, sometimes these things happen," she said. "Try not to make yourself crazy."

I couldn't help but feel guilty. I was the one who'd opened that morning. I had maybe two or three visitors to the shelter, but all had come after I did the first head count, when I first noticed I was one cat short.

I couldn't sleep and after two hours of driving myself crazy in bed, I gave up and headed back to Keno's. I was very careful to be quiet when I slipped inside the vestibule door. Primo greeted me at the door by kissing my hand until I gave him a few belly scratches, but then I sat down on the couch and let everyone settle down. Less than a minute passed before I could hear mewing coming from somewhere over my head. It was then I looked up at the ceiling and said, "Son of a bitch."

I took out the aluminum stepladder I kept in the bathroom, listened for Sonny's mewing again, and then set the ladder under a group of tiles near the front door. I climbed up onto the stepladder and pushed one of the tiles up. Soon as I did that, I could hear Sonny scurry to another area of the ceiling.

"Fuck me," I said.

I got off the ladder, moved it, and tried the same thing again, with the same results. Sonny was too skittish in the dark environment to stay put.

This happened another few times before I tried removing a few tiles near the fluorescent fixture in the center of the room. This time when I looked up into the ceiling, I could see Sonny was just out of reach. Two wires were in the way.

I went back down the ladder, grabbed a wire cutter and headed back up. I cut one wire, but I still couldn't reach. I cut the second wire and the entire ceiling came down. Afraid the fluorescent lights might land on one of the animals, I made a quick move to grab one end of the fixture. The move collapsed the aluminum ladder and down we went, me and the fixture.

I could barely breathe from the bruised ribs I gave myself, but when I looked up from the mess I'd just made, there was Sonny on the top of the couch looking at me as if to say: "What did I do?"

How none of the animals were hurt was a miracle, but the place was a complete mess. I spent the next five hours putting the damn ceiling back up, which wasn't easy with badly bruised ribs. This time, however, I used a tube of superglue I kept in the junk drawer to seal all of the tiles that abutted the walls. If Sonny had plans of getting back into the ceiling again, he'd have to use a fuckin' rocket launcher.

To help support Keno's, I decided to run a couple of fund-raisers where we could promote the adoption of our rescues. I did most of the promoting out of our store, The Diamond Collar, whenever people brought their dogs in for grooming, but I also used social media and good old neighborhood word of mouth.

We held the first event at Milestone Park in Brooklyn. Aside from providing food and entertainment, we staged a "best-dressed dog" contest, with cash prizes given to the top three dogs. The costumes some people created for their dogs were truly incredible, but even more incredible were the dogs' owners, because not a single one of them took the money they won. They each donated the money right back to Keno's Animal Rescue, making the day worth all the effort.

Our costs almost exceeded the donations, but it was a great time for all involved. At end of day, Keno's was up close to $300. At first I felt disappointed; I had hoped for more going into the event. One of the things that often trips me up is when I think back to my past when I made shitloads of fast cash, albeit illegally. Working, really working for a living, isn't easy. It takes real guts to earn a legitimate income. The day-to-day grind of a five-day workweek is a lot tougher than sticking someone up. As usual, it was Lena who set me straight. Our $300 wasn't a ton of money, but it would pay for a month's worth of food for our rescues, and I was very grateful to all the people who showed up and contributed.

We ran a second fund-raiser almost a year later on May 2, 2014, with two great performers, Erin Sax and Brad Cole, at the Cutting Room in Manhattan. It's a great venue with a big stage and seating areas. It was a packed house that night. Our fifty-fifty split with admissions was enough to pay half a month's rent at the shelter. Everyone who showed up had a great time, and I couldn't thank Erin and Brad enough.

The work that goes on behind the scenes of fund-raising is substantial. What it's taught me so far is that fund-raising events need to be spaced out and preplanned long in advance. The Cutting Room fund-raiser involved much less of my time and effort than did the event we held at Milestone Park in Brooklyn a little more than a year earlier. It also netted the shelter more money.

Although we accept donations at Keno's, I don't go out hawking for money. We have a website and a Facebook page with all the relevant information for those who want to donate, but I don't believe in selling the place with ads. Keno's is a lifetime investment for me. Whether funds are donated or not, I will keep it afloat no matter what happens. For now, profits from our store, The Diamond Collar, keep Keno's on a very tight budget. Sometimes when I'm short a few dollars, whether it's because of medicines my rescues require or because the business was a little slow, I find a way to pay the bills.

I came from the streets and I can always return there. I have no qualms about doing whatever is necessary to keep my rescues safe, happy, and healthy at Keno's. So long as I'm alive, Keno's will be around.

The New York City Fire Department showed up for a routine inspection one morning, and it was pretty funny once I let them inside Keno's. The two guys who walked in first nearly ran out when they saw Primo and 66. I had to step around them to clear a path.

"Sorry," I said, then reassured them that both dogs were tame. "The big one is a teddy bear," I said. "The pit bull is just playful."

"I guess you'll never have to worry about being robbed in here," one of the fireman said.

"Unless they make it inside," I said.

One of the firemen was petting Primo at the time. On cue, Primo rolled onto his side for a belly rub.

"See?" I said.

The fireman laughed. "Still," one of them said. "Who'd take the chance and come inside. He's as big as a lion."

They were nice guys, and at the end of their inspection, they commended me for opening the shelter. They each donated a $20 bill. It meant a lot to me then and it still means a lot to me. These are guys in the business of saving lives. Maybe they understood the concept of a shelter more so than the average Joe. In any event, I was grateful for their donations.

Two years ago, I decided to get a tattoo of my Princess. It's a big tattoo that covers my left rib cage. As mentioned previously, Princess was a tough dog to socialize. It took a lot of patience, perseverance, a few hundred bites, and the help of a few strippers, but once she was amenable to the larger world around her, she was perfect. Even after I added Primo to our daily routine, Princess never showed signs of jealousy.

About eight months ago, Princess started to show signs of slowing down. She seemed a little less anxious getting in and out of my truck. She also didn't eat as much as she had in the past. She was no longer a young dog, so some of her slowdown was to be expected. Unfortunately, her deterioration continued over the next two months. She was eating less and remaining stationary for longer periods of time than was her norm.

Six months ago, after we returned home for the day, I noticed Princess was acting very strange. I immediately had a bad feeling and kept my eyes on her. When I saw her stagger as she tried to urinate, I picked her up and rushed her to the BVG. I wasn't sure if there was anything they could do, but I never had the chance to find out. Princess suffered a fatal heart attack in my arms within minutes after I walked into the BVG office. It was another very emotional time for me, something anyone who loves animals would understand.

Princess had been getting sick for a while, and I knew her end was coming, but her passing still left me heartbroken. She had been my best pal for so many years. There isn't a day when I don't think of her. Every morning I kiss my hand and touch her tattoo.

The day-to-day workings at Keno's have fulfilled my life in ways I never could've imagined. My routine hasn't varied much at all. I'm up early with Lena to help feed our house animals. I shower, spend a few extra minutes combing my hair until it's the way I like it, and I head out of the house for Keno's to feed my rescues. I stop for my espressos along the way, downing the first two at the counter of Cafe Isabella, and I take another few with me for the short ride over to Keno's.

Primo is always the first to greet me when I first step inside. The big mush's cropped tail wags like a little machine. If it were a metronome, the band would be playing full speed.

I say, "Good morning, Primo. Good morning, my babies."

And my rescues make a rush to me like I'm made of dog bones and catnip. The mewing and barking begins and it doesn't end until after I've fed all of my animals, Primo first.

Weekdays, I'm there all day to keep the place clean, address potential adopters, and field rescue calls. Weekends, I start the day at Keno's but then spend the bulk of the rest of the day at The Diamond Collar, just half a mile away on Seventy-first Street and Thirteenth Avenue. I return to Keno's for the evening feeding and to clean the place before heading home for the night. On good nights, if I'm home before nine o'clock, and if Lena isn't bushed from handling the thirty or so animals we have at home, I eat my spaghetti and we get to relax on the couch with bowls of ice cream while watching a movie.

Each morning the process begins again, and it is repeated every day of the year. God willing, it will keep going until the day I die.

Back when I was still living in Richmond Hill, Queens, before I was convicted and went away to prison, my wife at the time wanted to see the Broadway play *Les Misérables*. She was a religious person and couldn't see that particular musical enough. I must've seen it with her three or four times, but the truth of the matter was, I never paid attention and really didn't know what the hell was going on. More than likely, I was stoned or drunk.

Some twenty years later, I saw that there was a movie version of the musical, which I later learned was originally based on a book that was written something like 150 or more years ago. This time when I watched the musical (in the movie theater), I wasn't jumping out of my skin jonesing for cocaine or a drink. I was sober and not only able to follow what was going on, I was interested in the story: a former convict is redeemed because of an act of kindness.

I'm no Jean Valjean, I don't kid myself about that, but my life was turned around from the love of a single person, Lena, and the relationship I developed with the abused and abandoned shih tzu we found tied to a parking meter some eight years ago now, my Bruno.

A priest bought Valjean's soul for God with a pair of candlesticks. I had Lena and Bruno, and I thank God every single day for the life I now live.

Epilogue

Lena remains the rock of my life. I'm convinced that it was her love and acceptance of me during my worst days that brought me to this point in my life. I know of no one who loves animals more, or who would so willingly give of herself for the sake of others. We may never have the money to obtain her ultimate dream, to own and operate an animal sanctuary, but Keno's Animal Rescue is, at the least, a big first step in that direction.

I owe her first and foremost for everything good that has come to my life.

Another person who has meant the world to me and my rescues is Dr. Salvatore Pernice. His devotion to animals remains unshakable. Sal has helped me from the first day we met, when he explained to me the horrors of puppy mills and what some people do to defenseless dogs for the sake of making money. He's been there every step of the way for me, for my rescues, and for Keno's. I owe him more than I could ever repay.

I've been given more chances than any one person deserves. At this stage of my life, it isn't difficult to see how life has been more than kind. At the worst times in my life, I was nothing more than a selfish addict-alcoholic in pursuit of my next line of cocaine or drink. Nothing or nobody else mattered. I found a love that helped me to conquer my demons. It is a love that provided light to a dark soul, a love that I can share.

Like they say, fuhgeddaboudit. My cup runneth over.

Visit the Diamond Collar website at: http://thediamondcollar.com/.

See our store Facebook page at: https://www.facebook.com /TheDiamondCollar.

Keno's accepts contributions through our animal-rescue Facebook page at: https://www.facebook.com/kenosanimalrescue /app_117708921611213.

Acknowledgments

For most of my life, I was consumed by the demands of drug and alcohol addictions. I ignored those who loved me, causing them great pain and anxiety. Immune to their feelings, my energy and focus was selfish and self-destructive. On the brink of suicide, Madelena Perrelli showed me love and compassion. The way she could never abandon an animal, she never abandoned me. She remains my love, my best friend, my rock. Anthony and Dorothy Guiliani, for supporting me when I needed them most. My best friends, George, Ralph, Mike, and Nicky (to name a few), guys who never turned their backs on me. Dr. Salvatore Pernice, for being a great friend and savior for me and my animals. The entire staff and doctors at the Brooklyn Veterinarian Group, Dr. Brett Levitzke, VERG Veterinary Emergency and Referral Group, and all the other animal care groups, for all they've done and continue to do for my animals. Dr. Fred Notarniccola, for keeping myself and Lena healthy. My 112 crew—brothers forever. My family who are no longer here, my mother and father, Maryann and Louis Guiliani. My brothers Joseph and Thomas. Always in my thoughts, I miss them every day. The shih tzu I named Bruno, for finding and saving me. Erin Niumata and the Folio Agency for taking my memoir to Dan Ambrosio and Claire Ivett at Perseus Books, for helping me tell my story. For Charlie Stella, for finding and writing in my voice like no other.

Mom, I hope I did you proud.